1995

To David Bales

Best wishes always

Sarah S. Zelzer.

Maurice Seymour

The Zelzers' Twenty-Fifth Anniversary, 1958

IMPRESARIO

THE ZELZER ERA
1930 to 1990

SARAH SCHECTMAN ZELZER

WITH PHYLLIS DREAZEN

Academy Chicago Publishers
1990
Our 15th Year

Published in 1990 by
Academy Chicago Publishers
213 West Institute Place
Chicago, Illinois 60610

Thanks to Ann Barzel for her contribution to this book; and to Marjorie Hassen, Music Librarian at the University of Pennsylvania, for permission to reprint portions from her master's thesis at the University of Chicago, "Harry Zelzer Concerts: A Study of Musical Taste in Chicago 1937-1977."

Printed and bound in the USA

Library of Congress Cataloging-in-Publication Data

Zelzer, Sarah Schectman. 1909-
      Impresario: the Zelzer era, 1930-1990/Sarah Schectman Zelzer with Phyllis Dreazen; an appreciation by Daniel Barenboim.
          p.   cm.
      ISBN 0-89733-351-9: $18.95
        1. Zelzer, Harry, 1897-1979. 2. Zelzer, Sarah Schectman, 1909-
3. Impresarios—Illinois—Chicago—Biography. 4. Music—Illinois—Chicago—20th century—History and criticism.
I. Dreazen, Phyllis. II. Title.
ML429.Z44Z4 1990
380.1'4578'092—dc20
[B]
                                         90-39549
                                       CIP
10 9 8 7 6 5 4 3 2   MN

For Harry, my partner, my friend, my husband.

CONTENTS

CONTENTS

I will never forget the shock of my first visit to Chicago. I was fifteen years old and had had the good fortune of hearing several concerts in Europe and Israel by such fine orchestras as the Vienna Philharmonic and Israel Philharmonic orchestras. However, the shock—and no word can describe my feelings as precisely as that—of the sound of the Chicago Symphony Orchestra playing Strauss' *Ein Heldenleben* with Fritz Reiner will always remain in my memory. Full of these feelings, I was invited to dinner by a gentleman who was the presentor of the recital I was to play the next afternoon, Harry Zelzer. His combination of humour, energy and irony made the rest of the evening extremely entertaining. He had the kindness (loyalty or maybe misplaced faith...) to invite me regularly to play recitals at Orchestra Hall and we inevitably dined together afterwards with his wife Sarah always there to calm his excesses of food or speech. These weekends became part of my life and contributed greatly to the affection I developed for Chicago—Harry Zelzer was one of the rare people whose musical "nose" was so extraordinary that it was enough for someone to play the first few notes of a recital for Harry to know the real potential of the artist. His tenacity and courage in presenting young artists contributed greatly to the knowledge of the public and Chicago, and therefore, all music lovers must cherish his memory with admiration and affection.

—Daniel Barenboim,
March 1990

HARRY Zelzer was unique in his knowledge of the Chicago audiences—in knowing what his music lovers wanted to hear and what he thought they should experience. His frequent visits to New York put the entire management field on notice—Harry's in town! What fun and what a pleasure it was to match wits with one of the smartest impresarios in the business!

—Kurt Weinhold
Former President
Columbia Artists Management, Inc.

IMPRESARIO
THE ZELZER ERA
1930-1990

I. PRELUDE

IT was January 21, 1989, my eightieth birthday. I stood at the entrance to the Lake Point Tower Club, greeting my guests. From the Club's wraparound windows, I could see all the lights—moving along Lake Shore Drive, shining in myriad windows, reflected in the glittering snow....They made me think of the thousands of people my husband and I had greeted during our nearly six decades in the concert business. I wondered briefly how many people that actually was.

If you attended an opera, ballet, recital, visiting orchestral concert or ethnic event from 1930 on, it was probably a Zelzer or Allied Arts concert—in short, one of ours. And if you did, you may have seen my husband Harry Zelzer, a small, dapper gentleman, or me, Sarah Schectman Zelzer, near the door of the hall as you came in. We were always there to welcome people, to solve problems of any kind, and, not infrequently, to let students in free.

The next day a concert by Ivan Davis in the Auditorium Theatre would mark the end of the second series of concerts—the Zelzer Series and the Zelzer Piano Series—which I had been running by myself, after a short retirement. But tonight was to be an elegant cele-

1

bration: an excellent dinner; the Paganini Ensemble, a fine string trio; a guest list including members of my family, new and old friends, musicians, managers from New York and other business associates, media people....

I was full of nervous excitement; I'm not sure why. It wasn't as if this sort of event was new or unusual for me. Ours had been, after all, a public life, with constant entertaining both here and at our home in Wisconsin. My associate, Noah Hoffman, had handed out press releases and photographs, but that too was a normal part of the way we lived.

But as I stood greeting people, I suddenly felt Harry's presence so strongly that I turned, expecting to see him standing beside me. But Harry had been dead for more than ten years. I knew that calendars don't lie, but I found it impossible to believe that he had died so long ago. It seemed as if it were only yesterday that we had greeted people at *his* seventy-fifth birthday party....

II. SARAH'S EARLY YEARS

MY life had always centered around music: after my first piano lesson in 1915 when I was six years old, my one ambition was to become a great pianist.

I was born in Philadelphia on January 23, 1909. I don't remember Philadelphia because my family moved to Chicago when I was three years old. I do remember I was wearing a pink dress and that my Aunt Dora cried when we left. It was raining hard when we got off the train and my father was not there to greet us. My mother bargained with the driver of the horse cab who finally agreed to take us to the place where my father lived. I remember climbing up two flights of stairs, being frightened by a cat which brushed past me. I was crying when I found myself in my father's arms; he comforted me and gave me a penny. He had apparently never received the telegram my mother had sent him.

I was the baby of the family; besides my parents, of course, there were my sister Lena, fourteen years older than I—she changed her name to Lovell—and my sister Annie, fifteen months younger than Lovell—she changed *her* name to Cynthia. There was another child who did not come with us to Chicago; his name was Sam and he was left at a school for retarded children in

Philadelphia. Nobody wanted to talk about him, and I did not know him. I got the impression that he might have been epileptic. He did not talk. I think my mother believed that my father had dropped him when he was a baby; it was something that she never got over. And then, to compound the tragedy, Sam died in Philadelphia during the great flu epidemic that followed the First World War. My father went to Philadelphia for the funeral. Mother always wanted to bring Sam's body to Chicago and I promised her that some day when I earned enough money we would do it. But somehow we never got around to it.

We sisters caught the flu too: I remember being delirious for three days. Dr Leviton was at our house continuously. They cut off all my hair and I remember the huge teaspoon of medicine that frightened me so I screamed. But I made a quick recovery. Cynthia was not so fortunate. She was an invalid for months.

I received my music-teaching diploma when I was thirteen years old. My family was very proud of me: Lovell and Cynthia gave me a huge glass sign with "TEACHER OF PIANO" in tall gold letters, to put in the window of our apartment on Fairfield Avenue, near Robey Street. My first pupil was a young man in his twenties whose family had just emigrated from Europe; I taught his two younger sisters too. I was so proud of the money I earned and of being a full-fledged teacher. Now I could put my hair up; I had been letting it grow for a year so it would be long enough to put up when I became a teacher. I had had a Dutch boy bob; Papa said that nothing would make me look older because of my haircut and my shape; I looked like "a rag, a bone and a hank-o-hair." But I didn't cut my hair again from that time until the '70s, when I had it cut in a fit of rage.

Harry always said he loved my long hair and that he did not want me to cut it, ever. But one day, right after we had moved to Lake Point Tower, Harry and I had a fight. I was so angry at him that I decided to cut my hair to spite him. So the next day I went to the beauty shop and told Marcello to cut it off. He was horrified; my hair reached to my waist. He told me to go home and think it over before I did anything I would regret. So I did, but I was still angry enough to go through with it the next day.

It was a really short haircut. As I looked in the mirror that Marcello held up for me, I began to get really nervous. What had I done? And what would Harry do? By the time I got home, I was a wreck. When Harry came home for dinner, I tried to blend in with the kitchen. But he looked closely at me.

"Did you cut your hair today?" he demanded.

I began to tremble. "Yes," I said; I started to add that it would grow out.

"Oh," Harry said. "It looks nice. You should have done it a long time ago."

I threw my shoe at him.

⨍

But to return to my early years. I went to Tuley High School; it was out of our district but my sister Cynthia worked for the Board of Education so I was able to get a special permit to go there, along with my best friends from Wicker Park: Theresa, who wanted to be an actress, her sister Ruth, who wanted to be a writer, and Rose, whose only ambition was to be a wife and mother. I had some writing ambitions myself; Miss Ferguson, my English teacher, encouraged me. During my senior year I edited the *Girls' Review*, the high school paper, and I won an essay contest sponsored by the *Chicago Daily News*. My essay was called "Washington Crosses the Delaware"; Miss Ferguson arranged for me to read it to the other English classes. (I have put it in the back of this book so you can judge it for yourself.) That day, filled with warm applause, has been my treasured memory for more than sixty years.

My music teacher too thought I had talent. With all this encouragement I really believed that I was capable of accomplishing great things: I dreamed of concert tours and applause and bouquets, and of writing important books....

And since I was the baby of the family, I had all the lessons that my sisters hadn't gotten or hadn't wanted. I even went to Hebrew School where girls were not admitted in those days. My father persuaded the rabbi to let me attend. I was the only girl in the class.

My father's health began to fail during my last year in grade school and when I was in high school I had to work on Saturdays at Iverson's Department Store on Milwaukee Avenue. I earned two dollars for the entire day. By the time I graduated in 1926, when I was seventeen, the family needed what money I could bring in, so I had to help out. I wasn't happy about it; I had always been pampered. After all, one of my sisters had once spent her whole paycheck on a dress for me. And I had been so sheltered that I was not allowed to go downtown by myself until I was in high school. Now at seventeen I had to find a job.

I went downtown to an employment agency. I was applying for office work, although I hated the thought of it.

"I don't have anything for you today," the woman said. "It's a pianist we're looking for."

Naturally I got very excited. "What do you mean, you're looking for a pianist?" I asked. "What are you talking about?"

"There's a woman in town from Chautauqua," she said, referring to an adult education program headquartered in Chautauqua, in upstate New York. "She needs a pianist to go on tour for her."

"I play piano," I said eagerly.

She looked at me in surprise. Then, after a pause, she said, "Well, all right. I'll set up an audition for you."

I had the audition and the Chautauqua manager was really pleased; in fact, she was delighted. She offered me $150 a week to go to Chautauqua with her. That was *big money*.

I couldn't wait to tell my mother. She knew how much I hated the idea of going to work in an office, but I had to do something; I wasn't making enough money teaching.

When I told her about my big opportunity, she said, "We'll ask Uncle Mendel."

My Uncle Mendel was considered an Authority because he was a musician who had a gypsy orchestra. When we told him about it, he said to my mother, "No. You can't let her go. She'll become a prostitute."

In those days—and actually until fairly recently—it

wasn't considered decent for a girl to live away from her parents' home.

"Even if you only make twenty dollars a week in an office, you're not leaving home," my mother said firmly.

Of course I obeyed her, because that's what you did in those days, but I've really never stopped thinking about it. It would have been such fun, and it would have been valuable music experience. But it would also have been $150 a week plus traveling expenses—and that would have been fabulous!

But on the other hand, since I had been so over-protected, I was afraid of everything. Maybe the travel would have been too much for me. Later, when I was working, I had another offer: my boss introduced me to a middle-aged man who wanted to take me to Europe to pursue my musical studies. He said he would get me the greatest teachers in the world and start me on my career. But my mother wouldn't let me go then either. And once more, I keep wondering what would have happened if I had gone.

So I took a job in an office on Crawford Avenue and continued with my studies at Struck's College of Music on the northwest side, in an area bounded by Milwaukee Avenue, Irving Park Road and Cicero Avenue. I worked in the office for a year and then, with some financial help from Cynthia, I relied on my teaching. When Struck's College was sold by Mrs Bertha Struck and her husband to a Mr Shreyer, I stayed with the school; its name was changed to the Master Conservatory. The Strucks eventually opened a new school a few blocks away.

The Master Conservatory became very dear to me; it

was my home away from home. Even now, if I close my eyes, I can call up the scene as it was there in 1926: the first thing that caught the eye was a huge electric sign extending from the front of the building, informing the passerby that the Master Conservatory taught all musical instruments, voice and dancing and that Mr Rose, the director, would be pleased to discuss all musical problems. The streets around the school were filled with people carrying their bundles, dodging cars, horses and wagons while the policeman's whistle split the air; there were children rushing home from school, wives hurrying home to prepare supper, men on their way home after a hard day's work. Inside the building, the office was crowded with teachers and students, like a happy family enjoying an evening at home. At first glance, the place may have seemed to be just another music and dance school, but to me it was very special.

I worked very hard there; I wanted to do everything I could to help the school become a success. I lay awake nights thinking up new ideas, making plans. And I stayed at the studio until eleven and twelve at night, sending out mimeographed promotion letters. I took care of the office, making sure it was tidy; I played piano for the dancing class, joined the regular orchestra, played drums in the All-Girl Orchestra and taught my classes. There was enough to keep me busy for more than a full day, and I loved every nook and cranny of the place. I didn't live like other people: when they slept, I worked; when they worked, I slept. I began to see less of people my age, except for my friend Rose. She and I would take long walks at midnight and exchange confidences. I got to know older people and I tried to learn to act older.

I led this life happily for six months until I fell in love with one of the music teachers there. He was a lot older than I was and even though I tried to act older, he really looked upon me as a child and treated me like one. My feelings for him eventually made it impossible for me to stay at the Master Conservatory and so I left. I was nineteen years old.

Now all my activities took place at the Esther Harris School of Music, also known as the Chicago College of Music. Esther Harris was a well-known pianist and teacher; she had a genius for bringing out special qualities in her students, and she turned out some remarkable pianists. I hoped to become one of them.

I owe a real debt to Esther Harris. If she hadn't been interested in me and helped me during those years, my life would have taken a different course. She not only gave me a scholarship for my studies, she gave me some students, including retarded kids no one wanted to take. There was one boy I remember especially. His mother begged me to take him.

"Please," she said. "Nobody wants to teach him."

I said I would try. I was really more interested in earning extra money than I was in her son.

I made a little progress with him. But finally I had to tell her that I thought I had taken him as far as I could. "I don't want you to waste your money," I said to her. "I know you're not wealthy. He can play a couple of scales and this little piece I gave him. I don't want you to spend money you can't afford."

But she said, "Please. Keep him. Any price is worth it."

I asked her why.

"Because he responds to you. From one week to the next, all he keeps asking is when is his next appointment with Miss Schectman. 'I like the way she talks to me,' he says. 'And I like her smile and she's so nice to me.' That's worth any sacrifice to me. Even if he never learns to play another note, it's worth it to me to see his face light up when he knows he's coming to you."

At that time, I was getting $3.50 a lesson. Esther Harris helped me out by telling some of her students that during the week they could take an extra lesson with me on technique and scales. She was using the Lechititsky Method: I didn't know it, but Lilian Raphling, another young teacher there, taught it to me. That extra teaching paid a dollar an hour.

Everyone at the school loved and admired Esther, although she was kind of a schemer. Once she lost her wallet on the El and asked me to pick it up at the lost-and-found office at the Ravenswood Station. I did, and, nosey as always, I looked through it. I saw that she had collected newspaper clippings about children who had won musical honors and awards. I noticed that two of them were outstanding students of hers, who were well on their way to concert careers. I learned later that when she read about these students in the newspapers, she had called their parents and offered them scholarships if they would study with her.

On Sunday afternoons the People's Symphony Orchestra gave concerts at the Eighth Street Theatre. This was a group of fifty musicians who presented classical music at popular prices. Our pupils got free tickets and I took advantage of this to attend these concerts regularly. I'd get the tickets at the box office and then take my mother with me to the performances. I really enjoyed these concerts; I was able to hear a lot of music by new local talent.

I saw Harry Zelzer standing in the lobby before one of these concerts; he was keeping an eye on the box office and the flow of the crowd. I knew that he was the orchestra's angel, but I really didn't pay much attention to him. Esther Harris told me she thought it would be a good idea if I had an audition with him; if he liked my performance he might let me play with the People's Symphony. She did actually arrange for me to play the Tchaikowsky Piano Concerto for him in his suite at the Harrison Hotel. But when she told me this, I balked. I certainly was not going to audition in any hotel room. The audition, I said, would have to take place at the Conservatory. The result was that I did not audition and I lost my chance to play with the People's Symphony.

III. HARRY'S EARLY YEARS

HARRY Zelzer was born in Warsaw, Poland, on April 15, 1897; he was one of a family of seven children. It was a family with a musical tradition: although Harry's great-great-grandfather could not read music, he had played the flute for Napoleon. And his grandfather was a fiddler, while his grandfather's brother, Harry's great-uncle, who had died the year Harry was born, was a dedicated musician; a friend of Meyerbeer and Halévy, a student of the violin with the famous composer Wieniawski, a composer himself of music for biblical Hebrew texts, and director of the Polish Theatre in Lublin.

Harry's father played the violin. But musical talent in that family seemed to have ended with the older generations. Harry himself had had violin lessons and his daughter Harriet was given music lessons, but neither she nor her children were much interested in music, much to Harry's disappointment.

Because of deep-rooted anti-Semitism in Poland, Harry's family decided to emigrate. Harry's sister Pearl had come over first. Then Harry came over when he was still a boy. He arrived in New York in 1909 and worked for his brother-in-law, Morris Malvin, who had a cigar and newspaper store. Harry lived with the

Malvins, saved his money and eventually was able to bring the rest of his family from Poland.

While he was working for Morris Malvin, Harry had an experience that made a deep impression on him. Morris sent him to collect a bill for cigars from a wealthy customer who lived in the Waldorf-Astoria Hotel. Harry saw the customer's furniture, his butler and maid; he was especially impressed by the man's printed dinner menu—that, Harry swore, was the kind of life he was going to live. From that time on, hotels were a symbol for Harry of success and the good life. That's why Harry and I spent most of our married life in hotels.

Although he worked hard, Harry didn't feel that he was getting anywhere in New York; he was very ambitious. He heard that there were better opportunities in Chicago. His family agreed with his decision to move there in 1919. He got a job as a teller in the City State Bank located on Wells Street. After nine months he was made a trust officer. He spent two-and-a-half years in the trust department; in 1923, at the age of twenty-six, he was made assistant manager. Two years later he was promoted again, to full manager of the bond department.

It seems funny, but it was through Harry's job at the bank that he became involved with the world of music. One day in 1923, a Mr Paulsen came into the bank and applied for a loan of six hundred dollars, offering his Guarnerius violin as collateral. No one in the bank knew anything about violins, so Mr Paulsen was referred to Harry. It developed that the customer, whose full name was P. Marinus Paulsen, was a composer and arranger of music; one of his compositions had won first prize in a contest sponsored by the Chicago Theatre, which was operated then by Balaban & Katz. In addition, Mr Paulsen was the sponsor and conductor of the People's Symphony Orchestra. He needed to borrow the six hundred dollars to meet the orchestra's payroll. After they had talked for a while, Mr Paulsen signed the note and Harry guaranteed it. As Harry said later, "I knew the value of that collateral and I was making good money anyway, since I was building up the bond department."

Mr Paulsen invited Harry to come and hear the People's Symphony, and right after Labor Day in 1923, Harry went to the performance. They played Liszt's *Les Preludes* and Beethoven's Fifth. Harry thought it was a good orchestra; he had been a regular attendant at the Chicago Symphony and the Opera House practically since he first came to the city, and he was eager to get more involved in music in Chicago. It seemed to him that the People's Symphony offered a perfect opportunity for him to combine music and business.

He called the woman who managed the Symphony's affairs into the bank and asked her what she did. She said she put an ad in the newspaper every week and sent out a release.

"What are you paid?" Harry asked her.

"One hundred dollars."

"Consider yourself relieved," Harry said, and that was the moment he took official charge of the People's Symphony.

He put one of his secretaries in an office in the bank building and told her to take charge of work for the orchestra. "I didn't know what the hell I was doing," he said later, "but I did it."

He raised money to meet the orchestra's deficit from the bank officers and customers. Most people gave about ten dollars apiece; one bank customer gave five hundred—a very large amount then. Somehow Harry managed to meet expenses. Running the orchestra was a hobby for him; he went to rehearsals on Sunday instead of playing golf.

Expenses were low. The musicians got fifteen to twenty-five dollars a concert; the conductor wasn't paid. Some of the best musicians were also members of the Chicago Symphony. The Eighth Street Theatre charged eighty-five dollars a session; the Orchestra got a free rehearsal room in the bank building. The soloists were local talent who got a showcase every Sunday. Students got in free. Harry also arranged for radio broadcasts of the concerts, earning fees of $250 a broadcast; he used his charm on James Petrillo, the hard-nosed boss of the musicians' union, to let the orchestra rehearse without pay. Harry helped select the programs which, he said, were "standard works, nothing avant-garde." That way he learned a great deal about classic symphonic literature.

Harry managed the Symphony and went on working at the bank until the market crash in October, 1929. The City Bank failed in November and Harry was the only officer who was not indicted, but he lost most of his money. The People's Symphony Orchestra no longer seemed to hold much promise and neither did the banking business. Harry had made a lot of contacts in the music world, though, and he decided to take a flyer at presenting an artist on his own: he made an arrangement with Beniamino Gigli, generally considered the greatest tenor after Caruso, for a concert which was held at the Opera House on October 15, 1930, under the aegis "Harry Zelzer Presents". The concert was a success, but Harry lost twelve hundred dollars. Nevertheless, he had learned something about concert management and he was considering turning his hobby into a full-time business.

But he was hampered because of the Depression and because his money was running out; and he had some personal problems. He went back to New York to be with his family and to try his luck at a business career there. After two years he became convinced that he had no future in New York; he came back to Chicago and to the music business that was his first love. To get back on his feet he took a job as manager at the Esther Harris School at twenty-five dollars a week.

IV. MARRIAGE

IT was in September of 1933 that Harry Zelzer joined the staff of the Esther Harris School of Music. Shortly afterward, he invited most of the faculty to a performance of the San Carlo Opera Company at the Auditorium Theatre. Much to my surprise, he asked me to have a late supper with him after the performance at an Italian restaurant, the Venice, near the theatre on Wabash Avenue. I was surprised because I had noticed that other women at the school were attracted to him and flirted with him. I wasn't really in their league; I was much younger than they and not at all sophisticated.

After that dinner, Harry and I developed a friendly relationship. He asked me to take on his daughter Harriet as a pupil. Of course I did, but although she had a good ear for music, I wasn't even able to teach her to play scales properly. She didn't want to practice; she wasn't interested. I enjoyed seeing Harry, although I didn't think my seeing him would make the other women on the faculty jealous. But it did, to the point of telling Harry unpleasant stories about me. Esther Harris herself offered me ten thousand dollars and a mink coat if I would drop Harry. I was dumbfounded. I didn't think Harry was that great a catch: he had lost most of

19

his money in the Crash, and I knew he wasn't earning much at the school. Besides, he had been married before and now his teenaged daughter was living with him. But I certainly wasn't about to drop him and I told Esther that.

Harry asked me to look for a furnished apartment for him and Harriet in my neighborhood. My friend Rose and I went apartment-hunting and found him a one-bedroom place on Rockwell Street in the Ravenswood area.

One evening when we were out for dinner Harry asked me if it was true that I had been living with a violinist. He told me that Esther Harris and several of the women teachers had told him that I had been living with this young man for two years. Of course I was upset, but I told him that he probably wouldn't believe my denials and that he would eventually find out the truth for himself.

He called me early the next morning. Could I meet him at the Capitol Building in an hour? No, I couldn't; but I could meet him at one-thirty before I was due at the studio.

When I got to the Capitol Building, Harry was waiting for me in the lobby; he had a marriage license. He wanted me to go upstairs with him to a jeweler and get a wedding ring he had picked out. Then he wanted us to go to a judge who was a friend of his and be married immediately.

This was too fast for me. I didn't want to be rushed like this, and besides I wanted a Jewish ceremony. Harry agreed and we were married on Hallowe'en night, October 31, 1933. Just before the rabbi arrived I went into a panic; it had all happened too fast and I wanted to change my mind. But my father said it was too late to back out. So I went through the ceremony with a heavy heart. The marriage, of course, was to last for nearly fifty years.

So the one-bedroom apartment on Rockwell Street I had found for Harry and Harriet now became my home too. I was frightened by all these new responsibilities. I was in love, but I was certainly not mature enough to be a mother to a thirteen-year-old girl. I didn't know how to make friends with a teenager and I resented being put in that position.

Another problem was that I didn't know how to cook. During the week we ate out, usually at the Venice, the Italian restaurant where our courtship had started, and where we could sign the tab if we didn't have money. On Fridays and holidays we ate at my mother's. And if Harry invited guests to dinner, my mother would come to our apartment and cook. Once Harry invited his lawyer to dinner, and he wanted to serve goose. "Call your mother," he said.

I called her and told her. "He wants a goose," I said. I didn't even know what a goose looked like, let alone how to clean one or prepare it. My mother told me not to worry. She and my sister Lovell came over; I told them dinner was set for six-thirty.

They worked for a few hours and then got ready to leave. Lovell said everything was ready and they had left it on a low fire.

"Why are you going?" I asked.

They pointed out that they had not been invited.

So I set the table and eventually served the dinner,

which was a great success.

I became pregnant almost immediately. I didn't tell anyone because I was afraid that the people at the Conservatory would think our hasty marriage meant that I was in trouble. Harry was not really happy about this pregnancy. I knew that financially it was not the right time to have a child, but it had happened and it had to be accepted. Unfortunately our child died soon after birth. It was a great disappointment, but maybe it was for the best.

Those Depression years were very rough. I had left my concert grand piano at my mother's house and now I was having trouble meeting the monthly payments. One day my mother called to tell me that the Kimball Piano Company had come to repossess it. Frantically I called Harry. He promised to take care of it, but he couldn't do anything, and I lost my piano. I was devastated. Harry promised me that he would make up for it some day. In the meantime we had fallen behind in rent for the apartment; we would have to move soon. Harry was paying rent on an office in the Auditorium building because he wanted to go back into the concert business. And my salary barely covered the food bills—a teenager is always hungry. But I was young, so I was hopeful and ambitious; I still dreamed of becoming a great pianist.

One night shortly after we got married, we went out to dinner with Arthur Wisner of CAMI (Columbia Artists Management, Inc.), an artists' agency based in New York, and his wife Frances. They came back to the apartment with us and Frances, who played, sat down at the piano.

Harry wasn't going to be outdone; he told me to

play the Tchaikowsky Concerto for them. I said no; I hadn't been practicing. But Harry insisted, so I played a few pages. And the next day Arthur called and asked me to come up to his office. He asked me to sign for Community Concerts with him; he said he could book me.

"Where were you before I got married?" I asked him.

And sure enough, Harry wouldn't let me do it. "Travel?" he said. "You're not going to travel. I didn't get married for my wife to spend time away from home."

So I had to tell Wisner that I couldn't do it. I really regretted that lost chance for a long time.

Marriage was a big adjustment—and not just for me. Harry didn't really know how to handle it either. One evening after we had been married only a couple of months, I finished teaching about seven-thirty and went over to Harry's office in the Auditorium building to meet him for dinner as usual. But the door was locked and the office was dark. I waited around in the hallway for about five minutes and then I went back to the Conservatory. I called home, but he wasn't there. Of course I imagined the worst. I couldn't eat and I went back to the apartment to wait. I didn't know what else to do.

About midnight Harry came home. He said he was sorry, but he had forgotten I existed. It had slipped his mind that he was married: he had gone to dinner with Jerzy Bojanowski and they had spent the evening talking about the possibility of producing the opera *Halka*. I was stunned, and frightened. This was a clear signal to me to stop and think about the rest of my life. It was a clear signal to me to go. But where?

So I stayed, but that was a costly decision. During the next few months I developed a mysterious illness which was to plague me and defy doctors for twenty years. Finally, after many diagnoses, many x-rays, many tests, many nightmares, I was told it was a food allergy.

But food is not the only thing you can be allergic to....

V. BIRTH OF THE ZELZER CONCERT MANAGEMENT BUREAU

WE had to move out of the apartment on Rockwell Street because we couldn't pay the rent. To be frank, we left the place at three in the morning without notifying the landlord. Harry was able to maneuver rooms at the Harrison Hotel on a due bill—that is, we traded off ads for the hotel in the programs of our attractions in exchange for rent.

Moving into a hotel was quite an experience for me; I didn't like it. We had no kitchen, of course—just a couple of rooms. True, I couldn't cook, but it was hard for me to get used to room service and eating out every night. Harry loved this kind of life—it was what he had wanted ever since he had called on his brother-in-law's customer at the Waldorf in New York. And we were to go on living in hotels for years. After a few years at the Harrison we moved to the Seneca Hotel and then to the Lake Shore Drive Hotel, which is now the Mayfair Regent. And then for over twenty years we lived at the Bismarck Hotel in the Loop.

But to get back to that summer of 1935. If Harry wanted to do anything in the concert business, he had to visit New York but we had no money for transportation. Fortunately he was able to arrange a ride; it was the only way he could get there. And it was a good thing he did it—he came back with contracts to present five artists in Chicago the following season: they were violinist Albert Spaulding, pianist-composers Ossip Gabrilowitsch and Percy Grainger, the Spanish dancer Argentina and another one whose name I have forgotten. I remember Argentina particularly because she was the first performer to put us in the black, even though we paid her the enormous sum of three thousand dollars. So now Harry was a full-time impresario in his office in the Auditorium building. He and I were both determined to devote our lives to the presentation of music. I was a little nervous about the future, but I had confidence in Harry.

He believed that the essentials of concert management lay in presenting worthwhile artists and finding audiences who would pay enough to cover costs. He knew that management could not depend on the dribble of single ticket-buyers at the box office. He conceived a plan to convince organizations to take sizable blocks of tickets or even whole concerts to sell to their supporters and members at increased prices. The organizations—usually non-profit art groups or charities—would profit, people who might not ordinarily attend a concert would have a valuable experience, and the artist would have the possibility of reaching a new audience. This procedure was to be called syndication.

To start, Harry got in touch with the League of Women Voters. He met with committee members and convinced them that they could raise a lot of money by sponsoring an Albert Spaulding concert. The women liked the idea and agreed to try it. They pushed ticket sales, the organization made money as Harry had said it would, their members and friends enjoyed a quality concert and Zelzer Management made enough money to justify its existence. We were able to pay our bills that first season; we didn't show a profit, but we broke even. Syndication was the way to go, Harry thought, and the history of music presentation in the next decades proved him right.

Harry wanted to keep his operation independent and self-sustaining. He never set up trustees or boards of directors. He depended on his own marketing ability and dedication. "What is a good impresario?" he used to say. "Some people say he's an exploiter of other people's talent. I say he's a gambler. If he ends the season in the black, he's a good impresario." He said too that his attitude toward Mr Public was like a banker's. "I have a fiduciary responsibility to give him what pleases him. One of the most important things for an impresario to know is the value of an attraction at the box office...I only really enjoy about half the concerts I stage, but I'm not in the business to cater to me."

Harry was so encouraged by that season that he decided to move his office from the Auditorium building to the Civic Opera House. Since the business failure of Samuel Insull, the public utilities tycoon who had built it, the Opera House was often vacant. The Opera House management offered Harry half of the fourth floor rent-free. The only charge was ten dollars a month for the cleaning woman.

The offices were huge, so Harry brought the publicity agency of Nathanson, Harshe and Jackson with him to share them. On Saturday afternoons the publicity men and Harry would play pinochle in the office— Harry taught them the game.

Most of the people we knew believed that this move to the Opera House was too ambitious: they predicted that Harry would fail. Our friend Fortune Gallo, the director of the San Carlo Opera Company, stopped me one afternoon on Michigan Avenue and told me to try and convince Harry that he was making a big mistake: the Opera House was too far off the beaten track; no one would go to concerts there. Gallo predicted that we would be out of business in a year. I told him that I would pass on his message, but I doubted that it would make any difference to Harry.

One afternoon when I had finished my teaching for the day, I came into the office to find Harry pacing restlessly back and forth. He was upset because his secretary had left the office early for some reason; he had two urgent letters to send to New York and he had missed the public stenographer. I told him I was starved, but he wouldn't leave until he could find someone who could get those letters out. I volunteered that I could type, although I couldn't take shorthand. I said that if he dictated very slowly, I'd be able to type the letters for him. And I did it. He was astonished and impressed at this evidence of my hidden talent and of course he decided on the spot that I had to come and take over the office. I really didn't want to give up teaching, but Harry was very persuasive. He offered to match my teaching salary. So I agreed, although reluctantly. Knowing Harry, I knew I had to agree—if I refused, it would have had a bad effect on our relationship. So I agreed—although I didn't want to.

Harry Zelzer and I were now in the concert presentation business—totally. And the pessimists were proven wrong. We stayed at the Civic Opera House until June of 1978. It became home to me; I did all my growing-up there.

ƒ

In private Harry called me "dear" and I called him "Cookie"—my sister Cynthia started calling him that because Harry loved to eat cookies—but we decided that in the office I would be called "Miss Schectman", and "Miss Schectman" I was, for more than thirty years. The Japanese say that in every marriage the husband should have a dream and the wife should help him realize it. In our business, Harry dealt with the big picture—the direction of the company, negotiations with artists and managers and the press relations. At first I did all the detail work; later I directed our staff. Harry and I were an effective team: he was the brains; I did the contracts.

Part of my job was dealing with customers. Harry always sent customers to see "Miss Schectman", especially when there were problems. One day a big commotion arose. A woman was raising hell because she wanted a refund for one main floor and one gallery seat.

We checked the orders and told her that we didn't even have a mail order from her; how could we give her a refund? Enraged, she began to shout at everyone. I told her not to talk to the girls that way.

"And who are you?" she demanded.

I said I was Miss Schectman.

She rushed off into Harry's office. "I want that girl fired," she screamed. "The one with the braids!"

"Oh, her," Harry said. "I can't fire her; she's a very valuable employee."

The woman said that if Harry did not fire me, she would never buy any more tickets from him. He told her that was her decision.

"The only reason you won't fire her," she said, as a parting shot, "is that you must be sleeping with her!"

"That's absolutely correct," Harry said.

It wasn't easy working with Harry: he was so demanding that I don't think I could have put up with him if I hadn't been married to him. He paid attention to everything, and there was a lot of pressure because we booked so many attractions and all the details had to be right: the printing, the programs, the mailings as well as dealings with the artists, the managers and the press. He wanted things done a certain way, and only a certain way, and he was always looking over everyone's shoulder to see that his wishes were being carried out.

But he was as generous with the staff as he was with all the people he liked—helping them to pay off their mortgages and their cars. "If you need anything, come to me," he would tell them. They often did, but they were not motivated only by what he could do for them: satisfying Harry was a challenge and succeeding at it gave them deep satisfaction.

They were loyal people: Thelma at the switchboard, Arlene Cole who kept the mailing lists up-to-date, Harold Nadeau who handled mail orders and subscriptions, Martha Schechet the secretary and bookkeeper, and the various sales people. Martha had come to us right out of school and I think we were the only employers she ever had. After she married and got pregnant, Harry would call her in bad weather at seven in the morning and tell her, "Don't take the bus. I'm sending the boy with the car."

Harold, Martha and I worked well together. There were some weekends in later years when we had attractions in every theatre in town. The three of us would send Harry home to get some sleep and we would stay in the office and work until one or two in the morning. What Harry started, we finished; we made his plans work.

VI. HARRY AND
BOX OFFICE REALITIES

HARRY'S business sense was as keen as his interest in music. He knew what the public wanted to hear and how much they would be willing to pay to hear it. His instinct for this was so good that he seemed to know in advance what each presentation would draw; on the actual day of a performance, he could tell within a few dollars what the box-office sale would be. If he didn't predict a profit, I knew we were in trouble.

There were two stories he liked to tell about the realities of the box office. One concerned, to quote him, "a good friend of mine, a famous violinist. It was during the Depression. He charged three thousand dollars a concert and he was only getting three concerts a year. Then he got an agent who told him he could get him many more engagements if he dropped his fee to a thousand dollars. The violinist agreed, and he played eighty-five concerts."

The other story was about Mischa Elman, who had been under Harry's personal management for a few seasons. Elman decided he wanted to double his fee. Harry told him he couldn't; box-office sales didn't warrant it.

"Isn't there any sentiment between us?" Elman asked.

"Yes, Mischa," Harry said. "In the first thousand dollars, but not in the second."

That was the end of Mr Elman under our management.

Of course, sometimes Harry took a gamble on bringing worthwhile attractions to Chicago. He thought that a box-office deficit on a fine musical event could never be a total loss—after all, the public would have profited. But he certainly had no desire to make a habit of losing money on good music. So he worked hard to develop brilliant promotional ideas. When something that had intrinsic artistic merit seemed to be deadwood, he searched for ways to interest the public in it.

A prime example of this was his promotion in the late '30s of the Original Don Cossack Chorus led by Serge Jaroff. The first announcement of this concert evoked almost no response. But Harry believed that Jaroff's group had the potential to rouse the public interest. Harry could be a really convincing salesman because he believed so fervently in the product he was selling. He convinced an executive of the *Daily News*, the Chicago afternoon paper, to sponsor the Don Cossack Chorus concert as a benefit for the paper's Fresh Air Sanitarium. The *News* saw the possibilities and mounted a sensational publicity campaign; they ran full-page photographs of marching Cossacks led by their pint-sized conductor. The public came, they loved the group, and Jaroff and his Chorus became a popular annual event in Chicago.

Harry used the Hearst morning paper, the *Herald*

and Examiner, in the same way, this time for the sponsorship of outdoor opera at Soldier Field: a spectacular *Aida* complete with camels, horses, a huge ballet and hordes of supernumeraries as slaves, soldiers and prisoners. It was a great success. People who would never support the elite art of opera in an indoor theatre flocked to the lakefront for entertainment at popular prices.

Of course everything could not work out that well. But Harry was the ultimate poker-face: he was always standing in the lobby of the theatre, greeting people and giving a feeling of confidence to the project. You could never tell from looking at him whether the event had been a financial success or failure. As I've mentioned, he often said that an impresario was a gambler and that you could tell how good he was by looking at his books at the end of the season. And that was what you had to do: look at Harry's books and not his face. Although he believed he had a fiduciary responsibility to his audience, his customers, he also had the supreme arrogance and love for danger of a high-stakes gambler. He could be a monster if things were not run efficiently, but he took his losses quietly and turned to the next toss of the dice, so to speak. There were no postmortems. He was prepared to lose money on an attraction he believed in.

He would give an artist two or three chances to succeed at the box office, as a rule. But sometimes he became committed to a musician and would stick with him no matter what happened. He took this attitude toward Segovia. We first presented the Spanish guitarist in the Civic Theatre; although it was a small hall, it was almost empty. But Harry refused to be discouraged: he believed that Segovia deserved a decent audience and he was convinced that he could raise it. He kept bringing Segovia back to Chicago: every year we recruited about a dozen new fans. Every year Andres would ask, "How's the box office this year?" And Harry would reply, "A little better. Don't worry, it will come." And it did.

Harry was always ready to work with little-known artists as well as big names. What Harry called the "backbone" of his operation was the subscription series, and that enabled him to present lesser-known artists. Our Piano Series was successful with both well-known and lesser-known pianists. "Year after year," Harry once pointed out, "there is a steady, fairly large audience for pianists. Around fifteen hundred out of a twenty-five hundred capacity always come." In addition to the Piano Series, we had a Guitar Series, a Music Series, a Dance Series and a Folk Series. "If," Harry said, "I tried to present lesser-known artists off the series, no one would come, but if the performers are on a series, we get an audience. People like ticket packages because they're good buys."

And no organization ever lost money in a co-presentation with us. If they ran into trouble, we would adjust the contract or even take over the promotion. And if they still lost money, the Zelzer office gave the organization credit for the next season so that it could make up any loss it might have incurred. We didn't worry about our loss because we could make it up on something else. The organizations understood that we were in business for the long haul and not to make a quick buck and disappear. They knew that Harry would always give them a fair deal.

And they respected his taste as well as his honesty. They knew that he knew music and that he had a sixth sense about talent. He could predict which artist would be a flash in the pan and which could become a star.

I have a couple of examples of this which date from 1948 and both of which involve tenors. The first was a tenor the managers picked for stardom; the second was a tenor Harry picked for stardom.

CAMI, the biggest New York management company, was very enthusiastic about a tenor named Ferrucio Tagliavini, whom they were planning to sign to a long-term contract. By 1948 Zelzer Management was called Allied Arts; we were involved then with the Chicago Opera Company where Tagliavini was scheduled to appear in *La Bohème*. Two CAMI managers, Fred Schang and Francis C. Coppicus, flew in from New York for the performance and invited Harry to come with them. I watched his face during the first act of the opera and I could guess what his opinion would be.

When we came out for the intermission after the first act, Schang and Coppicus were waiting for us. "Well?" they asked.

"Pleasing voice," Harry said, "good looks. But just another utility tenor."

We booked Tagliavini for a few seasons. He was big box office at first but he quickly petered out.

Then that summer Herbert Fox of CAMI called Harry to tell him that he had a great tenor he wanted him to hear. The singer was on his way to California but if an audition could be arranged, he would stop off in

Chicago. Harry said he would listen, but he didn't want to be in Chicago during the hot weather. At that time we had a summer home in Kenosha, Wisconsin—about which more later—so he arranged for the audition to be held at Pierpoint, which was the name of our house.

So one Sunday in August Herb Fox and his wife Ulla arrived in Kenosha accompanying the tenor, Mario Lanza and his wife Betty. As usual, our house was filled with guests: Harry's sister Regina was visiting from New York and our friends Sylvia and Ted Levitt were there too. The Lanzas and Foxes arrived in time to join us for a huge Sunday breakfast and a swim. Then we ate lunch. As we sat around with drinks, feeling relaxed and full of food, Harry decided that it was time for Mario's audition. I accompanied him. And what a glorious voice! Harry was deeply impressed.

Then Herb Fox explained that the Lanzas had just been married; they were on their way to Hollywood where Mario hoped to get a break in the movies. They were broke and they needed three hundred dollars for train fare to get to California. Herb Fox hoped that Harry could think of some way to help them out.

Harry was ready to oblige. He called his friend Jack Siegel, a community activist. "I've just heard a magnificent tenor," Harry said to Jack, "a second Caruso. He would really provide first-class entertainment for your organization."

Jack said that as a matter of fact the organization was holding a dinner at the old Morrison Hotel in Chicago the next evening, Monday.

"Good!" Harry said. "I'll give you the privilege of being the first to present the great Mario Lanza and for only three hundred dollars."

Jack Siegel agreed.

For the rest of the day we discussed Mario's future. Harry said that he would present him in an Orchestra Hall concert.

On Monday night Mario sang at Siegel's dinner to great applause. Then on Tuesday he and Betty left for Hollywood. Of course I don't need to say that he became a very popular movie star.

And Harry kept his promise. On April 7, 1951, he presented the singer—who was famous by then—in concert at Orchestra Hall; it was sold out as soon as it was announced. And it was a sensation! Betty Lanza was there with her mother and her sisters. She had asked me how to dress for a serious concert—after all, she had been living in Hollywood! I told her to be chic but simple. I saw her face while she watched her husband from her box seat, and my own eyes filled with tears. She obviously worshipped him. I understood how she felt.

Harry advised Mario to take a leave of absence from films and from Hollywood; he told him he could build a major career for himself if he would take time to learn some repertoire and opera roles. But Mario had tasted big money and he couldn't bring himself to turn his back on that. He wanted what money could buy for Betty, for his children, for his parents.

He was always fun to be with; he was a warm-hearted, good-natured man. He and Harry had a warm relationship—Harry especially enjoyed introducing him to gourmet foods.

Fate played a cruel trick on Mario Lanza, robbing

him of the years in which his great talent could have been really developed and appreciated. He destroyed his health through too much indulgence in the good life and other things, and died young.

VII. OPERA

ARRY and I both loved opera. I had been an opera lover since childhood; my first opera was *Hansel and Gretel*, presented for schoolchildren at the Auditorium Theatre. When I was a music student I took my mother to performances at the Chicago Opera Company where teachers and students could buy tickets for a dollar. My mother would wait outside while I exchanged the two coupons at the box office; I didn't want anyone to notice that she was not really entitled to the dollar ticket. I fell in love with opera and with the Opera House simultaneously.

For four decades, starting with the Chicago City Opera in 1935, we presented opera at the Opera House, the Arie Crown Theatre in McCormick Place, the Civic and Schubert theatres among others, and outdoors at Soldier Field. We brought the San Carlo, the Metropolitan, the New York City Opera, Sarah Caldwell's American National Opera and others as well as local companies. And we put on New Year's Eve galas and arranged the annual opera nights for the Covenant Club.

Before I talk about our experiences with opera, I think I should give some information about the Opera

41

House and the Chicago Music Foundation to provide background for Chicago opera.

ƒ

In 1929, attempting to boost local opera, Samuel Insull and others organized the Twenty Wacker Drive Building Corporation; its purpose was to erect a forty-two story building with an auditorium and office space. The Corporation got a $10 million first mortgage from the Metropolitan Life Insurance Company and issued nearly 100,000 shares of stock, of which over 90,000 was sold to the public for about $9 million. And 101,000 shares of stock were issued and given to the Chicago Music Foundation, a non-profit organization for the advancement of musical art and education in Chicago. The Foundation was also given about ten percent of the total issue of preferred stock.

The trustees had the right to provide education and training in various branches of music—ballet, chorus, orchestra—and in the design, building and decorating of scenery, to establish schools and to create scholarships in these schools or in any schools in any part of the world.

Insull and his associates hoped that the income from this would assure the future of opera in Chicago so that there would be no need to continually urge the public to contribute.

But after the market crashed in 1929, the future was dark for opera in Chicago. No dividends were paid on the preferred stock; the common stock was worthless.

Owen Coon, chairman of the board of the General

Finance Corporation, stepped in with a generous proposal to purchase the interest of the Chicago Music Foundation. The trustees received permission from the state to sell the assets and GFC acquired them in July, 1943. The Foundation got $266,000 and GFC took control of a property worth millions and saved on taxes too. Insull's dream of a permanent Chicago opera company was dead; the Music Foundation's stock was in the hands of men who knew a lot about finance, but nothing about opera companies.

Those stockholders who were not frozen out or persuaded to trade, were given certificates of beneficial interest in a trust which would receive building earnings and the proceeds of the building assets.

On November 30, 1948, the building was sold to Lumbermans Mutual Casualty Corporation. One of the provisions of the sale was that the Foundation would secure a ten-year lease on the Opera House for a period not to exceed eight weeks of each year and that the Wacker Company would not dispose of the considerable scenery, costumes, stage equipment and other opera paraphenalia stored in a specially constructed building at Twenty-sixth and Dearborn.

Opera produced in 1942 had resulted in a deficit of $28,000 of which $21,000 was made up by contributions. The remaining $7,000 was to be considered a proper charge against the trust. The trustees, as lessees, had the privilege of designating in writing the company or companies which would produce or sponsor opera for any given year and the period of the performance. In addition, the trustees, as lessors, had the sole right to produce opera, or have opera produced, in the Opera

House during the ten-year span.

In 1943, '44 and '45 the trustees designated the Chicago Opera Company to produce opera and contributed about $77,000 to liquidate deficits. In 1946 the Chicago Opera Company was designated again, but although the public contributed $30,000 the trustees were asked to come up with the remaining $50,000 of the deficit. They petitioned the court to supply $25,000 which they had on hand and another $25,000 advance on the $125,000 coming from the Wacker Company on the installments due on the purchase balance of $25,000.

Since its 1947 quota had been used to meet the 1946 deficit, the Chicago Foundation issued a statement: "The Trustees of the Chicago Music Foundation in conjunction with the officers and directors of the Chicago Opera Company have devoted constant study and thought to building a permanent resident opera company for Chicago..." But this aim, they said, could not be met before 1948 and the San Carlo Opera Company would be its 1947 designee under the direction of Harry Zelzer and Fortune Gallo.

In September of 1948 Charles Aaron, who was the lawyer for the Citizens Committee for Opera, and who had been the lawyer for the trustees in their suit to dispose of the Foundation assets, enlisted the support of fifty-four leading businessmen and professional men for the formation of a new opera organization. He had roused the enthusiasm of the New York City Opera Company for the idea of coming to Chicago to help form a new opera company; he had the support of the Chicago Music Foundation with its $100,000 capital fund for the building of scenery, for scholarships for promising young singers and for promotion of music and music education and the support also of GFC's Owen L. Coon.

Mr Coon unfortunately died before the plan could be implemented, but his brother Byron helped to provide the guarantee required by the New York City Opera and paid off the deficit of the 1946 season.

The New York City Opera Company, with Laszlo Halasz as artistic and musical director, signed a three-year contract to present twenty-three performances at popular prices of four dollars a ticket plus tax. All the ballet and half of the orchestra would be recruited in Chicago. Halasz reported that the Chicago Music Foundation had $23,000 available for the first year and $30,000 for the next two years. And there would be $30,000 remaining after the expiration of the New York contract. His breakdown of the Foundation's $23,000 for the three-week season included $10,287 for orchestra rehearsals, $2,232 for chorus rehearsals, $515 for ballet rehearsals, $7,500 for preliminary expenses of training staff and $5,000 for managerial and office staff—a total of $25,535.

The assets of the trust were dissipated. The Chicago Music Foundation became a memory.

While all this was going on, James C. Thompson and Herb Carlin decided to book the Opera House themselves; they would deal directly with the companies we had been booking and they would book only one-night stands. Thompson's new rental policy required that Zelzer Management relocate its attractions for the following season. So after ten years at the Opera

House we had to move our presentations to Orchestra Hall.

Soon after we were married, Harry became the business manager of the Chicago City Opera Company, which was headed then by Paul Longone. It was really exciting attending rehearsals, learning scores and being involved with everything. But it was also nerve-wracking—Longone and Harry never knew from week to week if they would be able to raise enough money to raise the curtain. Longone always kept a suitcase packed and ready in case he had to make a quick getaway.

One Saturday afternoon the curtain for the two p.m. performance didn't go up. Harry had invited some friends to this performance and I was sitting with them. Two-fifteen came, then two-thirty. The audience began to grow impatient. Finally, at a quarter of three things got underway. During the first intermission, I caught up with Harry and asked him what the trouble was. He said not to worry, everything was under control. He said there was no money to pay the salaries but he had promised the staff that they would be paid by Monday. I don't remember anything further about that performance. I was too busy worrying. I couldn't imagine how he was going to be able to come up with that money by Monday.

But we were saved by a miracle: Alderman Jacob Arvey gave the Opera Company fifteen thousand dollars in return for a promise that his protégée would sing in the performance of *Lucia di Lammermoor*. She did sing, but unfortunately in the final note of her main aria, her delightful but small soprano voice cracked and that was the end of her operatic career. What a season that was!

The following year—1936—Jason F. Whitney became president of the Chicago City Opera Company; Paul Longone was general manager. On April 2, Mr Whitney wrote to Harry to tell him that the Company was dispensing with his services. The board of directors had asked Mr Whitney to take over the business management of the company to save money. "However," he wrote, "I can assure you that we are very grateful for your wonderful help during the past season and wish to extend...our thanks and...our deep appreciation. Enclosed you will find a check in the amount of one hundred dollars due you for your work during the last week of the 1935-36 season."

As early as 1935 Harry had arranged for the City Council to pay a fifteen-thousand-dollar broadcasting permit to the City Opera for a program called *Opera Theatre of the Air* to be broadcast over radio station WAAF every Sunday from five to seven p.m. Giovanni Cardelli was the general manager, producer, commentator and annotator; Giacomo Rimini was the artistic director; Harry Zelzer was the business manager and Sarah Schectman was administrator. Our intention was to present works, both classical and modern, which were not part of the standard repertoire of major American opera companies, but which were internationally recognized as worthwhile and holding audience appeal. These works were presented in English by carefully prepared young casts. The intensive rehearsals created a freshness and an ensemble discipline that was not possible under the prevailing transient-star system. Our motto was "Opera in Chicago for Opera's Sake." We presented Mozart's *Abduction from the Seraglio*, Puccini's *Tosca* and on Sunday evening, June 1, 1947, the American premiere of Benjamin Britten's *The Rape of Lucretia*, with Paul Breisach conducting. Our cast included Carlos Alexander, Edward Kone, Regina Resnick, Emile Revon, Frank Rogier, Belva Kibler, Alice Howland and Marguerite Piazza.

Unfortunately *Opera Theatre of the Air* lasted for only two seasons.

ƒ

I can't talk about opera in Chicago without mentioning the role played by Fortune Gallo and his San Carlo Opera Company, which was also known as the Dollar Opera Company because one dollar was the top price for any ticket. Gallo was Harry's age and he became a good friend to both of us. I had gotten to know him and the San Carlo while I was still at the Esther Harris School: although the Company was based in New York, it toured the entire United States. Gallo had some superb singers. I particularly remember Armand Tokatyan, and two women who were wonderful Carmens: Winifred Heidt and Coe Glade, the most outstanding Carmen I have ever heard. (No, Gallo didn't do only *Carmen*.)

ƒ

The year 1943 was a significant one both for opera in Chicago and for us. Harry and Fortune Gallo decided to produce outdoor opera in Soldier Field. I've already mentioned the *Aida*. Harry and Gallo also produced *Il Trovatore* and one *Carmen* which I've never forgotten. It starred Jan Kiepura and Gladys Swarthout. For some reason Kiepura and Swarthout were at swords' points all through the performance. Finally at the end of his aria in the smugglers' cave scene, Kiepura picked up Swarthout and literally *threw* her down onto the stage with all his strength.

I remember gasping. It was horrible. I have never seen anyone look so enraged as Swarthout did at that moment, and her anger was certainly justified. She finished the act but she would not take a curtain bow. I rushed backstage. When he saw me, Kiepura said, "I didn't do it on purpose. It was an accident."

"But you did," I said. "I saw you do it."

It was typical of Kiepura that he would want complete attention when he was on stage. Luckily that was a single performance. Swarthout was furious when it was over and I'm sure she would never have done a second performance with Kiepura.

In another memorable Gallo/Zelzer *Carmen*—this time at the Opera House—Micaela was sung by Virginia Pemberton, a local soprano with a very rich husband. In the scene where shots are fired at Micaela, someone in the audience could be heard lamenting, "Too bad they missed her."

Outdoor opera had its own pitfalls, of course. *Il Trovatore* was set for a Sunday evening in Soldier Field. On Sunday morning Monte Fassnacht called us at our house in Kenosha and asked us if we knew how bad the weather was in Chicago. We told him it was really beautiful in Kenosha. He said he was at Soldier Field setting the stage for that night's performance and the winds were so high that nothing could be tacked down; even stronger winds and heavy rains were predicted for later on in the afternoon and evening. He wanted to know whether we should go on with the performance. There was a dilemma: if we cancelled the performance by four p.m., we could give it the following night. But if we didn't cancel and we got rained out before the first intermission, we would have to refund the ticket holders' money *and* pay the cast and musicians as well.

We told Monte to call Fortune Gallo at the Congress Hotel and tell him that we were taking the next train into Chicago. We met Monte and Gallo at Soldier Field and spent the afternoon discussing the situation. Gallo tried to get me to make the decision but I refused; I said the decision was up to him and Harry. Finally they decided to take the chance and go on with the performance. We met with the cast before the opera started and told them that we were going to abolish intermissions and the narrator and that the tempo should be speeded up and the performance raced through as rapidly as possible because the weather report called for heavy rains to begin by ten-thirty.

That was a performance to remember! By the time the first act began, the winds were up and props had to be removed; by the end of that act the winds seemed to be at gale force. The heavy winds and real thunder and lightning created an impressive camp scene. Theo Mc-Coy and I ran from one box office to another to tell the men on duty there to close up so people couldn't come by and ask for refunds.

The opera ended at exactly ten-thirty and as the audience was leaving, the rain began to come down in torrents. We breathed a collective sigh of relief. We had barely escaped a catastrophe—we could not have afforded the loss. That night we celebrated with a champagne supper at which we vowed never to do any more outdoor opera. It was too nerve-wracking. But it had been a wonderful experience all the same.

The Chicago Music Foundation designated Gallo and Harry to produce opera at the Opera House to take the place of the Chicago Opera Company. When the San Carlo Opera Company came for the 1947 season, on October 20 the opening curtain of *La Bohème* was delayed for fifteen minutes. The audience became impatient. Harry was feverishly working behind the scenes to get that curtain up: he had been called earlier, at five-twenty, by James Petrillo, the head of the musicians union, who told him that the forty-three-piece orchestra could not play because James Thompson, the manager of the Wacker Corporation, had locked out the eight-piece band for the performance of *The Late Cristopher Bean* at the Civic Theatre. Thompson's argument was that this was a play, not a musical, and he did not have to pay the band. Consequently the union branded the entire building "unfair to organized labor": if there was to be no band for the play, there would be no orchestra for the opera. Harry presented *his* argument, which was that the orchestra could play because the union had an existing contract with the opera company which would not expire until October 26, the last day of the run.

Finally at ten minutes after eight word came from New York—presumably from Petrillo—that the union had conceded and the performance could go on.

Another labor disagreement occurred during a 1952 performance of the New York City Opera production of *Madame Butterfly*. The New York City Opera had first come to Chicago in 1948 with Harry as Chicago manager, and it came again from 1949 to 1953 and from 1963 to 1965. In 1951 we bought their opening night performances of *Manon* and *La Bohème*.

During *Butterfly* the conductor, Laszlo Halasz, apparently displeased with the orchestra's performance, suddenly threw his baton at the first violinist and concertmaster. It struck the violinist in the face. As a consequence at the next performance James Petrillo was standing at the entrance to the orchestra pit when the musicians were about to file in to perform *Carmen*: he announced that the orchestra would not be allowed to play until Halasz apologized.

"I would apologize," Halasz said. "but I didn't hit him."

For some reason, Petrillo was willing to accept that answer, and the performance went on.

There was another eruption during a New York City Opera performance of *Carmen* in 1953. This time Joseph Rosenstock was conducting. At a dramatically critical moment in the last act. David Poleri, the Don José, suddenly interrupted himself and shouted in English, "Finish the opera yourself!" He stalked off, leaving Gloria Lane, the Carmen, alone on the stage with no one to stab her. Walter Fredericks, a singer who happened to be in the audience, was pressed into emergency service and sang from offstage. The Opera Company fired Poleri.

Harry tried to smooth things over, saying that it was simply a matter of tempo against temperament. Rosenstock wouldn't budge. Harry told the press: "Poleri is one of the few great tenors in the world. We regret the necessity of severing his connection with the company, but the honor of opera demands that discipline be maintained."

But over the weekend Poleri apologized to Rosenstock and to the company and was reinstated.

In that 1953 season Harry announced that the New York City Opera Company had earned $113,101.43 in its thirteen performances: an average gross of $8,750 per performance and $13,000 more than anticipated. Attendance was up almost seven percent over 1952.

No talk about opera is complete without a mention of Maria Callas. Although we never presented her in an opera, we did present her in a concert with an orchestral accompaniment. She required that an orchestra accompany her. This orchestra was to be conducted by Karl Böhm, and the rehearsal was held at Orchestra Hall because the Opera House was not available at the time. After the rehearsal Böhm called Harry from the Drake Hotel. He was very upset; he wanted Harry to come to the Drake immediately. He had to talk to him.

Harry asked him what the problem was.

"I'm not going to conduct the Callas concert," Böhm said. "This woman is impossible. She doesn't stick to tempos; you never know what she's going to do next. And besides the orchestra is scheduled to do only the opening number. I will not be a mere accompanist."

Harry reminded him that he had known from the start that that was the arrangement.

But Böhm was fuming. "I don't care," he said, "I want out. I'm not doing any symphonic numbers. I don't want this concert."

Harry said he would see what he could do about it. I was in the room when he hung up and I asked him what he had in mind. He said that the only one who could get along with Callas, with her tempos, no matter what she did in rehearsal, was Fausto Cleva.

I pointed out that Fausto Cleva was conducting at the Met in New York.

Harry said he would call Rudolf Bing and see what he could do. So he called and explained to Bing that he was in a predicament, and Bing said that Cleva was supposed to conduct the night of the Callas concert, but since he owed Harry a favor he would change the schedule and Harry could have Cleva on that night. And that is what happened. Cleva came to Chicago and conducted the concert. And Callas was on her best behavior: she didn't make any special demands or throw any of the tantrums she was notorious for. It might have had something to do with Harry; a lot of these artists who tried things with other managers were on their best behavior with Harry. They kept their temperament under control while they were in Chicago.

We brought Callas back on another occasion for what was her last concert in Chicago at the Opera House. She and Giuseppe Di Stefano were to appear together. That was another potentially disastrous evening but not because of Callas. In fact, this time she was graciousness personified.

I had barely gotten home to change for the concert when I got an urgent call from Harry.

"Come back to the office as fast as you can," he said. "I need you to type a release for the critics. Never mind why; I'll tell you when you get here."

I knew it had to be something serious so I rushed back to the office.

"Di Stefano is ill," Harry said when I got there. "He can't perform."

"What are you going to do? Who's going to read this announcement?"

Harry said, to my surprise, that Di Stefano would read it. "He's enough of a ham that once he gets on the stage he won't want to get off," Harry said.

And that is what happened. Di Stefano read the announcement and then he said to the audience, "I don't want to disappoint you—I'm going to try and start the performance as scheduled."

He did the opening part of the program. Then Callas did a section. Then they sang some duets. Finally his voice gave out and he couldn't continue. Callas finished the program alone.

$$\int$$

In May of 1950 we brought the Metropolitan Opera Company to the Opera House for the first time. We underwrote the engagement and we were overjoyed that there was a big advance demand for tickets. Interest was so high that afterward the *Tribune* commented:

> ...opera lovers poured $138,684.52 into the Civic
> Opera House box office to attend seven performances of
> the Metropolitan Opera last week. Harry Zelzer, manag-
> ing director of the Allied Arts Corp., sole guarantor of
> the Met's Chicago engagement, was already several
> days into negotiations with the New York company for a
> longer engagement next season.

Harry did not want to hear praise; he disliked being told that he had pulled off a real coup. When people said things like that to him, he leaned back in his swivel chair, frowned until his black eyebrows almost met his Charlie Chaplin moustache and growled, "Don't try to make me a martyr. They kill martyrs. I'm a business-man. I know my customers and all I do is give them what they want." He attributed the big advance to sev-eral factors—among them the fact that it had been sev-eral years since the Met had come to Chicago and that this was the last time it would come under the aegis of Edward Johnson. The repertoire that year included *Tosca* with Ljuba Welitch as Tosca, Alexander Sved as Scarpia and Jussi Bjoerling as Mario. I have never for-gotten that *Tosca*. When Sved threw Tosca on the couch he did it with so much energy that his foot became tangled in her dress and he couldn't get up.

$$\int$$

Rudolf Bing, who was to take over management of the Met, came into town to discuss plans for the follow-ing year, but he came unannounced because he didn't want to distract attention from Johnson's farewell appearance.

We brought the Met to Chicago for seasons from 1951 to '52 and '54 through '58 and in '61 and '62. In order to get them for '52 Harry had to offer them a $100,000 guarantee for one week. And this was in the days of very low ticket prices: in 1954 the main floor went for seven to ten dollars, the balcony from six to eight dollars and upper balcony for four and five dollars.

The *Chicago Daily News* said in an editorial, "A tribute is due to Harry Zelzer, the impresario who brings the Metropolitan Opera Company annually without benefit of guarantors and civic donors. Music is not a business, but the staging of it is, and Chicago is a far richer place musically for Mr Zelzer's willingness to assume these risks."

Harry did not take a risk on the Met only. In 1952, while civic groups were talking about reviving opera in Chicago, Harry produced *Rigoletto* for a New Year's Eve gala at the Opera House, funding it himself without donations or subsidies. He did not want to describe the occasion as a test run for Chicago opera, but he thought that Tulio Serafin, the conductor for that evening, might like to head a Chicago company. Harry estimated that a four-week season would need a guarantee of $150,000. If he, Edward Johnson, the former manager of the Met, and Frederick Chramer, the owner of the Kungsholm Restaurant and its little marionette theatre, could raise that amount, they could put on a four-week season in 1953. Unfortunately this idea fell through, because they were not able to raise the money.

The *Rigoletto*, which starred Uta Graf and Robert Weede, contained another of those unforgettable moments I like so much. This one occurred near the end of the opera when Sparafucile drags poor dead Gilda across the stage in her sack, and dumps her out. Probably because she had felt cramped in the sack, Miss Graf forgot she was supposed to be dead and stretched her legs. This sight was too much for the audience. The tragic ending disintegrated into comedy.

In 1954, from February 5 to 7, *Don Giovanni* was produced at the Opera House by Carol Fox, Betty McAllister, Lawrence Kelly and Nicholas Rescigno. This was Carol Fox's bid to establish an opera company; the bid was successful enough for the group—minus Betty McAllister—to announce a season for 1955. Thus Lyric Opera was born.

At this writing, Lyric Opera is Chicago's official opera company. But along the road there were bitter disputes among Carol Fox, Larry Kelly and Nicholas Rescigno; they finally parted company and Carol Fox became head of the company. Wheeling and dealing, she controlled her board, raised money and, along the way, introduced some great artists and presented some great productions.

Her office was at first next to ours on the second floor of the Opera building. We were not on friendly terms with her. In fact, Harry built a private washroom so we wouldn't have to meet her. He was furious because she had taken C. H. Kirchway, our ticket man and bookkeeper, away from us. And she had no love for us either. We heard that one year, at her company Christmas party, Carol Fox proposed a toast to the de-

struction of Harry Zelzer and Allied Arts. She believed
that anyone who was successful as an entrepreneur in
the music world was depriving her company of funds
which she deserved. In fairness, I must say that she did
not single us out; she felt the same way about the
Chicago Symphony Orchestra.

And yet, when Rudolf Bing resigned as general
manager of the Met, Harry recommended Carol Fox for
the job. I couldn't understand it. But Harry did it because he thought she was better qualified than anyone
else available.

In 1967 Carol Fox cancelled the Lyric season because
of a disagreement with the musicians' union. So Harry
presented Sarah Caldwell's American National Opera
Company in Lyric's place. On October 19, 1967 the
Chicago Sun-Times editorialized:

> This is the time of year when we usually welcome a new
> opera season to Chicago. This year the Lyric Opera
> season was cancelled because of unreasonable demands
> by the musicians' union, but thanks to Harry Zelzer, the
> impresario, the cultural void will be filled with five more
> performances after last night's opening.
>
> The Opera House is coming alive with presentations
> by the American National Opera Company of Puccini's
> *Tosca*, Verdi's *Falstaff* and Berg's *Lulu*. Sarah Caldwell,
> director of the company, will conduct the performance
> of *Falstaff*.

As I write, Lyric Opera is still in existence. It is very
successful, grows more successful every year. Carol Fox
is dead; her former secretary, Ardis Krainik, heads the
company now. I subscribe to the Monday evening series, but I have a long memory, and because of that

Christmas toast, I do not contribute to the Lyric.

The Metropolitan and the New York City opera companies no longer come to Chicago. At present there is no local manager who can afford to bring them here. Both have priced themselves out of the market. We are fortunate to have the Lyric Opera. But it would be good to have the opportunity to hear the great New York companies.

$$\int$$

The Twenty North Wacker Building, the home of the Opera House and the Civic Theatre, is now owned by Dino d'Angelo. The building calls itself a performing arts centre and maintains an agreement with the Lyric Opera. It books its own attractions and gives the impression that it has always been responsible for every presentation that has ever appeared there. No one talks about the fact that Allied Arts Corporation booked outstanding artists and companies. Now this newest regime has mounted a drive for membership to defray the costs of presenting major artists: in other words, they are asking audiences for donations so that the audiences can have the privilege of paying to attend these concerts. I call that a culture tax over and above the price of the ticket.

VIII. FRIENDS AND COMPETITORS

OVER the years we had a fair number of competitors who failed. Harry said that the reason we survived and they didn't was that "they thought the public would like whatever they liked and would dislike whatever they disliked. I, on the other hand, have a fiduciary responsibility to give them what *they* like." He often said, "If the public as a whole will not subscribe, the foundation falters."

Harry valued worthy competition. Although Sol Hurok was not really a competitor in Chicago, he did in New York what Harry did here, and Harry commented that Hurok was "always ahead of me." Hurok had started in 1911, almost twenty years before Harry entered the field. The two men met for the first time in 1930, although in 1926 Hurok had come into the bank where Harry worked to cash a check and had offered the cashier a ticket to the Russian opera. The cashier had suggested Hurok give it to Harry instead and Harry had gone to the opera.

Hurok was arranging extensive U.S. tours for prime artists in the '30s and naturally he looked for a Chicago connection. At that time Zelzer Management was the only organization with enough stature to present

Hurok's artists. For decades we presented ninety-nine percent of them in Chicago. Harry and Hurok's business relationship, which they used to say was "based on friendship and not on franchise" went on until Hurok died in 1975 and after that the relationship continued with the Hurok organization.

Harry called Hurok on the phone every Sunday. If for some reason Harry didn't call him, Hurok would call Harry on Monday morning and say, "You don't talk to poor people any more?" They exchanged gossip, discussed box-office receipts, artists' fees, what the New York agents and their publicity people were up to, and speculated about the future of the concert business and what could be done to stabilize it.

Harry had a lot of admiration for Sol Hurok, who had set out in 1906 to earn his fortune—an eighteen-year-old Russian immigrant with no English and no education, working for three dollars a week—and who, before he died at the age of eighty-five, lived a royal life in a virtual palace on Park Avenue. He was a great influence on American cultural life and the effects of his taste are still felt. Harry said that his death "got as much publicity as King Faisal's...Hurok was just like a German shepherd dog. He would sniff out what people would want to hear." And Harry said that ninety-five percent of the time Hurok guessed right. He especially loved ballet and the artists of his native Russia. He was Chaliapin's first manager—and Harry was the last manager to give the Russian bass a contract, in 1934, although Chaliapin died before Harry could present him.

Harry enjoyed Hurok's sense of humor. He often quoted the older man's comment: "If they don't want to come, you can't stop 'em." Every musician, all the conductors and violinists, wanted to work under Hurok's banner; they knew he would do a good job for them. And Hurok fought against the outrageously high artists' fees which were ruining the business: for instance, he presented groups of artists and not just soloists. That helped make money for a while. But when Hurok died, Harry said, "There will be no more Huroks." He knew the day of the impresario was passing.

To digress for a moment, I want to point out that in the early days there were quite a few local managers throughout the country. In 1948, at least seventy independent impresarios and managers banded together to form the National Association of Concert Managers. Harry was one of the founding members. The organization's purpose was primarily to lower artists' fees, although it also created the opportunity for exchange of information and ideas and the working out of arrangements for block booking. When the NACM was not able to control the fees charged by artists, Harry became disenchanted with it; he said he thought the members were a bunch of dilettantes who wanted to come to New York to party rather than to get things done. But he did not resign from the group. Instead he helped to form another group, the International Society of Performing Arts Administration while keeping his membership in the NACM. The International Society was no more able to control fees than the NACM, however.

As the years passed, there were fewer and fewer independents. By the time Harry retired, he was virtually the only one still operating with his own money.

To return to Sol Hurok: as I said, he was not a

competitor of ours, because he and Harry worked together. And Harry considered Hurok his friend. (Harry often said that he valued a genuine enemy because he could learn from him.) But our real business competitors were mostly people without business acumen or professional know-how. Harry called them "would-be's." And often they had questionable taste. They were attracted, as their modern counterparts still are, to the glamour of the business. And usually they didn't—and don't—last long.

One of the first was Bertha Ott, who had worked with Samuel Insull to present musical events. After the Crash and the collapse of Insull's business in 1929, she tried to continue alone. She concentrated on presenting local talent and arranging debut concerts in various small halls around Chicago—in the Studebaker Theatre, Curtis Hall, Kimball Hall and—very occasionally—Orchestra Hall. She was not really successful and after 1930 was known more as the local correspondent for the old *Musical America* than as a presenter of talent.

Another "would-be" competitor was Grace Denton, who presented many worthwhile attractions at the Auditorium. She had taste and flair, but she lacked business sense, so she was always in financial difficulties. She hoped that an Auditorium concert by Rosa Ponselle, one of the leading singers of the day, would bail her out. Unfortunately, she didn't calculate properly and that concert finished her off. She owed everyone and she had no money to pay them. She turned to us for help. We took her to dinner, listened to her story and Harry told her he would try to help her. All he really could do in the end was try to persuade Rosa Ponselle's manager not to sue Grace. He phoned him and said in effect, Don't waste your money. Even if you win, you won't be able to collect. Harry's practical, down-to-earth manner convinced the man and he didn't sue.

Grace Denton left town after that. Her business was taken over by Warren Thompson and Edgar Goldsmith, who had done publicity and public relations for her. Their organization was called Allied Arts. Thompson had an academic orientation and he planned events in conjunction with the University of Chicago—a "History of Enjoyment of Music" Series, for instance. This was a pre-concert lecture series for which students could receive credit. Allied Arts had half of the business in Chicago; Harry had the other half. Some New York managers tried to use the competition between the two businesses to fuel bidding wars. Harry understood this strategy; Thompson and Goldsmith did not. Harry shrewdly turned down attractions whose fees were out of line with what he knew they would bring in at the box office; he didn't want to sign up an artist who might have an impressive name, but whose booking would cause a financial loss. Some of the managers tried to pressure him by threatening that Allied Arts would book them if Harry didn't.

"Be my guest," Harry said. And Allied Arts did pay the high fees and take the name attractions. It was inevitable that this policy would bankrupt them as it had Grace Denton and as it would bankrupt others in the future. By 1947 Goldsmith and Thompson were, for all practical purposes, finished.

Harry sent J. Charles Gilbert, the manager of the Opera House and the Civic Theatre, to negotiate a buy-out for us. Gilbert didn't tell Thompson and Goldsmith the name of the potential purchaser; all he told them was that he had an interested buyer. Gilbert handled the sale and Allied Arts passed to Zelzer Management for a ridiculously low price. We took over their contracts for the following season and re-negotiated the fees.

Zelzer Management was a private ownership; Allied Arts was a corporation so Harry gradually transferred Zelzer Management into Allied Arts. By 1950 all our business was being done under Allied Arts Corporation. Harry was president and I became treasurer. Harry liked to tell people that after the Allied Arts purchase, "I was *the* Chicago impresario. I incorporated and became the Allied Arts Corporation. My wife—who was once a piano teacher—and I own all the stock." New York managers now had no choice; if they wanted their attractions to appear in Chicago, they had to deal with Harry Zelzer. When we renegotiated the old Allied Arts contracts, the managers had to agree.

In 1959 to 1960, Byron Belt came apparently from nowhere to present a music series which included artists he thought should be given a chance to be heard in Chicago. Calling himself Chicago Concert Management, he booked a vocal series and a Music of the Baroque series into the Civic Theatre. But he didn't make any money, and he soon closed up shop and left town.

Then there was Mrs J. Dennis Freund. She was a competitor on a different level from Byron Belt; she wanted to be a public benefactress, and money was not her primary interest—she didn't care about making a profit or even about covering her expenses. She

founded the Free Concert Foundation to present concerts in Simpson Hall, the auditorium of the Field Mu-
seum, known then as the Chicago Natural History Mu-
seum. She contracted with avant-garde musicians like
Pierre Boulez, before he became a world-renowned conductor, and distributed tickets to students who couldn't
afford the city's professionally-presented events. Mrs
Freund, aware of the appeal which the avant-garde held
for the socially and intellectually prominent, reserved
sections of the hall for special guests. But despite the
policy of free admission, attendance at these events was
underwhelming and the enterprise was dropped after a
couple of seasons.

Another threat to Allied Arts—although not a major
one—was Community Concerts. This was a part of
CAMI administered by Ward French. It operated in the
Chicago suburbs and in communities throughout the
country. Community Concerts would approach a group
of culturally-aware people and suggest that they pull
together a committee to oversee a subscription series—
three to five musical and dance events to be presented
throughout the year. Subscription was the key here;
there would not be single ticket sales at the box office.
There would be performances by a pianist or a violinist,
a singer or singing ensemble, a small instrumental ensemble and/or a small or medium-sized dance troupe,
presented usually in the auditorium of a local high
school. After World War II some high school auditori-
ums were built with good acoustics and the rent for
them was low. The community committee, usually
made up of influential citizens, would volunteer their
services and organize on a tax-free non-profit basis. Of

course, the local media would fall all over themselves to promote the subscriptions which could be offered at bargain prices because expenses were low and the concerts were pre-sold.

These Community Concerts were a boon to the boondocks but a threat to all local managers. Professionals who had to pay the costs of offices, staff, promotion and so on could not compete with these ticket prices. Harry began to fight fiercely against these concerts in the late '40s. He said that this practice could put local managers out of business, and he convinced agents that the entire music field would be badly damaged if there were no local managers to present top artists, world-class musicians. Harry prodded CAMI into allowing him to join with them and help them to organize viable series in the Chicago suburbs in a non-competitive, carefully monitored way.

In 1952, in response to a request for a change in arrangements from Community Concerts, Harry wrote them a letter detailing his relationship with them:

> Sometime during the year 1947, Arthur Wisner [of CAMI] informed me that he had decided to organize all the suburban towns adjacent to Chicago. I at once protested to him that this would be very detrimental to my business in Chicago. Wisner did not pay much attention to my protests and began to organize Community towns in surrounding suburban areas.
>
> I protested Wisner's policy to Mr F. C. Schang II, pointing out to him that places like Evanston and others are just an extension of Chicago and contain the best element of citizens who have been patronizing my attractions. Shortly after my conversation with Mr Schang on this matter, he happened to be in Chicago and arranged a conference with Wisner and myself and the

three of us discussed this matter at length. As a result of this meeting, I entered into an arrangement with Community Concerts to receive five percent commission on all Community Concerts Association's net artist budgets within a twenty mile radius of Chicago.

I was not very happy about this arrangement, because the better class of people then as now were moving out to the suburbs from Chicago in great numbers and the competiton of the low series prices in the suburbs was very unhealthy for my series. However, this was a deal I had to accept under the circumstances. I want to bring out at this point that the compensation of five percent was accepted with the express understanding by both parties that this was a deal as long as Community Concerts Ass'n was doing business in the...area. Upon acceptance of the agreement, Mr Schang said, "Harry, we now consider you an ally."

The five percent payments continued until 1952 at which time I was asked by Ward French at one of our conferences in New York to turn in my original letter in exchange for a letter dated September 22, 1952, calling for seventy-five dollars per month instead.

Since Community came into being in my vicinity, my records show that the subscription business has suffered a fifty percent loss largely due to suburban competition.

I feel that Community Concerts has no moral or legal right to abrogate an agreement entered into in good faith by both parties. I want to point out that any deviation from the agreement by Community Concerts Inc. will not only result in a loss to me, but perhaps a greater loss to Columbia Artists Management.

I am certain you gentlemen are all aware of the hardships existing today for the local manager due to an age of television; no replacements for the names of the past; skyrocketing fees for artists who carry small resemblance to former box-office giants. All these factors have created a constant erosion in our business during the last decade. I believe it is good business on your part to cooperate with the few local managers in the country who are still solvent.

I urge you not to alienate the friendship of a client and an ally of your corporation.

This letter didn't succeed in getting the percentage arrangement restored. Harry accepted the seventy-five-dollar payment which went on until his seventieth birthday when CAMI put him on a small pension.

Despite Allied Arts' base in Chicago, Harry did present events in nearby towns. He wasn't interested in branching out and he didn't want to expand his influence, but he was often invited to arrange concerts for a municipality. Or sometimes an artist or his manager or agent asked Harry to arrange a concert in a midwestern city. During the '40s and '50s, Harry booked concerts in Grand Rapids, Milwaukee and Indianapolis. In Milwaukee the Arion Club, which presented concerts, ran into trouble and asked Harry for help. He entered into an agreement with them and helped them set up a subscription series which he told them would give them stability. I went to Milwaukee to set up arrangements and commuted every week after that to get the project off the ground and keep it on course.

Harry kept up on what was going on in the territory outside Chicago; he knew about the demand for quality music in those communities. Many music lovers were reluctant to travel into Chicago from the suburbs or even from outlying Chicago neighborhoods. To serve these people, Harry booked a mini-series in the auditorium of New Trier High School in Winnetka and in several Jewish temples on the North and South Sides.

ƒ

Harry was helpful too to young inexperienced sales-men from the booking agencies who worked in what may well have been the least glamorous aspects of the business. Harry showed them how to assess the value of the artists they were trying to book; he explained to them that each city had to be studied carefully because what sold in one city might not sell in another. Harry told these men that they should not bleed local manag-ers by asking fees that could not be realized at the box office. And, especially, he explained that loyalty was important: continuity and experience eventually paid off, he said, and it wasn't a good idea to seek new presenters constantly because many an "instant impre-sario" would not last for more than one or two seasons.

Harry did not give these young men advice only. He listened to their problems too and often helped an un-happy salesman move from one agency to another. He always knew what was going on in the business and he could often use his information to help these men find better salaries and more congenial surroundings. His motivation wasn't altogether altruistic: it was also an investment in the future of our business. He created pockets of good will for Allied Arts throughout the concert field.

ƒ

Private entrepreneurs were not our only competi-tors. Managers of concert halls began to produce their own ventures. The Auditorium Theatre, for instance, had been virtually abandoned over the years and had fallen into serious disrepair. Roosevelt University took over the Auditorium building in the late '40s, and Edward Sparling, the University's president, did not want the historic theatre converted to classroom use as the rest of the building had been. He told Harry the theatre was going to be completely renovated and asked him whether he would be interested in moving his subscription series back into it and managing it after it was done over. Harry turned this offer down; he was too independent to tie himself to the management of a theatre and to be forced to report to an employer—in this case the Board of Roosevelt University.

At this point Beatrice Spachner entered the scene. She had been active in presenting Community Concerts in Highland Park and now she set out to rally public support for the renovation of the Auditorium Theatre as a Chicago landmark. She headed the Auditorium Theatre Council which did skilful public relations work for the project: soon the newspapers were filled with articles about the importance of the Auditorium Theatre as the masterpiece of the architects Adler and Sullivan, about its former grandeur, its fabled acoustics.

It was an effective campaign; Mrs Spachner was tireless and dedicated. Money came in and the renovation began. The roof was repaired, seats replaced and the interior cleaned. However, the lobby remained a dark dungeon and there was a mess backstage: the dressing rooms were barely habitable and the bathroom facilities were a disaster—and not just backstage either.

But Mrs Spachner wanted to revitalize the Auditorium in every way. She announced that the theatre was going to revolutionize the concert business in Chicago, offering the best in music and dance—artists and programs not booked by Allied Arts—and at prices low enough for students and anyone who couldn't afford tickets to Orchestra Hall and the Opera House. Mrs Spachner began to raid our artists, paying them enormous fees. CAMI and some other New York managers jumped on her bandwagon. At first even the Hurok office responded to her: Sheldon Gold and Walter Prude of Hurok made some moves in her direction but Hurok called them off, and made it clear to them that he wanted to continue his long association with Zelzer. Years before he had dealt on a very small scale with Edgar Goldsmith and Warren Thompson and later with James C. Thompson and Herb Carlin and his experience had been that his attractions were safest in the hands of Harry's Allied Arts.

Mrs Spachner called Hurok, but he refused to talk to her. And as he had foreseen, the Auditorium operation began to lose money. The Auditorium had attracted renters when it reopened—that is, groups that presented their own programs, schools with large graduation classes, and jazz and rock concerts. As time went on and the expensive concert and dance attractions did not cover their expenses, Mrs Spachner had to rely on these rentals to make up her deficits.

In 1980 Mrs Spachner died, and the Auditorium Theatre Council changed the arrangements so that bookings had to pay their own way. Of course that reduced their number to a minimum. The large attractions were self-producers who merely rented the facility.

Now things are changing again at the Auditorium. The current regime booked *Les Misérables* for a long run in '89 and in 1990 brought in *Phantom of the Opera*. Shows like this put money in the coffers, but they mess up dates for other events and change the direction of the Council.

The Arie Crown Theatre was another competitor. It had been opened in McCormick Place in the '60s—in fact, Harry had opened the theatre with a performance of the Metropolitan Opera Company. And after the disastrous fire in 1967 that destroyed McCormick Place, Harry was also the impresario who presented the show that reopened the rebuilt Arie Crown. The Arie Crown is attractive and it is an excellent house for ballet performances because the seats are built at one and a half steps instead of the usual one step, so the sightlines are very good. However, although the Arie Crown acoustics serve full orchestras, anyone who needs a microphone has a problem there. Singers and string quartets tend to be lost in this large theatre.

Despite these drawbacks, the management of the Arie Crown made an attempt to enter the concert business. Once more the New York managers were intrigued; once more Sol Hurok remained loyal to Harry. Then the Arie Crown turned to show business: the Nederlander organization, which owns chains of theatres and is based in New York, rented the Arie Crown for a number of touring companies for Broadway productions—among others, *The King And I, Annie* and *Peter Pan.* And Nederlander also booked popular entertainers into the Arie Crown who had previously been presented by Allied Arts—people like Liberace, Johnny

Mathis and Victor Borge. Nederlander was able to get them because it did block bookings—that is, booking attractions into all the Nederlander theatres around the country.

The Chicago Theatre also got into the act. In 1987 it was renovated at great cost and opened in a barrage of publicity. But the theatre ran up enormous debts and did not give concerts for more than a couple of seasons. The acoustics are bad in that theatre too. Every two or three months now it is rented out to organizations for concerts, but these are not classical music concerts; they are popular music performances.

By now—1990—almost every hall presents its own series. There are too many concerts being given and too little coordination. So virtually everyone involved in these presentations loses money.

IX. A TYPICAL DAY AT ALLIED ARTS

E VERY morning Harry left for the office at six-thirty. During the years we lived at the Bismarck Hotel, he would stop off at the Bakery there and buy rolls and coffee cake for the staff. He was at his desk by seven-thirty.

Thelma, our switchboard operator, arrived at nine and the rest of the staff—Earline, Shirley, Michelle, Gail—came in about nine-thirty, and Harold and Martha about ten, because they had worked late the night before and would probably be working late again the rest of the week. I usually got to the office between ten and ten-thirty

Between seven-thirty and nine a.m. Harry would concentrate on studying box-office intakes, promotional ideas and calls to New York managers at their homes. This was hard on the managers' wives. They pleaded with me to tell my husband not to call so early in the morning. It was no use. Harry insisted that his best deals were made with the managers before they arrived at their offices.

The staff were busy opening the mail and recording intake on each attraction—we kept a daily tab on the mail orders. Then Harry would make a decision about placing ads for the week based on the intake report. I typed and mailed press releases to the newspapers—confirmation of artists' arrivals, details of hotels where they were staying, etc. I would check rehearsal times with the theatres, proofread programs, check delivery times for programs and for pianos, if necessary, set up appointments for piano tuning, and make decisions about the mailing of circulars to various lists.

At eleven a.m. Harry would send out our errand boy to pick up lunch for everyone—no one ever went out for lunch. Every day gourmet lunches were brought in and while they ate, staff would answer the phone, wait on customers who preferred to come to the office to buy advance tickets rather than go to the box office. That was good for the customers—they enjoyed talking to the staff and it was good for us because it helped us learn the customers' preferences and complaints. There was a good relationship between the office and the ticket-buyers.

Harry ate lunch in his private office and he usually invited someone to share it with him. Sometimes it was a social lunch hour, sometimes it was a business lunch. When that was over, Harry would take a nap on his brown leather couch. During that time all his calls were transferred to me.

After his nap, Harry's phone was glued to his ear. He was talking to "Bill"—William Judd of CAMI—or "Max"—Marks Levine of NCAC (National Concert Artists' Corporation)—or other managers, shopping for artists in New York, our source of supply. To plan a series of concerts, he had to maneuver dates, artists, fees, like an expert chess player. His annual budget for artists was the largest in the country for a manager of a single city.

He didn't put his preferences on the Series or the critics' preferences, but what he knew the public would like. He would have been happy listening all day to Bach, but he knew the public's taste did not run in that direction. The Series began with pillars of the music and dance community—Rubinstein, Serkin, Brendel, Heifetz, the Philadelphia Orchestra, the New York Philharmonic, Flagstad, Schwarzkopf, the Jooss Ballet, the American Ballet Theatre, the Bolshoi Ballet—and then newcomers. Outside the Series—Mantovani, Borge, opera companies, Toscanini and so forth.

The public was slow to accept new talent.

At four-thirty in the afternoon the day's reports were handed to Harry—cash intake from ticket sales and the totals from benefit and group sales. After five o'clock, when things quieted down, tickets were sent out to mail-order customers. But the phone kept ringing. No matter how late we stayed in the office, ticket buyers would call for information. Our office was open until ten or ten-thirty and sometimes even later on evenings when attractions were running, because we worked with managers drawing up statements for ballet and opera runs.

Some days were taken up with battles with unions—the stagehands' union, the box-office union. There was never a dull moment. Everybody had to be continually alert to make sure that everything was in place for a perfect performance. Sometimes we had more than one performance on one day. One weekend I remember there was a ballet run at the Arie Crown Theatre, a ballet at the Opera House, a concert at Orchestra Hall and a duo piano concert at the Studebaker Theatre.

Harold, Martha and I ran from theatre to theatre, making sure that house programs had been delivered, checking box-office statements at intermission. We were all tense and naturally felt great relief when each performance ended with no casualties.

Then the morning after the performances we were busy reading the critics' reviews, re-checking box-office statements and then back to the routine for next week's presentations. We were the Allied Arts family, led by Harry, and we were dedicated to keeping culture alive in Chicago. Our personal lives came second; we gave as much attention as we could to the attractions and to the ticket-buyers. Harry was always there to hear the troubles of each member of the staff and to lend them money when they needed it.

It was a wonderful staff, day in, day out.

HZ in Baldwin, Long Island in 1913.

HZ in the lobby of the Civic Opera Building.

SSZ at the piano.

Above: Marta and Jan Kiepura.

SSZ and HZ.

(Maurice Seymour)

HZ at the box office
of the Civic Theatre.

This Performance
Sold Out

HZ at Pierpoint, 1938.

(Dr Max Thorek)

Lily Pons

Grace Moore in 1934.

Lily Pons and Andre Kostelanetz; from their Christmas
card in 1938.

"...another in a series of souvenirs of First Ladies of Music..." from
Humphrey Doulens' Christmas card; (l to r) Gladys Swarthout,
Jeanette MacDonald, Lily Pons and Grace Moore.

Nelson Eddy

SSZ and Judy Garland in Chicago.

Judy Garland with her husband, Sid Luft, and HZ.

HZ and Mischa Elman.

Edward Johnson with HZ in May, 1950.

Maria Callas with Giuseppe Di Stefano in the 1960s.

Jussi Bjoerling clowning around with HZ.

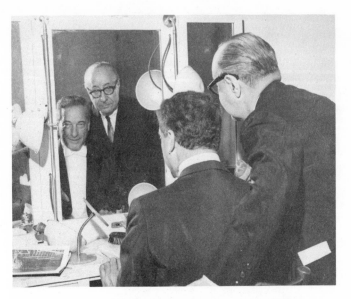

Victor Borge and HZ before a concert in the 1950s.

To Harry and Sarah Zelzer — I just don't know two more wonderful friends in the world — The very best of everything in life always from

Mario Lanza

Mario Lanza

Maurice Chevalier and HZ.

HZ and Serge Jaroff of the
Original Don Cossack
Chorus.

HZ and Ezio Pinza score a big hit.

Tito Schipa, 1938.

Arthur Fiedler and HZ.

X. HARRY'S HANDS-ON STYLE

THE '50s and '60s were golden decades for us; the first twenty years had been the hardest but all that work was rewarded. The biggest reward of all, for Harry, was Allied Arts' presentation of Arturo Toscanini and the NBC Orchestra at the Opera House on May 17, 1950. From his earliest professional days, Harry had dreamed of three-sheets that read, "Harry Zelzer Presents Arturo Toscanini." There were only a few names on Harry's list of "the greatest of the great"; there were Caruso, Kreisler, Elman...and the name of Toscanini, who was eighty-three in 1950, was at the top.

The words "Presented by Allied Arts; Harry Zelzer, President" constituted a magic entry to the concert world. This was brought to the attention of the public by Roger Dettmer, the music critic for the *Chicago American*, in his column for April 26, 1959.

> While anyone today can give a concert here, in the hall of his choice, under any of several managements, it's a fact of musical life that few artists have any Chicago box-office power without support from one or another of Harry Zelzer's package series. It is a rare artist who can ignore Mr Zelzer and make it pay these days. A number have tried, almost the exact same number have failed.

Although his contracted artists came first, Harry tried to help self-produced artists as well. These are performers who are not presented by an impresario with a contract, but whose personal agent has rented a theatre and attempted to act as manager. Often these agents would ask us to supervise the engagement, providing advice and dealing with sticky chores like arrangements with stagehands and the musicians' union, seeing to transportation of properties and similar things. Most of the ballet companies relied on us to oversee things in Chicago; they had faith in Harry's expertise.

Harry had a "hands-on" style. He threw himself into everything and had a lot of fights: he fought the unions—musicians, stagehands, teamsters—about outrageous charges and irritating rules. He fought with the artists' managers about excessive fees. And he fought with critics. He thought that he knew at least as much as any critic, and he felt his taste was more reliable than theirs. "We're interested in the public," he used to say. "Critics are not. I call them the wrecking crew because instead of building an audience, they tear it down. A critic once told me, 'If there ever is an apocalypse, you'll present it.' And I said, 'If I do, you'll pan it.' Critics very often don't like an artist the public adores and then they review the public as well as the artist. Maybe this is sour grapes on their part. Or maybe they use it as a tactic to hold onto their self-imagined importance. Someone should review *them*. History is full of misjudgments and stupidities they have come up with; some very entertaining books list them.

"My favorite story concerns Paderewski when he

first came to America. He gave a concert in Carnegie Hall. There were few people and he got a bad write-up. This didn't scare him; he resolved to make good. He talked Steinway into giving him another concert. This time the audience was double the first. Eventually he played to sold-out houses and the critics changed their minds and decided he was a great pianist."

This makes me think of the time we had Liberace here for two performances. The pianist was not flamboyant in his private life, but he knew that showmanship paid off at the box office and he knew how to put on a good show. Claudia Cassidy, the *Tribune*'s music critic, really hated his concert and reviewed it in acid.

The next day Liberace said to me, "Mrs Z, I'm going to make an announcement right before the intermission, and I want you to be sure and be in the theatre so you can hear it."

This made me more than a little nervous, but I made sure I was there.

Just before the intermission, Liberace addressed the audience: "Ladies and gentlemen, I'm glad we have a full house tonight in spite of the review in the *Tribune*. I want you to know that it really didn't affect us—Harry Zelzer and I cried all the way to the bank."

That was the real origin of what has become a legendary phrase.

Chicago critics had a national reputation for being tough. Some artists actually stayed away from Chicago because of the critics—many, like Nelson Eddy, for instance, suffered terribly from the reviews. And there were those who wanted to sue. Arthur Rubinstein was one.

In March of 1951 Claudia Cassidy reviewed an Allied Arts Rubinstein concert. "It was as if," she wrote, "he tucked us absentmindedly into a busy schedule, rushed into town, glanced hastily at the 'by request' program, played it briskly with some startling areas of monumental bluffing, collected his check, and galloped off again."

The morning after the review appeared Sol Hurok called Harry. "You'd better talk to Rubinstein before he leaves," he said. "He wants to sue the *Tribune* and Cassidy."

Harry immediately got Arthur Rubinstein on the phone.

"Listen," he said to him, "you're not going to gain anything fighting the *Tribune*. What the hell's the difference what she said? You've been booked every year. You're coming back next year. Leave it alone."

Fortunately for everybody, Rubinstein took this advice. Basically, he was a very amiable man; he rarely gave us any problems. But he did give us more than a few gray hairs because he never arrived at Orchestra Hall more than a minute before his performance. If it was a three-thirty concert, he made his appearance at three-twenty-nine.

Harry asked him why he always waited until the last minute.

"Because I like to come up and go right on," he said. "I don't want to warm up or hang around backstage. If I do that, I get nervous."

He was always kind to young artists. He gave Willi Kappell a lot of help when Willi was starting his career. And of course Janine Fialkowska—in many cities he would not agree to give a concert unless the presenter booked her also. We would not do that. We did present her later, but we would not do it under pressure.

The last concert that he gave for us nearly wasn't. He wanted to cancel it because he had begun to lose his sight.

"You can't cancel," Harry said to him. "You've got a sold-out house."

"But I can't see, Rubinstein said.

Harry said he had a solution. (My husband always had a solution.) "We'll change it to an all-Chopin program. You know Chopin by heart. You don't even have to see the keyboard."

Rubinstein agreed to try this. He did the all-Chopin program, and it was a sensational success.

We operated on the principle of "balance the artists to balance the books." The sellouts—Mantovani, Johnny Cash and Arthur Fiedler's Boston Pops, for instance—helped to carry chamber music and lieder recitals. I don't know whether Harry was the first to offer arranged series to subscription audiences, but he made that innovation the cornerstone of his marketing plan; he demonstrated its value to successful business. It provided stable, predictable audiences and it gave these audiences definite dates and savings over single admission tickets. We offered special interest series: Lecture, Music, Dance, Guitar, Travel, Folk, and ethnic events. And then we had mixed-style series, like our Saturday night Zelzer Series which included Pop concerts and which we continued for a couple of seasons after we bought Allied Arts Corporation, with a different mixture of programs.

Our Piano Series, which presented, over the years, everyone worth hearing, existed because Harry felt it should be done to help pianists. We presented talented young artists as well as established pianists; some of the young ones were debuts and most of those lost money. It took us a few years to build the Young Pianists Series, partly because we sold the tickets very cheaply, but we wanted to enable students to attend and to attract music lovers venturesome enough to give novices a hearing. Harry would say to me, "If I book some of these pianists on our Series, the people west of Chicago will book them too and that will give them a chance to make a living." There were many local managers then who always watched what Harry was booking. And there was our Society of American Musicians Contest: we always put the winner on the Piano Series, giving him or her a free concert at Orchestra Hall. And we paid the pianists for it; we never expected them or anyone else to do anything for nothing.

Harry never considered a box-office deficit on a worthwhile event to be a real loss because the public profited. Of course, on the other hand, he didn't make a habit of losing money on "good music". It was Harry who decided who he was going to book for the Series. Of course he talked to me about it; he might ask my opinion and some of my recommendations might eventually rub off on him, but it was his show basically. Many nights very late—about three o'clock—Harry would say to me, "Come on, I've opened a bottle of champagne and put the caviar on the table. Let's talk." We never shared these talks with anyone else, and if something didn't work out that I had expressed doubts about, I never said, "I told you so," because I knew how much he wanted to help these musicians and especially the pianists.

XI. RELATIONS WITH
SOME FAMOUS ARTISTS

AFTER we moved our offices to the Civic Opera Building, we went on presenting events in Orchestra Hall and the Eighth Street Theatre in addition to the Opera House and the Civic Theatre. In those early years we presented, among many other attractions, the New York Philharmonic, the Vienna Boys' Choir, the Kurt Jooss Ballet, Lincoln Kirstein's Ballet Caravan, Jascha Heifetz, Mischa Elman, Grace Moore, Nelson Eddy and Jeanette MacDonald, Martha Graham, Carmelita Maracci and the Minneapolis Symphony Orchestra conducted by Eugene Ormandy.

We presented Eugene Ormandy for the first time on January 23, 1936. That concert has remained in my memory for three reasons, two of them having to do with radio. The weather had turned cold; it was about twenty below zero, and radio announcers were warning people not to leave their houses. The announcement was also being broadcast that Ormandy had been chosen to take over the Philadelphia Orchestra, which was quite a feather in his cap.

In those days it was customary to dress for concerts. I sat in the front row, in a long dress, and I applauded like mad. Afterwards we went backstage. Ormandy came up to me, gave me an appraising look and said, "Oh, you're the one. You were sitting in the first row."

"That's right," I said.

At that time he was still married to his first wife, who was one of the musicians in the orchestra and who had a reputation for being rather jealous. I felt her eyes on me all the while Ormandy and I were talking; it made me feel uncomfortable.

The orchestra left town the next morning and a few days later I got a letter from Eugene Ormandy in which he said he had left an autographed picture for me; he had tried to look us up in the phone book but he couldn't find us—we weren't listed in those days—so he had left the photograph in the receiving room of the Congress Hotel.

We brought Ormandy many, many times over the years. He always took Harry's advice about programs and audiences. If he was considering playing this or that, Harry would tell him whether it suited the audience. On one occasion, he was giving a concert in Evanston and he thought he would give the same program he was giving in Chicago. Harry advised him against that. "What you play in Evanston is one thing," he said to him. "What you play in Chicago is another. They're two different audiences." Ormandy substituted a lighter program for Chicago.

Artists took Harry's advice because they felt he knew what Chicago audiences would like to hear. Sometimes, when we had sold-out houses for benefits, for example, Harry would tell the artists what to play, and the sensible ones listened to him. Often they took his advice about other things as well. For instance, I remember that in the early years of her career, when Elisabeth Schwarzkopf was staying at the Bismarck Hotel where we were living at the time, she borrowed my iron so that she could get a couple of dresses ready to show Harry; he was going to pick the one she would wear for the concert. Elisabeth became the personification of elegance when she was established, but I will always remember that afternoon.

Jascha Heifetz

Heifetz was another artist who always accepted Harry's suggestions for a program. If Harry told him to change something, he changed it. I never got to know Heifetz well; I was always a little in awe of him. We presented him year after year. He was always polite, always pleasant, but remote, almost impersonal. Heifetz and Harry respected each other: Harry of course recognized Heifetz's artistic eminence and Heifetz knew Harry's expertise and professionalism. He always praised Harry to the tour management and commented that all local managers could learn from Harry.

In 1947 the Heifetz concert was scheduled for the Opera House. Whenever Heifetz arrived in Chicago he always called us to tell us where he was staying. This time he told Harry that Mrs Heifetz had come with him to Chicago for the concert; Harry invited the couple to dinner and they accepted. At that time Hiefetz was married to Florence Vidor, the silent-movie actress. She was one of my idols. I had seen all her films; she had been my ideal of what an "older woman" should be. (When I was young I considered any female over the age of twenty-five to be "an older woman".)

After the concert we went backstage to ask the Heifetzes whether they wanted to go back to the hotel before dinner. I was tingling with excitement: I was going to meet Florence Vidor in person! But meeting her was a disappointment. She was aloof, cold to well-wishers and annoyed by the autograph seekers. Heifetz, cordial as usual, said they would meet us at the restaurant.

And thank goodness, in the intimate atmosphere of the restaurant, Mrs Heifetz was a changed woman. Gone was the coolness she wore as an armor in the midst of a crowd. At dinner in the Sarong Room she was relaxed, friendly and gracious—a delightful companion. The Sarong Room featured East Indian food and Balinese and Javanese music and dance; it was operated by Tony Malevitch, who managed a troupe of Bali-Java dancers headed by Devi Dja. We had presented the troupe in concerts; they were on tour when the war broke out and they were consequently stranded, so they opened the Sarong Room.

That evening in honor of our party they presented both special food and a special program. The Heifetzes were pleased with both the dinner and the performance.

After dinner Harry and Heifetz excused themselves and moved to an adjoining table to discuss business. Mrs Heifetz and I had our fortunes told by a resident fortuneteller and after that we had a relaxed, intimate talk. Florence Vidor said she had real problems when her husband was on tour: when she stayed home with the children, she worried about him, and when she joined him on tour, she worried about the children. She was a devoted wife and mother, and I admired her for that.

Later, when we got home, Harry told me about the business discussion. Heifetz, it seemed, wanted a higher fee, but he felt shy about bringing it up. When he heard mention of more money, Harry got nervous: he thought his model artist was going to ask for an exorbitant amount.

Heifetz made a logical argument. He said, "If you had a file clerk working for you for as many years as I've been working under your management, you would certainly agree it was time for a raise, wouldn't you?"

"How much are you talking about?" Harry asked cautiously.

"Two hundred and fifty dollars."

"Agreed," said Harry.

What a contrast this presents to current conditions in the performing arts, where every contract provides an occasion for unreasonable demands. Here was one of the greatest violinists of our century—not greedy, making a reasonable request of a local manager. Year after year Heifetz returned under our management.

During the Korean War, there was much movement westward and travel conditions were difficult. Before one of his Chicago concerts, Heifetz called Harry to ask for a favor: could we possibly get a train reservation for a friend of his who was leaving Chicago for Los Angeles after the concert? Last minute reservations were impossible to get in those days but Harry was able to secure one through his connections. After the concert, which was held in Orchestra Hall, I found out who Heifetz's friend was.

I was on the deserted stage talking to Emanuel Bay, Heifetz's accompanist; suddenly a woman who had been pacing back and forth came up to Bay and began to criticize the performance. I thought she had a lot of nerve. Then in a flash I realized that she was the "friend" for whom Harry had gotten the train reservation. Later when Heifetz and Florence Vidor were divorced, the violinist married this woman, whose name was Frances.

Some three years after that first encounter, Harry and I had dinner with Heifetz and the new Mrs Heifetz. I decided that my first impression of her had been correct: she was an officious, outspoken woman. Of course I resented her because I liked Florence and Frances was very different from her. Heifetz had a son with Frances; there was a lot of publicity about this child, far more than about Florence Vidor's two children by Heifetz. But time passed. There was another divorce. Frances, too, left the scene.

Once Heifetz came in town a day early and expressed a desire to see Carol Channing in *Gentlemen Prefer Blondes,* then playing at the Palace Theatre. I had already seen the show, but of course we bought the tickets without telling Heifetz that; he might have insisted on going elsewhere just to be polite. We had dinner at the Bismarck Hotel and then went to the Palace, which was next door. The musicians in the pit recognized Heifetz and gave him a standing ovation. He thanked them.

After the show we stopped for coffee at the Swiss Chalet. Heifetz turned to me. "Confess!" he said. "You've seen this show before."

I admitted that I had, but I said I had really enjoyed it this second time too. The next day I received a dozen long-stemmed red roses from Heifetz, with his thanks for a lovely evening.

Jascha Heifetz understood the problems faced by local management. There was the time, for instance, when Marian Anderson cancelled one of our concerts because of a sore throat. Heifetz had a concert scheduled for the next afternoon. But not until it was over did he tell me that he was going right back to his hotel and get into bed; he was running a 102 temperature. He had gone on despite his illness because he knew we had suffered a loss in the Marian Anderson concert and he did not want to add to our woes. Despite his health he gave a glorious concert. Of course, probably predictably, his wife Frances complained that he should not have jeopardized his health just out of consideration for us.

In 1956 at what was to be his last concert, we noticed the first signs of his failing health. As he was playing, just before intermission, he paused suddenly, holding the bow in midair. It lasted an instant only, and no one realized that anything was wrong. He finished the piece. But the intermission was unusually long. I hurried backstage to find out what was happening. Dr Maurice Cottle, a close friend of both Heifetz and Harry, had rushed off to his office to get his medical bag. After thirty minutes, the violinist felt strong enough to resume his concert and he finished it with his usual perfection. Although we squelched the inevitable rumors that followed this concert, we believed that this was an early warning of heart trouble.

When Heifetz returned to New York, we heard from Bill Judd of the tour management, that he was not going to tour any longer. What a loss that was to the world of music!

After Harry died, there was some talk that Heifetz might come out of retirement to give a concert in Chicago in Harry's memory. Unfortunately, Heifetz himself died before that pleasant possibility could be realized.

Grace Moore and Other Snobs

Grace Moore was a talented, good-looking soprano with a svelte figure; she was a definite improvement over the portly opera stars of her day. Throughout the 1930s, Gracie, as she was called by all who knew her, was a member of a concertizing quintet that included Frances Yeend and George London. Then she starred in the popular film *One Night of Love* and became an overnight box-office sensation.

I was still giving piano lessons at that time. One day Harry's secretary was out and he asked me to take his phone calls because he had an important meeting outside the office. Of course I agreed to help, but only until three o'clock when my first lesson was scheduled.

The phone rang at twelve-thirty. It was a woman's voice, asking for Harry.

"Who is this?" I asked.

"Grace Moore," she said.

It was true that Harry had scheduled her to sing a solo concert in Orchestra Hall. It was our slow season and we needed the money from what would be a sellout. But the Chicago papers had reported a few days earlier, to our great dismay, that she was ill and had cancelled her concerts in the South. I decided this call was someone's idea of a joke, but I answered her politely. "Mr Zelzer won't be back until two o'clock. Can he return your call?"

"Yes," she said. "I'm at the Blackstone. I want him to take me over to Orchestra Hall to check the facility."

"But I thought you were ill," I said.

"Well, I'm not, I'm here. Give Mr Zelzer my message when he returns."

She banged the receiver down in my ear. I was in a state of shock. I counted the minutes until Harry came back. He immediately called her at the Blackstone and arranged to meet her at Orchestra Hall. It turned out that she was in excellent health: she had cancelled the concerts in the South because she just hadn't felt like singing them. Two evenings later she must really have felt like singing again, because she gave a wonderful concert for us. It was the first of Grace Moore's engagements in Chicago under Zelzer Management, a relationship marked by splendid performances and erratic incidents.

By the summer of 1940, when we booked her into Grant Park where she drew a tremendous crowd, Gracie had developed into a nasty, temperamental star. At her last concert for us she insulted her accompanist to the point where he left the stage. Jussi Bjoerling and his wife Ana Lisa were our guests at that debacle. After the performance Harry suggested that we go backstage—the usual custom at such occasions. Jussi would not go. He said he could not honestly tell Gracie that it was a good performance and he refused to lie. So Harry, always gallant to his artists, went alone, and we waited for him. When he returned, he told us that Gracie had invited him and Jussi to have dinner with her and Mrs Charles B. (Bobsie) Goodspeed, a local socialite, at the Blackstone Hotel. Obviously neither Ana Lisa nor I was included. Ana Lisa was not happy about this, and she told her husband he should not join them.

As usual, Harry had a diplomatic solution. We walked together the short distance from Orchestra Hall to the Blackstone and we waited in the lobby while Harry went to meet Gracie. He explained that he was with his wife and the Bjoerlings. Gracie made no attempt to include his whole party. Instead she asked him to have a drink with her and Bobsie. Harry declined politely and returned to us.

Bobsie was just as rude as Gracie. In May, 1950, we were presenting the Metropolitan Opera: the Women's Board of the Cancer Research Foundation was sponsoring a performance of *Salome* starring Ljuba Welitch who was also appearing in an Orchestra Hall concert a month earlier. The benefit committee of the Foundation decided that the Welitch concert would offer a good opportunity to hold a press conference and a cocktail party to announce the Foundation's participation in the opera season.

Bobsie Goodspeed hostessed the cocktail party; Harry promised that Ljuba Welitch would attend. Mrs

Walter Wolf, a dear friend of ours who was president of the Women's Board of the Foundation, said she would meet us at Bobsie's apartment after the concert. I told her that only Harry had been invited, despite the fact that our party included the Arthur Wisners and Ward French of Community Concerts, who had flown in from New York for the concert and who had booked Welitch. Ward French was furious at the snub; he felt that if our party wasn't invited, then Welitch shouldn't attend the party either.

Harry, who had promised the committee that she would appear, thought of a solution. He and Ljuba would appear briefly at the cocktail party and meet us half an hour later at Jacques' restaurant. We were skeptical, but we went on to Jacques. Twenty minutes later Harry and Ljuba joined us. What had happened? Harry had whisked the singer into the Goodspeed apartment, and told Mrs Goodspeed that his wife and Miss Welitch's managers, who had not been invited to the party, were waiting for them for dinner. "I promised you Ljuba Welitch," he said. "Here she is. And now goodbye." They politely withdrew.

Gracie always carried a hot plate and coffee pot with her on tour. Hotel managers were not happy with her: she invariably blew fuses in the hotels she stayed in; when she was threatened with eviction, she always promised not to use her "instant kitchen". But of course the next day another fuse would be blown.

Gracie had her good points: she was not an ungenerous person. Dorothy Kirsten was her protégée: a young girl with a good voice. Gracie helped Dorothy, who copied her mentor right down to her bitchiness toward the wives of local managers. Fred Schang of CAMI, who had been Gracie's personal manager, took Kirsten under his wing and got her a contract at the Met.

Humphrey Doulens, a publicity man for CAMI, often traveled with Gracie. Once, when they were in New Orleans, Gracie said she had heard a lot about the city's red-light district and she wanted to see it. She gave no peace to Humphrey and her accompanist until they hired a car and drove there with her. Her curiosity was only whetted by the sight of the street: she insisted that the two men go inside a house and give her detailed reports of their experiences. They weren't too happy about this assignment, but finally they agreed to go inside. What followed, Gracie would have confided only to Humphrey Doulens. Gracie waited, prowling up and down the street. She spotted a pretty young girl standing in a doorway and went up to her.

"How's business?" Gracie asked.

"How can it be," the girl said, "when someone like you is giving it away free?"

Gracie was very quiet on the trip back.

Grace Moore was killed in a plane crash in 1947. Although I was obviously not fond of her, I was saddened that her brilliant career had been cut short in that brutal way.

Nelson Eddy

Nelson Eddy, an American-trained baritone/concert artist/movie idol, was an even bigger star than Grace Moore. When he appeared in Chicago under our management, as he did from the early '30s to 1949, his concerts were always sold out; there was an atmosphere of wild excitement. His audiences, mostly women of all ages, worshipped him; the critics, however, were never very kind to him, which hurt his feelings. Harry always told him not to pay any attention to the critics; "The audience," he said to him, "is the important thing. You've made millions happy. They worship you. That's real success."

And his admirers were truly devoted. Once a young fan came up to our office to buy a ticket for his concert: the top price for a seat on the main floor at the Opera House was three dollars and thirty cents. She gave us the money in pennies. While everyone was watching her counting them out, she said, "I've saved two years to buy this ticket. I could only do it by throwing my pennies into a jar; I just have to hear him."

"That's okay," I said soothingly. "Don't worry about it, dear."

"This is all the money I have," she said. "I don't have carfare home. But it's worth it."

She said she lived on the South Side. Of course I gave her the bus money to get home.

For years a woman and her nurse followed Nelson from city to city on his tours. When they came to Chicago they stayed at the Bismarck Hotel, where we were living. One night Harry struck up a conversation with them in the dining room; he was curious about why they followed in Nelson's footsteps like that. The woman, whose name escapes me, said that his concerts gave her pleasure, a basis for fantasizing, a reason for being alive.

When Harry asked her if she would like to meet Eddy, her reaction can be imagined. Harry said he would arrange it; we would be having dinner with Nelson and his manager the next evening in the Bismarck restaurant at seven o'clock. He would introduce her to the singer.

Harry told Nelson about it; he agreed to be a good sport and make these women happy.

The next night we gathered for dinner. The women weren't there. We ate, talked, and sat for a while waiting. The women did not come.

The next day we saw the companion. She said that her employer had become hysterical with excitement and could not go through with the meeting.

A similar thing happened later. Before every Eddy concert in Chicago we received an anonymous gift of a delicious chocolate cake which we had for dessert at our post-concert suppers. Nelson always joked that I should taste the first piece in case someone was trying to poison him. After a few years we discovered the identity of the cake donor: our daughter Harriet hired a nurse when her second son was born, and when this woman found out about Harriet's relationship with us, she revealed that she had been sending these cakes to our office for Nelson Eddy each time he appeared here. I offered the nurse a ticket for the next concert and told her to meet me at the box office afterward and I would take her backstage to meet her idol. She was really excited and I felt certain she would take especially good care of our grandson.

I waited after the concert to take her to Nelson, but she didn't show up. It must have been another case of hysteria.

Nelson thought these things were funny. "You see what I do to people?" he said. One evening while we were having dinner, two girls came to our table to ask for his autograph. I was sitting next to him and one of them turned to me. "Mrs Eddy," she said, "do you enjoy living in California and do you have a hard time buying stockings?" It was during the war when nylons were scarce.

I opened my mouth to say that I was not Mrs Eddy, but I felt Nelson kicking me under the table. I said I loved living in California and I could get nylons occasionally.

When they left I asked Nelson why he had done that.

"Why not make them happy?" he said. "They're happy thinking they met my wife. And it's okay for you—anyone would be glad to be mistaken for my wife."

"Maybe," I said, "but I'd rather be known as Harry Zelzer's wife."

Although I liked Nelson and admired his singing, I wasn't ga-ga over him.

But he certainly captivated his audiences. Critics or no critics, he was a great artist. I still get a thrill when I watch his old movies on TV and I miss the excitement of his concerts: the near-hysteria of his fans waiting for hours backstage afterward at the Opera House to catch a glimpse of him or to touch him. We would take him up to our offices on the second floor of the Opera House and then leave through the building entrance away from the fans and go to the Bismarck for our late snack. Once Harry and I went back to the Opera House after supper, just for the fun of it. It was two in the morning, but there were still people waiting. Harry told them to go home; Nelson Eddy had left hours ago. "But come back next year," Harry said. He gave them the date of the next concert.

For some reason, Nelson Eddy gave up his concert tours in the '50s and went the nightclub route. We caught his act when he appeared at the Palmer House and he had the same Eddy charm. I have precious memories of the concerts, the dinners, the laughter. They are unique and I will always cherish them.

XII. JUDY GARLAND

I N July of 1958 Harry got a call from Sid Luft, Judy's husband and manager; he wanted Harry to present her in concert at Orchestra Hall during the first week of September. Harry had never seen Judy Garland movies and knew very little about her. I, on the other hand, had admired her for years and I told Harry I thought she would be a terrific draw.

He called New York while he was trying to decide. Some of the managers there told him not to get involved with that project. They told Harry that Judy had a lot of problems, not the least of which was her reputation for cancellations. And Sid Luft was not to be trusted, in their opinion. They told Harry to forget it.

But in the end he listened to me. "After all," I said, "she has never appeared live in Chicago. It would be worth the gamble."

We announced Judy as "Miss Show Business" to appear for seven performances at Orchestra Hall, September 4-14, 1958, with Alan King; the orchestra was conducted by Nelson Riddle. The advance sale was stupendous. There did not seem to be any problem with Sid Luft.

Harry spent the last weeks of August in New York closing deals for the coming season with the managers there. While he was gone, Sid Luft called me on a Monday morning. He was in Chicago and he said he wanted an advance on the box-office receipts.

I asked him why he hadn't talked to Harry while they were both in New York the previous week. He didn't respond. It crossed my mind that Luft might think it would be easier to get the money from me than from Harry. I told him that according to our contract, there was no advance; we settled up at the end of the run.

He went on to California. He was to be back with Judy for a press conference scheduled to be held at our apartment at the Bismarck Hotel a few days later, September 3, at two o'clock in the afternoon. On September 3 Harry and I and the staff gathered, feeling very tense. We weren't sure that Judy would show up.

Two o'clock came: no Judy. Two-thirty. Three o'clock. Still no Judy. The apartment was crowded; reporters milled about impatiently. They were getting ready to leave.

While I was looking around, I suddenly saw Judy and Sid Luft. They had arrived, but no one seemed to recognize Judy. She looked completely different from the Judy Garland I had admired in the movies. She was very heavy, and seemed shy, bewildered and uneasy. I hurried to get Harry and we rushed her into the adjoining room where the reporters were eager to pounce on her. Despite her altered appearance, she handled herself very well.

And her opening night was a tremendous success. But for the rest of the week we were on tenterhooks until we saw her walk on the stage. There was both a matinee and an evening performance on Saturday, and Sid Luft suggested that we persuade Judy to stay at Orchestra Hall between the two performances. I was elected to convince her that since it was a hot day, she would be more comfortable in the air-conditioned Hall than anywhere else. I told her she could take a nap, and I would bring her her favorite chicken dinner. "Save yourself for the show," I said. I succeeded in selling her this bill of goods and the week's run ended in a blaze of glory, financial and otherwise.

Early in '59 we presented her again for one performance in the Opera House. This time I spent a lot of time with her and we became good friends. She suffered from many phobias—claustrophobia for one—and she was often nauseated. Harry told her that I had suffered from nausea for years and had overcome it. I sat and talked with her in her dressing room and tried to distract her from the fact that it had no window, while I fed her soda crackers and tea. She told me about her days in the studios when she was still a child: they started giving her pills, she said, to keep her awake during the late night shooting hours and then they gave her other pills to help her to sleep. And pills to keep her weight down.

When she was married to Vincent Minelli, she said, she was taken to a sanitarium during the night. When she got out of the car, she had to walk across the lawn to the front door. She kept falling and of course everyone thought that she was under the influence of pills and liquor. But the next morning they found out that she had been tripping over the lawn sprinklers.

She talked frankly and the more she talked the sorrier I felt for her. I realized, for one thing, that she had been truly in love with Vincent Minelli. Perhaps she sensed that I really cared about her and I understood her problems. I wanted to help her, to assure her that she was wonderful.

Her wedding anniversary occurred during one of her later appearances in Chicago. Harry wanted to hold a dinner party for her. No, she said; she wanted only the cast and us and the Kupcinets (Irv Kupcinet the columnist) to come after the performance for some dinner and drinks in her apartment at the Ambassador East. We ordered in the food and then, after the performance, Judy sat cuddled up in one of the big armchairs, wearing Sid Luft's robe. She looked like a little girl waiting to be loved. She was charming and it was a wonderfully pleasant evening.

In May of 1959 Harry and Sid Luft decided to tour "Judy and Company" in opera houses across the country. The tryout was to be in Cleveland; the first stop was scheduled for the Metropolitan in New York and the other cities besides Chicago were Los Angeles and San Francisco.

Trouble started on May 14. Herman Krawitz, the administrator of the Met, didn't want to rent the Metropolitan Opera House to Judy. He felt, as he put it, that she would "stink up" the place—that she wouldn't show or that she would create problems if she did. Rudolf Bing interceded and said Harry could have the theatre for a week and that the staff would cooperate in every way. There would be no charge if a performance was cancelled. But there was a high rental and Krawitz insisted that we carry the entire stagehand crew whether they were needed or not.

Opening night was a benefit for the Children's Asthma Research Institute and Hospital. Things were very hectic. The stagehands wanted a week's pay in advance and so did the musicians. The benefit people got an injunction to freeze the box-office receipts until after opening night. The day before I left for New York, Harry called to tell me that he had persuaded the unions to wait for payment until after the run, but to get that concession he had to guarantee payment. He told me to bring some of our stocks as collateral.

I was staying with his sister Trude in New York and I got there after the banks were closed. Trude and I decided to hide the stocks under the carpet so they would be safe for the night. We ripped up a piece of carpeting, put the certificates under it and moved the sofa on top of it.

Harry spent the day of the performance at the theatre. Tension was building; we couldn't be sure the performance would go on. At about four-thirty in the afternoon, Harry called to tell me not to come down until I heard from him again. He kept calling me every hour on the hour. Finally at seven-thirty that night I decided that Trude and I had to leave for the theatre, no matter what. When we got there, there was no sign of Harry. I was growing more and more worried. Finally, one of the box-office men said that Harry was in the bar across the street. And sure enough, there he was. He hadn't changed into his tuxedo and he was a sight. Anyone could see that he had had a very trying day.

Trude and I went back to the theatre. It was a sold-out house. It seemed like an eternity before the lights went off and the performance started. What a relief! "Judy and Company" was a huge success, thank God.

The opening night ended and there were only seven more nights to go. Two nights later Harry called us about two-thirty in the morning. He and Luft were at the hotel with Judy, who was sick; he wanted us to get a doctor. It was the usual nausea and fears. I told Harry to give her tea and crackers and to keep talking to her. I told him not to leave her alone and to call me in the morning.

Trude and I went back to bed, but it was a restless night. In the morning Harry called and told us to bring him a change of clothes. When we got to the hotel, we found Judy asleep. It was another trying day. Trude and I went to the theatre that evening but we left as soon as the performance started. And that was our pattern for the remaining performances: how many times can you sit through the same show with your heart in your mouth, hoping it will run to the finish? Performances were sold out for the week, but expenses were so high that there was practically no profit.

We went on to the Opera House in Chicago. Now we were on home territory at least and Harry was in charge completely, with no interference from anyone. Still, it was another strenuous week. I tried to maintain my sympathy for all of Judy's neurotic fears, but I was beginning to lose patience with her. The run in Chicago was a success. When the company went on to California, I was so exhausted I went for a rest to our house in Kenosha. The Los Angeles show did not produce a profit and when the company arrived in San Francisco, Sid Luft reneged on payments to Harry. With the help of a friend, Harry attached the box-office receipts. The tour seemed to go on forever, but it finally ended. We were able to recoup our initial investment and meet expenses, but no one made a profit. Poor Judy. She had so many fears and she worked so hard, and there was no money left for her.

In 1961 Judy appeared for us again at the Opera House and in 1962 we presented her at the Arie Crown; that was the theatre where she gave her last Chicago performance on May 7, 1965. That was a catastrophe. She was separated from Luft by then and was being managed by David Begelman, later of *Indecent Exposure* notoriety. Harry persuaded her to stay at the Astor Towers where we were living at that time.

The second night after her arrival, there was a terrible thunderstorm. The desk called us at four in the morning to tell us that Judy had moved to the Ambassador East. When we heard that, we knew we were in for trouble. For the next few days she remained shut up in her suite, refusing to see anyone. Her current young male companion sat drinking all day in the bar.

Then I heard through the grapevine that Judy's daughter Liza Minelli had arrived. The whole thing sounded very serious to us. Begelman assured us that Judy would give the concert, but we didn't believe it. The concert was scheduled for nine o'clock; nine came, and there was no sign of Judy. We kept calling and we were told she was on her way. She finally arrived, one hour late. And what a sight she was! Her eyes were staring, she was swaying and she couldn't talk. She walked onto the stage and opened her mouth, but no sound emerged. The orchestra stopped playing, and then started again. She opened her mouth wide again but again no sound came out. The audience began to applaud, to coax her to sing, shouting, "Come on, Judy! You can do it!" She stared at them wildly. Finally she began to talk the first lines of the song. Occasionally she sang a word. The whole evening went like that. No one left the theatre. No one asked for a refund. Her audience loved her whether she sang or not.

After the performance a man came up angrily to Harry and demanded to know whether it was greed that had impelled him to allow Judy to sing in her condition. "Can't you see she's ill?" he shouted. Heated words were exchanged. The next thing I knew this man was shoving Harry up against the wall and Harry was trying to punch him in the nose. Bravely, I tried to separate them. A small crowd had gathered around us. Finally I was able to persuade the man to stop making a scene; I told him that if he left his name and address with us, I would see that he got a refund. He finally left.

Needless to say, that was the last time we engaged Judy. She went from bad to worse. Her downfall was chronicled in the press. She owed money to everyone; her young husband spent every last dime of hers. She went back on alcohol and pills, and behaved in the most self-destructive way. She was her own worst enemy, and she couldn't blame anyone but herself, at the end. And she did blame everyone but herself for what finally destroyed her; her refusal to take responsibility for her actions caused me to lose the complete sympathy I had felt for her when we first met.

I cried when she died, but I had expected her death;

there was no other way out for Judy. She had nowhere to go.

XIII. PIERPOINT

THESE days when Kenosha, Wisconsin, is mentioned, people think of discount shopping malls, but when we went there shortly after our marriage, it was just a quiet beautiful town on Lake Michigan, far enough away from the hustle and bustle of downtown Chicago to provide a different kind of life and close enough at the same time to be an easy commute. Harry wanted to be able to commute daily. The Northwestern Railroad offered wonderful service, one hour from door to door. If Harry took the 8:45 a.m. train, he could be in the office before ten. Later when we had a staff, I would come in on Fridays to do payroll.

I don't remember who told us about Kenosha, but I do remember that we fell in love with the area immediately when we first saw it and we wanted to spend time there. We didn't have much money but it didn't cost much to rent a cottage in 1935 when we rented a house from the Pritzker family, with an option to buy. And we did buy it in 1937. We named it Pierpoint and we enjoyed it for forty years. Since our friends the Weinsteins had the house next door, it was a friendly as well as a comfortable place for us. Up until the '60s we had no musical attractions during the summer so we were fairly free from May to October.

Of course I was hardly idle because we entertained all the time. Friends, artists or business associates came up regularly for Harry's famous weekly card games. Sometimes Harry would call from Chicago to say that he was leaving the office and bringing twenty people home to dinner. It probably won't surprise you to learn that although he had a well-deserved reputation as a connoisseur of food and wine, Harry could not cook and never went near the kitchen and he ate only certain foods. When he brought people for dinner I created two different menus: one for our guests and one for him. "You don't have to eat it," I'd tell him, "but when you have people over, you have to cater to them too."

He liked to go grocery shopping, especially in Kenosha. Maybe that was because I didn't learn to drive until the late '60s, after Harry had his heart attack. In 1963 after the attack he got a driver, but up until then he had done all the driving. The minute we arrived in Kenosha he would make the rounds to see if any new shops had opened or any old ones had closed. He bought a lot of the foods he enjoyed—raspberries, for instance. When I complained about the amount he bought, he would say, "Don't worry. They'll keep in the refrigerator." I tried to explain that we couldn't eat enough of them and they would spoil even in the refrigerator if you kept them too long. But he never could understand that.

We had five acres which ran from Lake Michigan to Sheridan Road, including a private beach. We spent a fortune on cement walls, because the lake was always threatening to erode the beach. Chester, our caretaker, was a character: he looked after the flower beds and vegetable gardens and hired gardeners over the weekend, but he insisted that I work along with him during the week because he said I had a special way of growing things. We had other help in the house, and Harold Nadeau and Martha Schechet came up from Chicago almost every weekend.

The house wasn't big, but it was comfortable and warm. It had two bedrooms, a living room, dining room, kitchen and a basement. Later we added a bedroom and bathroom and paneled the walls with mahogany. But my favorite place was the guest house. It was a long, narrow building where we did a lot of entertaining. We barbecued and ate at one end and there was sleeping space on the other. Martha often slept there when she came out to work on the weekends. I could have lived there all the time, especially after Harry built me a sundeck where I loved to curl up with a book. As I write these words, I can almost feel the sun. We used to joke that we had "his" and "hers" houses.

Once we held a "Polish weekend" and invited some people from the Polish consulate and Polish cultural organizations. We had a special relationship with Chicago's large and influential Polish community; Harry had been born in Poland, his first language had been Polish and he had a nostalgic feeling for Polish artists and culture. He produced two of Moniusko's operas, *Halka* and *Strasny Dwor*; he helped organize a Chicago-based Polish ballet in 1940 with Felix Sadowski, a dancer with the Polish Ballet who had been stranded in Chicago when the Second World War had begun. Sadowski and his partner Janina Frostovna, born in America and trained in Warsaw, came to Harry for help and they set up a company of Chicago dancers which did Polish ballets choreographed by Sadowski. The company performed in the Opera House before making a tour of the midwest. Both the performance and the tour were successful. Later Sadowski was the choreographer for *Polka-Go-Round*, a popular national television show that ran for several years.

On this beautiful summer Sunday afternoon, Sadowski relaxed in a lawn chair while I prepared dinner in the guest house. I went back and forth constantly to the big house to get supplies; so did Harold, Martha and the various helpers. Felix watched all this with interest. Later he said to me, "Sarah, you have the most wonderful neighbors. You're really lucky."

"How do you know?" I said puzzled. "You haven't met them."

"Oh, I can tell," he said. "No, I haven't met them but I see you going in and out of their house as if it were your own. They must be very nice people."

I couldn't help laughing while I tried to explain to him that both houses were ours. I'm not sure he believed me.

$$\int$$

Little by little the business developed into a twelve-month concert season. I think this was a mistake, both financially and artistically. Many artists work now without taking a break for rest, reflection and learning new repertoire. I think audiences get tired too. The start of a new season is not special now that the old one never really ends. But be that as it may, the season got longer and longer, we spent less and less time at Pierpoint and more and more of the summer in Chicago. Since we were using the property less and less, we sold off the back half and the two side lots, although we kept beach rights.

Finally in the mid-'70s I told Harry that it didn't make sense to keep Pierpoint any longer. It had served us well for forty years but it no longer had a place in our lives. We sold it to a professor of criminal law at the University of Wisconsin-Parkside in Kenosha.

A couple of years later, after Harry died, I was in the area with friends. We drove up and stopped to indulge in memories. The new owner spotted us and came out.

"Mrs Zelzer," he said, "how are you? Would you like to see your old house?"

Foolishly, I agreed. The flower beds were gone, the main house had been remodeled and the guest house had been torn down. He was proud of his improvements; I was heartbroken at the destruction of so much of my past. Of course the house was his now, he could do whatever he wanted with it, but I realized that I shouldn't have gone to see it. When something is over, it's over except for memories, and those should remain undisturbed.

XIV. BLACK ARTISTS

IN the days before the civil rights revolution of the '60s, black artists were discriminated against in every way. If was difficult for them to travel and to find places to stay. In those early days we had no problem with audiences: people recognized that these were great artists and came to hear them. Our own problem when we booked black artists was with hotel reservations. For instance, when Dorothy Maynor was coming to sing for us, we had to beg the owner of the Bismarck Hotel to let her stay there. He finally agreed on condition that she would use room service and not eat in the restaurant.

Marion Anderson was always self-conscious when she was invited to eat in a restaurant. We always took her to Jacques, where we engaged a private room. We told her not to worry. They knew us there, and they knew who she was. There was never any problem.

We booked Paul Robeson in those early years before he spent most of his time in Russia. He always said that Russia was kinder to his children than the United States.

I remember Leontyne Price's first concert for us; it was her debut in Chicago. Her sorority took a block of tickets and they wanted to give a reception for her after the concert. They had to clear everything with Harry because he wanted to be sure that Leontyne would have a first-class reception and he was dubious about where that could be held. They chose a hotel somewhere on the South Side, I forget just where, but it was a wonderful affair, done by the best black caterers, with ice sculptures and beautiful flowers. Leontyne was really pleased and everything went off without a hitch.

The last time I presented her at Orchestra Hall, when I was still running Allied Arts Association, Keith Miller told me that Leontyne had come in a day early to try out the hall and that she was asking for me.

I went backstage to see her after the concert.

"So," she said, "you finally arrived." I reminded her that I never bothered an artist before a concert.

"You know who's missing from this concert?" she said.

"Yes," I said. "Don't start with me or I'll start to cry."

She began to reminisce. "I still remember that first concert when we had that great reception," she said. "You know what I miss most, not having him here?"

"No," I said. "What do you miss?"

"Well, you know, I was always afraid of him."

That surprised me. I asked her why.

"That one eye. The way he looked at me with that one eye. It wasn't a squint. It was more hypnotic. Like he could see right inside of me."

"But Leontyne, he was always so fond of you," I said.

"I know."

"Remember that concert at Arie Crown," I said, "when the critics wanted to know if we had microphones and what kind they were? Remember what he told the critics?"

She remembered. "He told them that I didn't need any mikes. Harry told them that I came with my own acoustics."

Leontyne never gave us any real problems; she listened to Harry's recommendations about programs, just as most of our artists did. Even Heifetz's contract said his program was "to be approved by local manager."

Leontyne never appeared in concert for us with her husband William Warfield. The only time she appeared with him after they were married was in *Porgy and Bess*. They were divorced in the late '50s or early '60s.

We were the first to present Cleo Laine and her husband John Dankworth to Chicago audiences, in 1973. Cleo is a great musician with a great range; she can do anything she wants to with her voice. And she is not only a great performer, but she was a pleasure to work with. She and Dankworth would come in days early to help us promote her concerts at Orchestra Hall or the Opera House.

Once during a concert at the Opera House, she developed some kind of bronchial trouble and couldn't go on after intermission.

"Now what?" Harry said.

"We'll just make the announcement," Dankworth said. "And the trio will perform the second half of the program."

"Oh boy," I said to Harry. "We'd better close the box office now; everyone will be asking for a refund."

But, you know, not a single person asked for his money back.

XV. PICKETS AND BOMBS

A FTER the war, Harry booked some artists who were accused of having Nazi associations. I wasn't too comfortable with Allied Arts' presentation of these people and Harry was attacked in the press for bringing them. But he insisted that music should be separate from politics and he had the courage of his convictions.

Kirsten Flagstad was booked for a Chicago concert in April, 1947. I was in New York at the time, so I didn't have to decide whether to attend. Because of a telephone strike, I couldn't call Harry to find out how things were going. Luckily, Fortune Gallo had just come from Chicago and Harry asked him to get in touch with me. Fortune took me and my sister-in-law Trude out for an evening on the town. We went out to dinner, to see Ethel Merman in *Annie Get Your Gun* and then for ice cream. He told me the Flagstad concert had been picketed, but the demonstration had been quiet.

Flagstad came again in 1951. This time she was booked for a concert series at New Trier High School in Winnetka as well as at Orchestra Hall. We were living then at the Bismarck Hotel and Harry booked a suite for her there which turned out to be right across the hall from us. I had refused to attend her concert in Winnetka; Harry excused my absence by saying that I was home with a cold which I didn't want her to catch. Flagstad liked to have champagne after a performance and Harry had chilled two bottles of her favorite brand. He kept going back and forth from her suite to our apartment, bringing me champagne. I wondered what she thought of all this.

Flagstad was one thing, but I was surprised when Maurice Chevalier was accused of being a Nazi—not only because of his charm, but because nobody had complained about him when he was in Chicago. The others—Flagstad, Gieseking, Karajan—had provoked protests and pickets. But not Chevalier.

He used only a piano in his performances; his accompanist was French. But the musicians' union insisted that we hire a full orchestra for him. It threatened to drop the accompanist, Fred Stomer, from membership in the union if he performed at Orchestra Hall. The union was so powerful that it could force a show to carry musicians it didn't need under the threat of being closed down altogether. That sort of thing is easing up now. Years ago ballet companies had to hire a certain number of musicians even if they were using a tape and didn't need them; today they can just use the tape.

Harry refused the demand to provide Chevalier with an orchestra. He said he would rather cancel the concert than be pressured into doing what he firmly believed was wrong in every way. Chevalier and Stomer, to their credit, said they would not be intimidated by the union and would stand behind Harry. Finally the union relented and let the show go on. And after that they never bothered Harry about that kind of thing.

In March, 1955, Herbert von Karajan and the Berlin Philharmonic were booked for three performances in Chicago. Immediately the Nazi question came up. André Mertens of CAMI called us at three o'clock in the morning. He was having trouble handling the press and he wanted Harry to come to New York and help him out of a bad situation. I wasn't delighted that Harry was getting involved in this thing, but since the Philharmonic was coming to Chicago, he undoubtedly felt some responsibility in the matter. I don't know what happened in New York, but when he got back, Harry said that he had helped to de-Nazify Karajan so that he could complete his American tour.

A delegation of rabbis called on Harry and asked him why he was bringing Karajan. Harry told them that in his opinion art had nothing to do with politics. And anyway if he didn't bring them, someone else would. I have since read, to my dismay, that Karajan was actually a card-carrying Nazi.

Once the Philharmonic arrived in Chicago, it seemed to me that I was being followed wherever I went, with or without Harry. At first I thought my imagination was working overtime; I hesitated to tell Harry about it because I didn't want him to call me stupid. But when I finally said something to him about it, he said I shouldn't worry; we were being protected by the FBI.

"Why should they do that?" I asked.

The answer was that our lives had been threatened. What a nightmare! Of course there were pickets in front of Orchestra Hall on performance days. And we had also been alerted to watch for bombs. You can't imagine the relief I felt when the performances ended and the orchestra left Chicago.

I was surprised at how well Harry and Karajan got along with each other. You have to understand that "getting along" isn't meant to imply that he and Harry were on a first-name basis. Harry never called these world-class artists by their first names. He was courtly and old-fashioned about it; he addressed them only as "Mr von Karajan" and "Mr Heifetz" and so on. But within these limits Harry and Karajan had a good feeling for each other—maybe they noticed that what they had in common was arrogance and the insistence of each on getting his own way. Once the German Consul General in Chicago gave a reception for Karajan after the Orchestra Hall concert; it was an extra-special occasion because the conductor had just gotten married again (for the last time). When we got to the reception we found out that Karajan was a no-show. We sent our chauffeur to his hotel to get him, but he couldn't reach him. So Harry went to the hotel, called him on the house phone and said to him, "I don't care if you're sleeping or what. Put on your pants and get down here. I'm waiting for you and I'm taking you to the reception."

Von Karajan appeared in the lobby a few minutes later. It was very unusual for him to obey an order like that. Harry was still mad, and he bawled him out: "You accepted the invitation and you have to show up!"

I believe the Berlin Philharmonic is the greatest orchestra in the world and Karajan was the greatest conductor, but I could certainly have done without all that tension which went with presenting a wonderful attraction. We brought the Philharmonic back to Chicago in 1956, '64, '65, '74 and '76, when our Chicago Symphony had just returned from a fantastically successful tour of Europe and were proclaiming themselves the greatest orchestra in the world. Just before the Berlin Philharmonic performance that year, the German musicians entered the lobby of Orchestra Hall and stopped to read the publicity on the Chicago Symphony. When they came to the sentence "The World's Greatest Orchestra" their laughter was something to hear and see. I have always regretted that I didn't have a movie camera with me at that moment.

In 1971 we booked the Moiseyev Dance Company at the Opera House for eight performances. Once more there were threats; tension grew from day to day. Opening night and most of the other performances were almost completely sold out.

On opening night the Emmett Dedmons (he was publisher of the *Sun-Times*) and Dr and Mrs Joseph Kirsner were my guests. The curtain rose to tremendous applause. Ten minutes later there was an explosion that looked like fireworks raining down from the gallery. At first we thought it was part of the performance, but as the theatre began to fill with smoke we realized that it was a bomb. I hurried downstairs. I couldn't find Harry. The FBI and the detectives were evacuating the theatre. Emmett Dedmon hurried out to call his newspaper. The theatre was evacuated in an orderly way. The bomb had landed on the main floor in the tenth row center. Two people were hurt badly enough to be taken to the hospital. The bomb had come from the gallery and the police were able to work out exactly which seats it had dropped from.

I suddenly remembered that no gallery seats had been sold at the box office; they had all been sold by mail order. With my assistants Harold and Martha I rushed up to the office on the second floor. We checked the mail orders and found the name of the person who had bought the seats. In the meantime the police had detained a suspicious-looking man wearing white gloves and were interrogating him in the room next to the box office. His name was on the mail order for the two gallery seats and he was taken to police headquarters. I don't know what happened after that.

We had planned a midnight supper for Moiseyev and Company after the performance, but we were all too upset to go on with it. Moiseyev was deeply depressed; he couldn't understand why a thing like that should have happened. We tried to explain how strong the feeling was against Russia, against its mistreatment of its Jewish population, to make him understand that this was an act of desperation. Certainly we agreed that his company of dancers had no responsibility for his government's actions. As you might imagine, he was extremely angry. He wanted to cancel the rest of the engagement but Harry and Sol Hurok—on the telephone from New York—persuaded him to finish. Harry actually persuaded him to add an extra performance so that the opening night audience could come back and we could avoid issuing refunds.

For the remaining performances extra security had to be brought in. All packages were checked and women's purses examined before their owners could enter the theatre. There were no body searches. And there were no more incidents—just relatively quiet demonstrations outside the theatre. Police kept the pickets across the street on Wacker Drive. All in all, it was a nerve-wracking week.

A delegation from the Rabbinical Council called on Harry and tried to persuade him to stop bringing attractions from Germany and Communist countries. As he always did, Harry responded that artists had nothing to do with politics. Music and Dance, he said, were ambassadors of peace and nothing would ever deter him from presenting them. He was accused of being greedy, of having no scruples when it came to making a profit. I knew this wasn't true; I knew that he cared about the mistreatment of Jewish people in those countries, but he insisted on fighting against that in his own way. He donated money to Jewish organizations and advised them.

In September, 1986, the Moiseyev Dance Company opened at the Metropolitan Opera House in New York. When I heard a *CBS News* report that the theatre had to be evacuated because of a tear-gas bomb, chills ran down my spine as I relived our ten-year-old experience.

XVI. AUDIENCES

ONCE I stood in for Harry at a luncheon given by a teachers association. He was due there at twelve-thirty and at twelve-fifteen he decided he wasn't going to go. He told me to go in his place and tell them that he had a high fever and couldn't get out of bed. So, under protest, that's what I did. They were very gracious to me; I was nervous: Harry was the speechmaker, not me. But after the talk, there was a question period, and someone asked why one artist succeeds and another doesn't.

I said that it had something to do with the chemistry of the artist's interaction with the audience. "There are some wonderful artists," I said, "who never draw anything at the box office."

And that is true. There were certain artists who I thought were tremendous, but who couldn't seem to draw an audience. We kept bringing them back anyway, hoping to build a following for them. But it didn't work. Of course many of the people who succeeded deserved to succeed, but there were some whose success was really undeserved—I could never understand why it happened.

I think it's worth noting that that percentage of the population which attends concerts has not increased since the 1930s when we initiated subscriptions. Subsidy has had no impact on the numbers of concertgoers. And the climate of culture in the television age is certainly not nourishing the interest of young listeners.

Harry estimated that out of an audience of 2,500 at Orchestra Hall, 500 are "feinschmeckers" or real connoisseurs, who love Bach, Mozart, Bartok and new music; another 500 are educated listeners who like music up to Strauss or early Stravinsky; the majority are people who deeply appreciate the classics but are wary of anything unproven; the last 250 would just as soon hear Sousa as anything else. They are not looking to be educated.

Chicago audiences go for big names, and preferably big names with scandals attached to them. Even so, once they've heard an artist they've heard him; they don't come back. They don't buy programs because, not knowing the repertoire, they only want to experience familiar works like *Carmen*, *Aida* or Beethoven's Fifth Symphony. They certainly will never risk hearing newcomers. I remember one of our Sunday afternoon piano concerts that was so completely sold out that I gave up my box and took an empty seat in another with two piano teachers whom I knew from my teaching days at the Chicago Conservatory. When the concert ended they asked me what I thought of the pianist. I told them I never discussed the merits of the artists we presented, but I asked them what *they* thought of him.

"We thought he was excellent," they said. "But we'll wait and read what the critics say tomorrow."

This lack of confidence in one's own judgement is sadly typical.

Another thing that comes to mind about audiences is the noise they make, coughing and fidgeting. Some concert halls now provide free cough drops, but the unwrapping is noisy. Segovia once interrupted his performance in Orchestra Hall in order to give the audience a lecture about suppressing disruptive coughing. Alfred Brendel once stopped his performance for the same reason and angrily told the audience that those who hadn't come to listen could leave.

There are people who talk, who rattle pages, who applaud between movements, who leave before the concert is over (they're usually sitting in the middle of a row) and there are those who don't enjoy the performance and blame the local manager for putting it on. And they all have their demands. They all want seats in the tenth row center. If they can't get them they feel cheated and they suspect the manager is playing favorites. "Why should subscribers get first choice?" is a familiar question. You try to explain that subscribers are buying a series of concerts and that often they have held the same seats for years. But it's like talking into a bucket; it's almost impossible to satisfy them even if they are people you know.

We knew our audiences. We were in direct contact with our ticket buyers during all the years we were in business in the Opera House. We kept our hands on everything that was happening. That is why we put in so many hours at the office and that is part of the reason for our success. Our staff was small, but they put in the hours with us. That was the only way we could manage when we had performances in five halls at once. We filled mail orders and subscriptions in our office; our customers were accustomed to coming up to our office even for single sales. I've mentioned the girl who saved her pennies to buy a ticket for a Nelson Eddy concert.

But that kind of direct contact with the customer— where the promoter knows his audiences and knows why they buy tickets—no longer exists. Today everything is done through Ticketmaster and computers. It's a whole different ball game nowadays, and it is not nearly so emotionally rewarding.

After the concert: SSZ with Ljuba Welitch, leading soprano of the Vienna Opera Company, who appeared with the Denver Symphony Orchestra in April 1953.

HZ and Charles Aznavour.

HZ and Igor Moiseyev.

HZ and Rudolf Bing of the Metropolitan Opera.

Elisabeth Schwarzkopf and HZ.

Cleo Laine and HZ, November 6,
1973.

"The Guys and Dolls": (l to r) Simon Seminoff, SSZ, HZ,
Sheldon Gold and Igor Moiseyev at the Arie Crown Theatre,
September 1974.

Eugene Ormandy,
1936.

Ghita Cottle, HZ, Vladimir Horowitz and Wanda Toscanini Horowitz.

(Philip J. Weinstein)

SSZ and George Balanchine at the Covenant Club.

HZ makes a point to Rudolf Nureyev.

Andres Segovia

Carlos Montoya

Andre Watts

(Don Fisher)

Sigmund Romberg in 1945.

(Don Fisher)

Mr. and Mrs. Vladimir Ashkenazy, January 20, 1980.

"The Czar and the Critics" at HZ's 75th birthday: Tom Willis and Claudia Cassidy, former music critics of the *Chicago Tribune*, with SSZ and HZ.

HZ, SSZ and Anna Russell in 1978 after the last performance at Orchestra Hall given under the auspices of the Allied Arts Corporation.

HZ with Paul Judy and John S. Edwards in 1979 at the merger of Allied Arts Corporation with the Orchestral Association.

THE KICK-OFF DINNER AT THE DRAKE HOTEL, CHICAGO, FEBRUARY 27, 1985

SSZ and Leonard Bernstein share a moment.

SSZ, Leonard Bernstein, and the late Mayor Harold Washington.

THE TRIBUTE DINNER, APRIL 15, 1985
GIVEN BY THE AMERICAN CONSERVATORY OF MUSIC

SSZ with William Warfield.

Victor Borge and SSZ.

Victor Borge at the piano.

ƒ ƒ ƒ

SSZ with Kerma Karoly, former President of the Chicago Chamber Music Society at a benefit concert honoring SSZ.

SSZ becomes a doctor...receiving an honorary degree of Doctor of Musical Arts from the American Conservatory of Music, May 19, 1985.

Jordan Katz with his wife Barbara and sons Jonathan and Adam.

The grandsons: (l to r) Jordan, Stuart, Dean and Barry Katz.

Roberta and Barry Katz with their children Jennifer and Jason.

America-Israel Cultural Foundation SSZ, June 20, 1978 at the Arts Club, Katz, Vicki and Stuart Katz, Barbara Harriet Zelzer Katz and her husband Marcus.

Stuart Katz and his wife Vicki with their children Brian and Amy.

SSZ and Harriet Zelzer Katz.

dinner concert honoring HZ and
Chicago: (l to r) Barry and Roberta
and Jordan Katz, SSZ and HZ,
Ernest, and HZ's sister, Trude

(Lee Balgemann)

Debbie, Josh and Robin Witt,
children of Howard Witt
(Lovell's son and SSZ's
nephew) at SSZ's 80th Birthday
Party.

SSZ's 80th Birthday Party, Lake Point Tower Club, January 21, 1989.

Ivan Davis with his manager, Maxim Gershunoff, and SSZ.

(Lee Balgemann)

SSZ with John von Rhein, music critic of the *Chicago Tribune* at her 80th birthday party.

(Lee Balgemann)

SSZ with Robert C. Marsh, music critic of the *Chicago Sun-Times* also at the 80th birthday party.

PIERPOINT

The main house.

The guest house.

XVII. HARRY ON MODERN MUSIC

I N 1968 Harry jotted down some of his thoughts about the state of contemporary music.

"Music washes away from the soul the dust of everyday life." Berthold Auerbach said. That was certainly always true, but now things have changed, and I am beginning to fear that 'the dust' is washing away much of the music we held dear. The music I'm talking about is, naturally, classical music, "highbrow" music at its best. There are two other types of music that I won't concern myself about; "lowbrow" (jazz, ragtime, rock, etc.) and "middlebrow" (pop music).

It's sad to realize that very little great music has been composed since the turn of the century—I'm talking about music acceptable to the classical-music lover. Since World War II, there has been virtually nothing composed in the grand tradition of the masterworks of Bach, Wagner and other greats. This is a sign of our times, a reflection of the tensions in this changing world. Would that it were changing for the better! As I see it, there's anarchy in the world and therefore there's anarchy in music.

Bad music is bred in tension. What we need is serenity—that's the soul of delicately flowering music.

The so-called "new music" lacks character and spirituality. Unless the mind works with the heart, we can't have good music. And unless the populace—the three billion people with more than one hundred governments—do not adopt as their common theme the idea of living in harmony, we will not have harmonious music.

If we are to appreciate life to its fullest, we must have music. It cannot be otherwise—this is something many artists know. As Leopold Stokowski once said, "Science helps us to understand many phases of the material and dynamic sides of life, but the highest reaches of music come thrillingly close to the central core and essence of life itself."

Centuries separate Stokowski from Plato, but their thoughts walk arm-in-arm. "Music is a moral law," Plato said more than two thousand years ago. "It gives a soul to the universe, a charm to sadness, gaiety and life to everything. It is the essence of order and leads to all that is good, just and wonderful."

Jascha Heifetz said, "Music is for the betterment and enrichment of the individual, just as education and reading are. When people come together to play music as they do to play bridge, civilization will have taken its longest stride forward since the beginning of time. Music is something to live with always, and the children should be taught to regard it as a close and inalienable friend."

I can't help thinking that we're losing this "enrichment of the individual" in this world of mass production, of disharmony, cacophony and atonal music. I'm convinced that atonal music will not replace the good music we have inherited from the masters. There will always be an elite who will not accept anything but the finest. What makes me sad is that this elite of good taste is so small.

I'm not a musicologist, but coming from a musical family, I'm steeped in the classical. As an impresario who has been serving musical feasts to the public for thirty-seven years, I've come to the conclusion that only three percent of the American public is interested in classical music. That's a sad commentary indeed on today's education, today's culture. There are some countries where this mournful state of affairs doesn't exist. In Israel, for example, fifty percent of the people can't live without great music—and they don't. In Israel concerts of great music are part of life. Here, they're an exception.

Television and radio aren't helping any. Turn on your TV or your transistor and what do you hear? More often than not you'll hear a steady crackling of shrieking rock 'n' roll or other loud noises sandwiched between the commercials. On such a diet, is it any wonder that we have become a world with musical dysentery?

We need a renaissance of great music. We must revise musical education. I've always thought that music is one of the most neglected subjects in our schools.

I agree fully with Oscar Wilde who said, "If one hears bad music, it is one's duty to drown it by one's own conversation."

And that's why I'm deliberately raising my voice. But it will take more than a single voice to drown out the discord of today's so-called music.

XVIII. HARRY'S
SEVENTY-FIFTH BIRTHDAY

HARRY was to turn seventy-five on April 15, 1972. Some of our friends who were active in cultural affairs—Judge Henry L. Burman, Judge Abraham Lincoln Marovitz, Harold Berc, Elmer Morris and Laurence Pucci—approached me with the suggestion that this birthday was an appropriate time for Chicago to honor Harry Zelzer, one of the country's leading impresarios. I thought they were absolutely right. But I knew that Harry would never agree to making his birthday into a public occasion.

But I did get him to at least listen to his friends. We all met for dinner at L'Auberge restaurant. I forget who brought up the subject of the testimonial dinner, but I remember being surprised at how well the discussion went. That is, it went well until Harry asked how this testimonial dinner was going to be paid for. Judge Burman said that the invited guests would be charged so much a person.

Harry exploded. "What! I should invite people to dinner, invite them to honor me and ask them to pay? Crazy!"

And he vetoed the whole idea.

That was the end of that plan, but I had become determined to have a bang-up seventy-fifth-birthday celebration for him. Our office staff and I decided to present him with an album of messages from artists, New York managers, family and friends. We worked on it secretly for months and had everything sent to Harold Berc's office.

I wanted more than the album. My heart was set on a celebration and I arranged three days of festivities: Friday, Saturday and Sunday. On Friday afternoon we had an open house in the office. This was the only party that Harry wanted, he said. Our staff was there, of course, along with critics, newspaper editors and whoever wanted to pop in. It was a jolly afternoon. Then, since Harry always insisted that family occasions called for private parties, I arranged a family dinner on Saturday evening in a private room at Jacques' restaurant. On Sunday we invited friends and VIPs to a concert by pianist Charles Rosen at Orchestra Hall, followed by another dinner at Jacques.

Harold Berc made a moving speech: "This afternoon Charles Rosen played the Goldberg Variations of Bach, but for Harry Zelzer the performance is one of a thousand variations on the theme of the impresario. That theme consists of gladdening hearts through cultural experiences...consisting of performances by violinists, pianists, cellists, flautists—there can be a duet, a trio, an ensemble, an orchestra, singers, guitarists, folk dancers, marching guards, ballets, musical comedies, plays. There you have a giant symphony with a thousand movements. It takes fifty years to play it and it is composed and conducted entirely by our birthday celebrant.

"Now there's Harry's title, 'Impresario'. It is a magic word...bring[ing to mind]...luxurious travel to the capital cities of the world. The Impresario is wined and dined in rich salons, enjoys private auditions and performances by...the great artists of the world...tens of thousands of obedient citizens race to the box office leaving untold wealth and ready cash for carefree disbursement to artists and Impresario alike.

"But hold on, friends, that's all fiction. The Impresario without subsidy must take chances, must promote, deal with unions. He must live a life of dedication to the performing arts, battling with critics, fighting to stay alive in a business which has few survivors.

"If there is a 'King of Culture' in the USA called Hurok, there is a powerful prime minister called Zelzer. In Chicago Hurok is happy to surrender his crown to Harry....

"Well, Harry, you say no plaques, no boasts, no toasts. You say you did it all for yourself. But no book has been written, no artwork drawn, no score composed or played that did not first have to be for the author, the artist, the musician himself. That's always the beginning. Later it reaches humanity.

"The larger truth, Harry, is that what you have done has been a service to mankind in our town. Your life justifiably endears you to relatives and friends, and more than warrants unmeasured recognition and acclaim. Happy Birthday from all of us to you."

XIX. AFTER 1972

HARRY did not consider his seventy-fifth-birthday celebration to be a retirement party. He continued to be active in Allied Arts for another five years, until 1977. But by 1972 the business was changing in many ways and for us these were not changes for the better. What we had glimpsed over the horizon was now reality. The Metropolitan Opera Company, the New York City Opera Company, the New York City Ballet and other major box-office attractions had priced themselves out of the Chicago market. The cultural exchange with the Soviet Union had been discontinued: that meant no more Richter or Gilels—Oistrakh was dead—and no more dance companies, no ballets—no Moiseyev, no Bolshoi.

We presented the Stars of the Bolshoi for the last time from August 6 to 11, 1973, at the Auditorium Theatre. One hour before the opening performance, Lillian Libman, the advance press agent from the Hurok office in New York, came to me in hysterics. The Russian stage manager had told her he was cancelling the show and probably the entire engagement. I cautioned Lillian not to upset Hurok with this news; Harry was on his way to the theatre and he would settle whatever problem had arisen.

145

When Harry arrived, the Russian manager told him that there was an ad in the program book for a film starring Rudolf Nureyev; since Nureyev had defected from the Bolshoi, the company considered that ad an insult to them and to the USSR. Harry and the manager had a long talk in Russian and worked out a compromise: we would tear the offending page out of the book and the company would go on as scheduled. Of course we refunded the advertiser's money—*that* was easy.

But this incident seemed to be an omen of things to come. The business was changing. Harry began to appear depressed and at first I thought changes in the business were depressing him, but then he began to lose interest not only in the business, but in everything else. He was so different from the man I had known for forty years that I became terribly worried. I talked to two doctors who were friends of ours, Joseph B. Kirsner and Bernard Levin at Billings Hospital, and they suggested that Harry see a neurologist at Evanston Hospital whose name I have blocked. He was extremely discouraging; he diagnosed the problem as stemming from deterioration of the brain cells.

I wanted a second opinion and Drs Kirsner and Levin recommended Dr Fred Plum in New York. We went there and Dr Levin went with us. Dr Plum's diagnosis was a great relief: he said there was nothing wrong with Harry's mind and certainly not with his brain cells. There was no question that he was depressed, but Dr Plum thought the depression would lift eventually. He prescribed medication, dietary changes, fresh air, exercise and fewer hours in the office. We returned to Chicago filled with hope. And sure enough, after about six months the depression lifted and Harry was able to stop the medication.

I see now what had caused Harry's depression. It had been clear to him for a long time—maybe twenty years—that the era of the impresario was ending. I realize in hindsight that that was the reason that he refused to take any of his grandchildren into the business.

The performing arts have been damaged by greed: exorbitant, spiraling fees, short-lived stardom based on jet travel, the desire of anyone with a hall or with an interest in music to become an instant impresario....All this along with equating the value of art with the size of the bottom line, is creating chaos in our world. Actually the '80s saw the end of what I call "the Era of the Impresario" in other fields too—in business and finance, for instance. The results of this are not encouraging: corporations get bigger and bigger until they literally burst apart. Look at Beatrice Foods; look at Campeau and the department stores. Unchecked greed is causing global disaster—the destruction of the rain forests is a good example—and is responsible in this country for insider trading and the sale of junk bonds. The short view is the only view taken; the future is being endangered.

Don't get me wrong. I'm not suggesting that greed and short-sightedness are new problems. But I can't remember that in the past they were institutionalized in the way they seem to be now. The savings-and-loan disaster will reportedly cost every man, woman and child in this country considerable money, and that's only *one* disaster.

Undoubtedly, Harry thought a great deal about the future of Allied Arts. While I was researching this book, I came across a letter dated December 2, 1958, which he wrote to Bea Spachner, chairman of the Auditorium Restoration Council, offering on his retirement to sell Allied Arts to Roosevelt University, the owner of the Auditorium Theatre. He pointed out that over the past thirty years he had brought "the finest artists and performers obtainable for the cultural benefit of the people of Chicago. It would be a great satisfaction to me," he wrote, "to have this work perpetuated. It is my conviction that the university with its great auditorium is in the best position to continue and further develop these services to the greater Chicago community of tomorrow...."

This came to nothing, but on October 22, 1970 an item ran in Kup's column saying that Harry was having discussions with the chairman of the City Council Committee on Culture and Economic Development, Alderman Edwin Fifielski, about Harry's offer of Allied Arts to the city on his retirement. Obviously this discussion didn't go anywhere either. It wasn't that there weren't plenty of people who wanted to buy Allied Arts. I urged Harry to sell, arguing that we had put our time, nearly half a century, into the business and enough was enough. But Harry discouraged buyer after buyer; he dismissed each one on grounds of musical or business inadequacy.

Three years later Harry offered Allied Arts to the Orchestral Association. The conditions were worked out with Stuart Ball of the Association: there was no cash investment or financial risk on the Association's part; Allied Arts guaranteed payment of any deficits incurred while Harry was running operations. Disbursement of profits was to be by mutual agreement and either corporation could terminate the arrangement on twelve months' prior written notice to the other. Allied Arts would become a not-for-profit organization maintaining its own offices. Harry would remain president and managing director as long as he was active in the business and John S. Edwards, manager of the Chicago Symphony Orchestra, would contract jointly with Harry for all soloists appearing with the Orchestra, an arrangement that would have saved substantial money for both organizations.

This agreement would not have brought us money; in fact, it would have cost us money, if it had been implemented, which it was not, in 1973. Harry was determined to merge Allied Arts with the Symphony; he may have been convinced that only large organizations could exist in the future, and/or he may have been acting out of a special feeling of respect and affection for the Orchestra and Orchestra Hall. He used to call Orchestra Hall his temple—music was his religion.

Five years later John Edwards called Harry to tell him that Paul Judy, a trustee of the Orchestral Association, was interested in Allied Arts. John arranged a meeting between Judy and Harry and the feelings on both sides were positive. Negotiations were progressing when the president of the Orchestral Association, Mr Joseph Burnham, died unexpectedly. Paul Judy was appointed to succeed him; this removed Judy from the negotiations with Harry because he would now have a conflict of interest. However Paul Judy could and did persuade the other trustees that acquiring Allied Arts would benefit the Association. Mr Judy pointed out to them that the acquisition would not only consolidate their position in the music field, but would help defray their deficit and give them buying power.

So the deal went through, although I had real objections to it. Peter Jonas, the Orchestra's artistic director, came to see Harry on March 3, 1978. He had planned to stay one hour but his visit lasted more than four hours. Harry showed him around the office and we both explained the ins and outs of our operation. The three of us were in general agreement on booking of artists, handling of fees and artistic matters in general. But after the merger it was going to be hard to deal with the differences in buying methods of the two organizations. Harry believed that the New York managers would not give the new entity the deals they had given him because the Chicago Symphony Orchestra was very much "up-market" and Allied Arts was "down-market".

In a long report, Peter Jonas wrote that Harry was worried about office management and operations. Harry had emphasized the importance of close monitoring of each day's mail, and of my supervision of the subscriptions and the progress of sales. Mr Jonas reported that we had shown him around our operation and that consequently he recommended a staff of three: one to take my place in supervising and coordinating the staff's activities, watching the daily returns, making effective liaison with the Orchestra Hall box office and to "funnel all information from different sources of sales, including benefits so that, as in Mr Zelzer's operation at the present time, a 'running budget' is in effect."

Harry had explained that "forward budgeting" was not important to Allied Arts; the whole "income, expenditure and profit profile" was fluid from day to day and release of benefits and other things were reviewed according to each morning's receipts. Mr Jonas reported that he agreed that this was "an effective way of constantly revising one's position and policies to suit the ever-changing selling situation of each attraction as it progresses from announcement to performance."

And Peter Jonas reported that Harry had emphasized the importance of maintaining separate office space for Allied Arts, and at the same time keeping it physically close to the Orchestral Association. And the importance of preserving Allied Arts' "different character" both "artistically and market-wise" from the Orchestral Association's activities, and formulating policy, both administrative and artistic, in order to continue Allied Arts' profitability and to "perpetuate the different attitude that New York managements have toward Allied Arts and toward the Orchestral Association."

It all seemed pleasant and reasonable, but I was against it, as I had been from the first moment Harry broached the plan to me. I felt that our organizations were too different in too many ways for the marriage to succeed. I didn't think that the Association would appreciate his gift. But that argument didn't sway Harry. So then I tried to talk him into selling—what difference did it make who the buyers were, I said, as long as they gave us a good price? We had put enough time into this enterprise and it would be wonderful to be able to relax at last, to travel, to be free of pressure. Let someone else struggle to make a go of culture in Chicago, I said to him. But Harry had his own ideas; he wasn't selling. All right then, I said, just leave the key in the door and walk away. No. He wanted to give his business to the Orchestral Association.

Of course I gave in. I was afraid, and unfortunately time has proved me right, that eventually Harry's name would be forgotten. The Allied Arts program today carries no mention of Harry Zelzer as founder of the series. But I'm getting ahead of my story.

We dissolved Allied Arts Corporation and became Zelzer Management. Our last independent presentation was on March 27, 1977, at Orchestra Hall. The artist was Anna Russell. She was very jolly and amusing, both onstage and off, and we had a good time together, especially when she had had a few drinks. I laughed myself silly whenever I was with her. And to make everything even better, we always did good business with her. When the evening ended on March 27, she announced that this was Harry's last performance and we all cheered him. I had to leave the box because I was crying. We had a little reception in the ballroom afterward and Anna chided me for not telling her earlier about the significance of the evening; she wanted to have done more for Harry.

So Harry Zelzer was made Honorary Impresario and Consultant to the new Allied Arts Association with new offices at 116 South Michigan Avenue (later they were at 332 S. Michigan) after four decades in the Opera House. Harry went to the new offices every day. He supervised the bookings and did some promotion, working with Carl Fasshauer who had taken over the daily operation of Allied Arts. By the end of the 1978-79 season Carl had left the Orchestral Association. Shirley Silver and Michelle Cuchiarro came along from our offices in the Opera House to handle subscriptions and mailings. Kathryn Jenkins was hired to help in the office and work on group sales.

Harry was partly retired and he enjoyed it. It was a wonderful year, that year that he was eighty-two. We moved into a large apartment at Lake Point Tower. We loved walking along the lake and we enjoyed the freedom from the pressure-filled routine. We had time to talk, to get to know each other in new ways. Harry went down to Florida for the first time to visit his sisters. We took our first non-working trip to New York. In May, Harry convinced me to go to Israel; he didn't want to go himself, but he wanted me to go and tell him about it. My sister-in-law Fay, who lived in Florida, went with me. It was a wonderful experience.

I returned on Monday, June 7, 1979. The following Saturday we were scheduled to leave for Poland, where we were to be honored for having brought so many Polish artists to Chicago and to make arrangements to book future performers. And after that, Harry was going to give me the European trip he had promised me when we had gotten married forty-five years earlier. "You see," he told me proudly, "I never forgot." What wonderful plans we made for the next two months!

But it was not to be. On Thursday morning we went our separate ways after breakfast. I had a Chamber Music Society board meeting and Harry had a luncheon appointment with Allan Stone and Sarge Ruck at the Bismarck Hotel. As I was leaving, Harry reminded me to pick up my visa at the Polish consulate. He was due home about two that afternoon and I said I should be back by two-thirty at the latest. It was a lovely June morning. At the meeting my fellow board members toasted our trip and then Pat Kemper drove me to the consulate.

When I got home, I was full of excitement. I was sure that Harry was home already because the front door was not double locked. I called out that I was home. There was no answer. I walked back to the kitchen. No Harry. Then I noticed that his bathroom door was slightly ajar and when I pushed it open, there he was, on the floor.

I called 911 and then I called Dr Levin at Billings Hospital. The paramedics were there in seven minutes, but they couldn't revive Harry. They rushed him to Northwestern Hospital where, at five-thirty that afternoon, he was pronounced dead of a massive cerebral hemorrhage.

$$\int$$

Harry had been as meticulous about arrangements for his funeral as he had been about arrangements he made in life. He left written instructions that he wanted to be buried in the suit he wore to afternoon concerts and that he didn't want to have a rabbi eulogize him. I followed his instructions about the suit but I couldn't do much about his second wish, although I did caution the rabbi, Seymour Cohen, not to paint a picture of Harry as a saintly husband, father and grandfather. Instead, the rabbi spoke about Harry and music.

The burial was on Monday, June 14, 1979. People

flew in from all over the country to pay their respects. John Edwards, who had flown in from a symphony orchestra managers' convention in California and had to fly back again, told me that there had been a memorial for Harry at the convention.

∮

Looking back, I wonder if Harry had a premonition that he was going to die, because in his last few days, he seemed to want to talk. We walked to Olive Park, across the street from our apartment building and looked at the lake and talked as we had not in all our years together. He told me things I had never known. He thanked me for putting up with all his *mishugassen* over the years and mentioned small things that I had never realized he had noticed. And he said all the things a wife or lover longs to hear during a relationship. If we had not had those talks, I would now have a different perspective about a number of things.

But soon the tumult was over and I was alone— alone, for the first time in my life. I had gone from my parents' home into marriage. And ours had not been the usual kind of marriage where the husband goes to work at a nine-to-five job and comes home for dinner which his wife has stayed home to cook. We were together all the time. There was the thinnest of lines between our work and our leisure. And now my partner, my companion, my love of forty-six years, was gone. All the memorials and tributes were meaningless to me. Harry was gone. I was alone. I had no one to share with.

I had been the impresario's wife, living in the shadow of a man dedicated to bringing the best of performing arts to Chicago. And he *was* dedicated; everything in Harry's life took second place to his business. I was caught up in this dedication of his, in the excitement of it. I was happy to share the problems, the gruelling hours of work to make each event a success—and sometimes I shared the disappointment of a failure. We would not have had the thrill of discovering new talent without Harry's genius; it was his determination and expertise which helped to bring success and recognition to many an artist. We had a partnership, a love for each other, that surpassed all obstacles. We were together twenty-four hours a day. We were friends in addition to being husband and wife. And I was content to be Mrs Harry Zelzer; although sometimes I was rebellious, I knew that only Harry could have made a success of the concert business. I acknowledged this and I was grateful to go along for the ride.

Many people thought Harry was callous, that he had no heart because he could not be crossed and he insisted on having his own way. Well, it was true that he was fiercely independent, but he had another side: he could be tender and sympathetic to others, he was a good friend and he would help his friends. He built many careers and never boasted about it. Yes—he was a kind of Jekyll and Hyde. I knew and appreciated both aspects of his personality. I loved the man—my husband.

Ironically perhaps, after his death I came into my own. I was determined to carry on where he had left off. I loved the publicity, the recognition and at the same time I was always aware that all this was happening because of him.

Some of my friends had encouraged me to seek recognition for myself. After all, they pointed out, I had always been a vital part of Allied Arts Corporation. I told them that although I knew a lot about the ins and outs of the business, I could never be the success that Harry had been. For one thing, I reminded them, times had changed, conditions were not the same, although experience stays the same and I did have experience. But I told them I wanted to live my life with fewer responsibilities—to enjoy my music, my books, my friends...just to enjoy being alive.

My close friends Lillian and Sydney Glickman, invited me to stay at their home in Colorado for as long as I liked; the mountain air would be good for me. I could be alone if I liked; no one would bother me. Convinced, I went. What a peaceful, lazy existence it was! I was pampered and I virtually stopped thinking.

But then from the Glickmans' I went on to spend a few days in Aspen with Bea and Bernie Verin. That was a mistake. In the late '40s Harry had been named a vice-president of the Goethe Bicentennial Foundation and he served as coordinator for the Foundation in the International Goethe Convocation and Musical Festival which went on in Aspen for almost three weeks, starting in late June, 1949. We had had a wonderful time. And now going back to Aspen without Harry called up all those memories. I tried not to show how upset I was. It was hard for me, but I think I put on a good show.

Then I couldn't put it off any longer. I had to go home and face facts. Where did I go from here?

XX. SARAH ZELZER AND ORCHESTRA HALL

I decided when I came home from Colorado that it would be good for me to remain active and it would be good for Allied Arts if continuity were preserved during the changeover; I wanted to carry on where Harry had left off. So I talked to John Edwards and we agreed that I should be an unpaid consultant to Allied Arts. I'm not sure that Harry would have approved. But it was a great challenge for me. Now I was on my own. And as I took my first tentative steps, I was surprised and a little embarrassed to discover that I loved the attention I was getting. That, too, was part of Harry's legacy to me.

I didn't work quite full-time, although it was more than part-time. The girls from the office were with me. Things went along smoothly. John Edwards and I had a good relationship; we respected each other and saw eye-to-eye on most things. He suggested that it would be a good idea for me to go to New York and see the managers there in person to make arrangements for coming events and just generally to do a little public relations.

I thought this was a good idea, so I went to New York and the day after I got there, Bill Judd, a manager, took me to lunch. We naturally talked about the artists.

"What about Andre Watts?" I asked.

"No problem," Bill said.

"Same fee?"

Yes, Watts was not asking for more money.

We went through the lists as dishes were served and removed. When we got to dessert and coffee, I said, "Why haven't you mentioned Serkin? He's been with us every year since the late '30s."

"I didn't want to mention him," Bill Judd said, "because I don't think you're going to want to pay his fee."

He said that Serkin's fee had doubled.

I gasped. "You're kidding!"

"I'm not kidding. You're a non-profit organization now."

I certainly didn't like that. "So what?" I snapped. "Why does that mean the fee has to go up? Double the fee—you're talking about twenty thousand dollars! No way I'm going to pay that."

He said he couldn't see why not, and I told him frankly that Serkin had never sold out on his own. Not once in all the times he was in Chicago. There were seasons when we had even lost a couple of thousand dollars with him. Harry had done everything he could to promote him. He had sold stage seats and he had discounted prices in the series. Rudolph Serkin could never sell out Orchestra Hall without the Piano Series. So why, I asked, should he get double what we paid him last year?

He repeated that we were non-profit now.

"But the box office doesn't warrant it! And besides,

doesn't he have any loyalty? He was with us all those years—"

Bill asked whether I could get one of the trustees to pay the bill.

I told him firmly that I wasn't going to spend other people's money that way. We would do without Serkin on the Piano Series.

I wondered whose fault this was. My gut feeling was that it was Serkin's and that Bill Judd didn't want to argue with him.

"I'll call John Edwards," Bill said. "He'll take him."

"Oh no he won't," I said. "John Edwards will not okay anything that I turn down. You've got the wrong idea. Whatever I decide, John Edwards sticks by me."

"I'll call him."

"Go ahead. It won't do you any good."

John Edwards called me that night at my hotel to ask me how things were going. He wanted to know whether I had eaten at any of the restaurants he had recommended and that sort of thing. I told him about Serkin and that Bill Judd was going to call him.

"If you told him no, Sarah," John said, "then that's it. I wouldn't go against you."

"I didn't think you would," I said. "But I wanted you to know about it. We can do without him on the Piano Series. It'll sell just as well."

When I got back to Chicago, Peter Jonas told me not to feel bad about not having Serkin.

I told him I didn't feel bad at all; I didn't think Serkin was worth that kind of money.

"Well," Jonas said, "we're booking him with the Chicago Symphony."

I was startled to hear this. "You're not paying that fee?" I asked.

"Oh no," he said. "We're dickering."

"You know, Peter," I said, trying to keep my temper, "the whole reason Harry gave Allied Arts to the Chicago Symphony to begin with was so that we could get together on fees and block-buying. I turned Serkin down, and so you shouldn't pay him that fee either. It's not right. That damages the purpose of combining Allied Arts with the Orchestral Association."

But nevertheless they made a deal with Serkin for the Symphony. I didn't book him again for the Piano Series while I was at Allied Arts. I felt this was a good example of why the two organizations should never have been combined.

$$\int$$

John Edwards hired Joyce Idema, from the Kennedy Center, to do public relations for Orchestra Hall and Allied Arts. Unfortunately the chemistry between her and me was all wrong; we never got along. It seemed to me that she had ambitions to take over Allied Arts and run it herself. She thought I was old-fashioned; I thought she was incompetent. But I tried for a year to work with her. It was an impossible situation, however, and I finally felt I had to ask John Edwards to dismiss her from Allied Arts. He did, and she was replaced by a young man who stayed for a year. When he left, I hired Keith Miller. Keith had begun working at Orchestra Hall through an apprentice program while Harry was still living. When John Edwards ran out of work for him, he sent Keith over to us at the Opera House, although he kept him on salary. When I took over Allied Arts, Keith applied and I hired him to be my assistant. He went to concerts to oversee them, handled press releases, publicity, benefits and subscriptions. He began to work for me early in 1980; he left a few months after I did.

In 1981 we celebrated Allied Arts' Golden Anniversary with a calendar of thirty-three outstanding events in Harry's memory. In October of 1980 John Edwards and I co-hosted an afternoon concert at Orchestra Hall by the Spanish pianist Alicia de Larrocha, followed by a dinner at five-thirty in the Hall's ballroom. This was dedicated to Harry. I invited the press, some New York managers, the president of the Orchestral Association and several of the trustees. I paid for the dinner, since that was an Allied Arts tradition: Harry had never believed in charging his guests to dine with him, and besides I didn't want to put the Orchestral Association to any expense.

The evening was a success, but the president of the Orchestral Association and the trustees did not come, and none of them sent any acknowledgement of the invitation. They had chosen to snub the man who had always said that Orchestra Hall was his temple. Now once more I had reason to regret bitterly that we had made a gift of Allied Arts to the Orchestral Association. But that deliberate slap in the face made me feel more determined than ever to make Allied Arts a success— and in spite of all obstacles, I really think I did do that.

One memorable experience I had at Orchestra Hall involved my booking of Vladimir Horowitz. We had booked him before his various retirements when he was still relying on his talent rather than his reputation and his press hype. I must say that after this concert and until his death in 1989, he played better than he did for us on that disastrous Saturday evening, April 16, 1983. Orchestra Hall was sold out that night and there were 170 seats on the stage.

I was really amazed that anyone, myself included, would take on the presentation of Horowitz, because dealing with him had become a real strain on everyone. As usual, he refused to make a commitment until three-and-a-half weeks before the concert. His mottos were "Keep Them Guessing" and "Wait Until the Last Possible Moment". Peter Gelb, his personal manager, sent a contract that was so full of demands that it was ridiculous.

Ridiculous it may have been, but I didn't laugh. I was furious. In Allied Arts' fifty-two years of concert presentation, no one had ever made such demands. If Harry were still around he would have torn up the contract. And I would have done just that too, if I did not have obligations to the Orchestral Association.

Trouble started right away. A real storm blew up over Gelb's refusal to accept credit card purchases of tickets. He said that Horowitz would refuse to allow the handling costs of the cards. I responded that we would not go on with the concert unless we accepted credit card charges because our Chicago audiences were used to that and it was the only way to ensure a sold-out house.

"All ticket sales for all attractions in theatres and concert halls are handled this way now," I said. I pointed out that the days were long past when a line would form around the block on the first day that a box office opened for a Horowitz concert. I really believed that these long lines at the box office were what Horowitz expected and wanted. And it couldn't happen. After all, I said, we knew the pulse of Chicago audiences better than anyone else.

But Gelb refused to accept that. He said he would get back to me about the charges. But of course he didn't. He went to Tokyo without responding. And far from responding to the credit card question, he didn't even give the go sign for the April 16 concert until March 27, the day our first ad ran in the Sunday papers. Just as I had predicted, on Monday there was no immense line waiting for the box office to open for sales. We had to make a decision about credit cards and since we hadn't heard from Gelb we went ahead and took the charged reservations, although we knew this would cause trouble later. We knew too that if we didn't sell out quickly Horowitz would cancel. Every day for the three weeks before the concert, Gelb's secretary called to get a report on ticket sales. By Thursday we had sold all but a few main floor and gallery seats. Now began the long wait for an answer to the question of selling stage seats.

On the Friday before the Saturday concert, Gelb and I had words once again. He wanted their money up front. I told him I considered this an arrogant demand; he didn't know how to deal with local management, I said. I reminded him that a manager who popped up overnight was one thing but managers who had been in business for fifty-two years was something else again. And we never paid an artist before a performance.

"You know, Sarah," Gelb said, "it's a matter of protecting everyone concerned. If Horowitz gets his fee the day before the concert, he's less likely to cancel."

"And if he decides to cancel even after he receives his check, what assurance do we have that he'll reimburse us?" I asked.

Gelb said that I could trust Horowitz.

I replied that I did not trust him. I pointed out that Horowitz had cancelled concerts with us twice before, the last time in 1980, and each time he promised to reimburse us for expenses and each time he had broken his promise.

"CAMI would reimburse you even if Horowitz didn't," Gelb said. "CAMI would never do anything to antagonize an important client like the Chicago Symphony and Allied Arts. You have my word on that."

Then the question of the service charges for the credit cards came up again. After a protracted argument, Gelb agreed to split that cost with us. "But Horowitz must never find out about it!" he cautioned.

A little while later, Horowitz arrived to try the piano. I sat in the last row of the Hall to listen; I didn't have any desire to talk to him. But watching him walk across the stage, I was deeply shocked to see how old he had become. And his playing reflected this: his control was gone, his fingers wouldn't obey him, he slipped notes and even passages. He attacked his fortes as though they were enemies he had to settle grievances with. His sound was unbelievably ugly and had no body. He did have some beautiful tones, but it was obvious to me that he was no longer a great pianist.

When Saturday finally came, the tension increased.

Would he cancel? And if he didn't, how would he perform? Well, he didn't cancel. He did play the concert, but his performance was no better than it had been in the run-through. Nevertheless the audience cheered him. Was it out of loyalty? Did they really hear what he was doing at the keyboard or were they cheering the legend, the Horowitz mystique? I really wanted to shout at them, "Dummies! If you knew what Horowitz really thinks of you, his public, you'd walk out and forget him!"

At intermission Gelb came up to me in a rage.

"There are one-hundred-and-seventy-five people on the stage," he said, "and you told me you had only sold a hundred-and-seventy stage seats."

"You're wrong," I said. "I've got the left-over tickets in my purse. I haven't even been to the box office yet."

"Then the usher took the money," Gelb said. "I was an usher once and I know all the tricks."

I called our head usher up and asked him to investigate. But naturally he wasn't able to find anything out.

When I gave Gelb a statement and a check for the balance due, he was still fretting over the stage seats. "I don't know if I should even sign this statement," he said. "It hasn't been corrected to my count of one-hundred-seventy-five."

In all my years of business no company manager had ever questioned my honesty. "Take it or leave it," I snapped. I wasn't going to budge.

"And don't bother sending me a bill for the service charges," Gelb said. "There wasn't any ad in today's paper saying that the concert was sold out."

I took a deep breath. "That's because we were not

sold out at the time of the deadline for placing the Sunday ad. There were still some seats available then." I had had enough of this. "I don't care to discuss this with you any more," I said. "I'm going to take it up with your boss. I want to tell you that Allied Arts can go on existing very well without Horowitz, but I don't think the reverse is true."

Gelb's boss was Ron Wilford, president of CAMI. After the concert I sat down and wrote him a letter, taking up points which Gelb had telexed to John Edwards on that day. He had complained about the Sunday ad, about the count of the stage seats, about the wording of Horowitz's biography in the program and about the credit card charges.

I explained that as far as the advertising went, I had told Gelb that Thursday was the deadline for Sunday ads for both Chicago papers and that at that time we had a few stray seats on the main floor and we were waiting for an answer from Gelb about whether we could put on fifty more stage seats. We had no answer from him by Thursday and we couldn't take a chance on putting in a "sold-out" ad which might keep people from coming down at the last minute.

I explained further that my assistant and I got three different totals when, from my box, we tried to count the people sitting on the stage. And that on Friday afternoon Gelb and I had agreed that 170 people would be accommodated on the stage, when the stage manager told us that 170 was the maximum number. Much earlier I had told Gelb's secretary that since our stage had been remodeled, we could probably seat more than 150 people and therefore I was printing an extra fifty tickets. I went on to write Wilford that on that Friday afternoon I gave Gelb the complete statement minus the additional stage seats, plus the manifesto from the ticket company and the check. I told him I resented being accused of dishonesty. No one had ever done that before in our fifty years of being in business.

I pointed out that Horowitz's biography had been sent to my assistant Keith Miller by Mr Gelb's secretary, Jo-Ann Siegel, and that Keith had checked with Ms Siegel that this was the biography intended for the program. I also pointed out that Gelb had left for Tokyo without getting back to us about the credit card charges. And the contract did not prohibit credit card charges.

By the time I finished the letter I was pretty mad: "I think it is time you spoke to the people who are representing you to learn how to treat local managers. Allied Arts has been in business for fifty-two years and I believe we know our own city better than you people in New York sitting behind your desks. Instead of being content to have received eighty percent of a sold-out house, all Peter Gelb was able to do was find fault, going back on his word, not telling the truth to either John Edwards or me about what we had discussed.

"In the future, Mr Gelb is not welcome at Allied Arts. I personally do not want him to call me and if circumstances ever came about that I would have to talk to him, I would only do so if someone else was to take dictation at the conversation.

"After all, Ronald, Allied Arts has been doing business with CAMI since the 1930s and at this stage of our existence, we will not take any abuse from your organization.

"We also know, through the grapevine, that Mr Horowitz's concert in Philadelphia was not a sellout and some papering took place."

I sent a copy of this letter to Peter Gelb.

Ronald Wilford's reply was a joke. He sent me a copy of a letter that Harry had written to Kurt Weinhold in May, 1968, and commented that it bore a striking similarity to the present situation. He said he was sorry I was having so many problems.

Despite all this, I was of course shocked to learn of Horowitz's death of a heart attack on Sunday, November 5, 1989. He was one of the great pianists of his day.

$$\oint$$

I was becoming upset at the way money was being spent; it was frittered away and I couldn't do anything to stop it. It was bitterly clear to me why Harry had never wanted any partners in our business; there can be only one boss or there's trouble.

Corporations give money to non-profit organizations and they want as much as they give in return. For the 1983-84 season, Merrill Lynch donated $100,000 to the Orchestral Association to be used for Allied Arts Music Section II. In return they required a certain number of tickets for each of the eight concerts, special circulars and posters printed with their name, a special cover for the house program, special ads and spot announcements, press releases and so on. Our non-profit organizations really know how to spend money. As I watched the money go down the drain at Orchestra Hall and other non-profit organizations, I squirmed. I tried to keep expenses down at Allied Arts, to run it as if it were still mine, in spite of the waste allowed by the Orchestral Association. But it was hopeless.

I didn't like the direction in which things were going. I didn't want to be involved any longer. We were now in our fifth season, 1984-85, which was to be dedicated to Harry, the founder. I told John Edwards that in September, 1985, after the first concert of the 1985-86 season, I would retire from Allied Arts.

On August 5, 1984—which I think was a Monday— Theresa Amling, John Edwards' secretary, called to tell me that John was in St Joseph's Hospital. He was incoherent, she said. Of course I rushed to the hospital. John smiled when he saw me, but I'm not sure that he recognized me. He didn't seem to know where he was. I went to see him every day. The following Sunday he had two strokes, one after the other, and was moved to intensive care. Four days later, early on Thursday morning, John died in his sleep. Mass was said at Orchestra Hall on Sunday. I couldn't face it—another dear, devoted friend gone from my life.

The following Monday morning the power struggle began. For the moment the Orchestral Association had no head, and the underlings hoped to take advantage of the situation to gain power for themselves. Allied Arts was one of the first targets. I called the Association's attorney, Stuart Bernstein, for an appointment so that I could ask him what to do about Allied Arts. Should I go on signing contracts as I had done when I was working with John Edwards?

He didn't know, he said, it was too soon to tell anything. He advised me to wait and see what developed. I realized that I was caught in the middle of an unpleasant situation. I decided not to take sides in the power struggle and not to give anyone the chance to drop the ax on me. It was time to tender my resignation formally. I wrote the following letter to Mr E. Norman Staub, president of the Orchestral Association:

There have been consistent rumors floating around during the past year that the Orchestral Association would like to abandon Allied Arts Association. At this time these rumors seem to be more definite: that the trustees would prefer I do not continue in my position as consultant of/to Allied Arts. I do not wish to be a part of the political intrigue amongst your various under-lings who are trying to gain power now that Mr John S. Edwards is no longer with us. You are blessed with a group of dilettantes who think they know how to run a symphony organization and a concert management bet-ter than anyone else. I hope they succeed. Their great accomplishment so far is letting money go down the drain.

I am hereby advising you that I am resigning my position as consultant as of December 13, 1984. The reason I have chosen this date is because of Allied Arts commitments to a few benefit organizations who have taken over several important performances in October, November and December. I have dealt with these orga-nizations for the past fifteen years and they do not want to deal with anyone else. I will therefore help them and us by staying on until December 13.

And now I want to point out a few facts regarding my participation in Allied Arts.

1) When my late husband, Harry Zelzer, and I turned over our Allied Arts to the Orchestral Associa-tion as a gift in 1978 we visualized a great future for it.

2) Harry Zelzer remained as consultant and honor-ary impresario until he passed away in June of 1979. Mr Edwards asked me to continue in the same capacity. I was very concerned about safeguarding our legacy. Al-

lied Arts and Harry Zelzer contributed enormously to the musical life of Chicago from 1930 to 1978. He was always ready to assist and advise the many conductors, presidents, etc., of the Chicago Symphony and the Orchestral Association. He was in the background, never pushed his way into your sacred and private territory.

3) In the four years I remained as consultant for Allied Arts...the Orchestral Association has treated Allied Arts as a stepchild.

4) In the fiftieth season of Allied Arts, which was dedicated to its founder, Harry Zelzer, the concert of Alicia de Larrocha in October was dedicated to Harry Zelzer, followed by a dinner in the ballroom. I, personally, angeled the dinner. The press, New York managers and friends of Harry Zelzer were invited, as well as the president of the Orchestral Association and your trustees. There was no acknowledgement from your Association in response to the invitation, no attendance, no message of any kind. John S. Edwards was the only one to do the honors with me.

I did not become involved in Allied Arts Association expecting any special recognition or honor from the Orchestral Association, but I did expect to be treated not as one of your volunteers, but as a vital part of your organization. This courtesy was never extended to me.

5) ...I knew you had hoped that Allied Arts...would be able to contribute greatly to [the reduction of] your deficit. I believe that Paul Judy oversold this idea to you. Yes, Allied Arts under the Zelzers was a very profitable concert management, and was the only one of its kind that existed without subsidy. It could have continued the same way under your auspices, but your trustees were unwilling to take chances, to present box-office attractions outside of the Orchestra Hall proper. I abided by your rules, but knew in the long run that you would not feel comfortable with this alliance. While Allied Arts has not been the profit-making alliance you had expected, it has held its own in spite of all the competition around us. I also know that we have been an asset for your fundraising. Corporations have considered the fact

that Allied Arts caters to a more diversified public. Merrill Lynch chose to support the Allied Arts Music Series, not your Symphony Orchestra concerts. One of our Piano Series subscribers remembered the Orchestral Association in her will and you received a substantial amount of that contribution.

6) I could go on with the advantages you have gained from Allied Arts Association. I may sound egotistical, but I know I have been able to keep Allied Arts a valuable asset for you. The New York managers have reckoned with me as always, and I have been able to keep the artists' fees down. I doubt whether anyone else in your organization would have been able to do this. You have not appreciated my services to you.

7) John Edwards and I have already booked the 1985-86 season. All the contracts will be in by the beginning of next week. I have given the list of attractions to Paul Chummers. I take for granted that you realize our word is our bond and that whoever is now in charge will honor these contracts. The New York managers booked their tours based on the Chicago dates and they are now very much concerned about these contracts. It would not be good business on your part to renege on these contracts.

8) Harry Zelzer called Orchestra Hall his Temple. I think he made a big mistake....

9) It was a pleasure, inspiration and a privilege to work with one of the great Symphony managers, John S. Edwards. He was a wonderful friend to my husband Harry Zelzer and to myself, since the day he arrived in Chicago. He has left a big void in my life. We had a unique friendship based on respect for each other.

10) I have two requests which I trust you will honor: a) to permit me to run Allied Arts until December 13th with no outside interference, as I have done for the past four years, and b) Mr Edwards had promised that when and if I ever retired from Allied Arts, that Box O, which I held for all Allied Arts concerts, will be mine, without charge, for as many seasons as I want it.

11) I would also like to remind you that I have

served Allied Arts...as consultant, booked the performances, promoted concerts, etc. without any compensation.

I wish you all the success in the future. May your
deficits decrease—may your Orchestra become more famous, and may Allied Arts Association continue to exist
under the proper supervision.

Please acknowledge receipt of this letter.

When Mr Staub received this letter, he called me
and we made an appointment to discuss things at my
office. Paul Chummers came to the meeting as well. Mr
Staub made no attempt to change my mind. He apologized for not being more aware of Allied Arts; he had
left it to Mr Edwards, he said. He regretted that I was
leaving with so much bitterness.

I told him I was more disappointed than bitter. He
agreed to my written conditions as well as to my request
that their public relations department refrain from issuing a release about my resignation. I would do that
myself when I returned from a trip I was taking to Spain
and Portugal.

There was a later meeting at my apartment with
Staub and Paul Chummers to discuss marketing suggestions Joyce Idema had given to Keith Miller. She had
four main ideas: a Pick-Your-Own-Series format; development of new mailing lists; abandonment of the *Chicago Magazine* season circular; and more and bigger ad-
vertisements.

I told Messers Staub and Chummers that I did not
think this plan would solve Allied Arts' problems. New
ideas are fine, but it is not wise to implement them in
place of old ones that are working. I pointed out that
syndication is still the big factor in promotion, but no

one at Orchestra Hall was equipped to do that. And incorporating Allied Arts without its present staff would give them many problems.

Mr Staub said that there would be no change for the present, but he couldn't promise anything for the long-range future. What eventually happened was that the Allied Artists office was sublet, and Allied Arts was absorbed into the Orchestra Hall bureaucracy.

One big problem for the Orchestral Association was that they could not book big box-office attractions in theatres larger than Orchestra Hall because if they made a profit on presentations outside the Hall they would violate the Chicago Symphony's non-profit status with the IRS. Why then did they take on Allied Arts, clearly a profit-making corporation? If Allied Arts could not report a profit, surely it offered no advantage to the Orchestral Association. They should have refused to take it, as they had turned down our offer in 1972.

I called critics Robert Marsh (of the *Sun-Times*), John von Rhein (of the *Tribune*) and Claudia Cassidy (retired from the *Tribune* but writing for *Chicago Magazine*) to tell them that I had resigned, that I was going away on vacation and that when I returned I would invite them to lunch and give them the complete story behind my resignation. I asked them not to release any information in the interim, and they agreed.

I went to Spain and Portugal with Ralph and Marge Ergas, although I really didn't feel like going. It was an interesting trip, but I picked up an intestinal bug in Portugal and came home feeling decidedly under the weather.

When I got back I found things at Orchestra Hall to

be more chaotic than ever. There was anarchy at the Orchestral Association. Paul Chummers had been appointed acting general manager while a search committee looked for a successor to John Edwards. The committee had not yet figured out where to start its search. I learned for the first time that, shortly before his death, the executive committee had asked several times for John Edwards' resignation. Now I vaguely remembered his mentioning the matter to me and my pleading with him not to resign. I told him that I and Allied Arts needed him, that he had to stay as long as I was there, and that I was sure he would be there long after others had gone.

If the Orchestral Association was up for grabs, Allied Arts was more so. Everyone wanted to run it: Joyce Idema, Evelyn Meine, Bill Rahe and Bob Zimmerman— these were only a few of those battling for the top spot. My decision to resign looked more and more justified.

I had my meeting with the three critics in October, 1984. I pulled no punches. In the *Tribune* on Sunday, November 11, 1984, John von Rhein reported, under the headline, "Another Old Concert Pro Bows Out. What is the Future for Allied Arts?":

> Like her late husband Harry, Sarah Zelzer has an old pro's instinct for making a grand exit and doing so at precisely the right time.
> It did not take long after the passing of Chicago Symphony manager, John S. Edwards, last August for Mrs Zelzer to make up her mind. She will retire as consultant to the concert series, leaving Zelzer's legacy entirely in the hands of the Orchestral Association.
> Without the direct involvement of a Harry or Sarah Zelzer, however, Allied Arts stands to become a very

different concert series from what the Chicago public
has known. Veteran observers will recognize the disso-
lution of the Zelzer empire as the end of an era, an event
that is bound to have far-reaching implications for Chicago music.

When Edwards died, Zelzer lost her principal ally at
Orchestra Hall. She also lost what remained of her authority to maintain a Zelzer-type concert business. The
problems that helped persuade Harry Zelzer to quit,
also nagged at her—escalating artists' fees; rapacious
managers; declining attendance for certain kinds of
events; competition from the Auditorium, Civic Center
for Performing Arts, Pick-Steiger Concert Hall and other
publicly subsidized ventures. Clearly it was time to get
out and leave the headaches to someone else.

Robert Marsh's article appeared in the *Sun-Times* on
November 18, '84, under the heading, "Outspoken
Sarah Zelzer Will Retire Soon":

Four weeks from now, a long and exceedingly important chapter in Chicago history will close when
Sarah Zelzer leaves the Allied Arts management which
her late husband, Harry, founded 54 seasons ago. Orchestra Hall without a Zelzer is going to be like City Hall
without Democrats. How can this be?

Allied Arts was a highly personal family business
that came from two militantly independent souls like
Harry and Sarah. They did things their way, and if you
disagreed, too bad. Outsiders might wonder how this
approach could possibly survive after the union of Allied Arts with a larger organization. The answer was the
late John Edwards, who as chief executive of the Orchestral Association, created a special situation in
which, as much as possible, Harry (and later, Sarah)
would be able to function in something approaching the
traditional manner. Although Sarah Zelzer has been
thinking about retirement for some time, the death of
Edwards in August was decisive. She did not want to go

on without him as her friend and ally. So, on the one hand, one must regret the passing of the old order; on the other hand, one must confront the fact that in a world in which change is constant and inevitable, Allied Arts lasted in its original form for more than 50 years. I find that remarkable indeed.

These two articles attracted a great deal of attention. I doubt that Staub and the board were happy about them, although I don't know their reaction. I for one was glad things were out in the open. Now it remained to be seen what the Orchestral Association would do.

The New York managers were upset by the news of my retirement. I assured them that they would soon find new people to sell to at higher fees and they would forget Allied Arts and everything it had stood for for so many years.

As for me, I had a whole new life. I was getting a lot of praise and publicity; I was becoming a celebrity and I loved it. Finally, my friends said, long-deserved recognition! In fact, I found myself seeking more and more publicity, just as my husband used to do, and I was more and more amazed at myself.

And then a catastrophe occurred. I went out to dinner on a Friday evening in November with Marge and Ralph Ergas. The dinner was good, but afterward I tripped on three stairs, hit bottom and landed in Michael Reese Hospital. I had broken the head of my femur. I had to have surgery and then I went home with a live-in nurse and a walker. I was shut in for weeks because I refused to go out in a wheelchair.

XXI. JAN PEERCE AND RICHARD TUCKER

I N December of 1984—the eleventh, to be exact—while I was deep in the doldrums because of my hip, I received word that Jan Peerce had died. Jan was one of the great American tenors, an opera star, a fine recitalist and a true friend.

It seemed like yesterday, but it was nearly fifty years, on October 13, 1937, that Jan had first appeared with us in recital at the Civic Opera House. He had just left the Radio City Music Hall to begin his classical career; Harry had been one of the first local managers to engage him. He shared the bill with Aaron Rosen, a twelve-year-old violinist who also went on to have an international career. After that first concert Jan drove around with us in our jalopy until the morning papers came out at three a.m. with the reviews. They were great!

Over the years in which we booked Jan, we developed a personal friendship. We had evenings of great music with him and of great conversation with him and his wife Alice. Once I told Jan that his recording of "Oh, Promise Me" always brought tears to my eyes. He was so pleased that he always sang it as an encore in his Chicago concerts, announcing that he was singing it for me. And I shall never forget taking part in a seder which Jan led one Passover in Florida. It was such an inspiration that that holiday held a new meaning for me from that time on.

When I think of Jan, I naturally think of the tenor Richard Tucker, because Jan's sister Sara was married to Tucker. The brothers-in-law, both tenors, were always competing with each other. And whenever I think of Richard Tucker and his wife, I can't be objective about them because we had a very unpleasant experience with them.

It started with an ill-starred engagement of the Met's *Tosca* in May, 1962, at the Arie Crown Theatre. All the singers—Robert Merrill, Victoria de los Angeles and Richard Tucker—became ill. Francis Robinson of the Met told Harry in confidence that Tucker had had a mild heart attack and had had to go back East. Harry always respected confidences but he was especially careful about this one because the Tuckers were personal friends of ours. He simply announced that due to illness Mr. Tucker would be replaced in *Tosca*. If mutual friends asked, Harry told them what Francis Robinson had said.

A few weeks later Harry called me at Pierpoint and asked me if I had read Kup's column that morning. I hadn't; I had been gardening all morning. "Read it and call me right back," Harry said. I got the paper immediately and read the item:

> End of a beautiful friendship: Richard Tucker, star of both the Met and the Lyric, has sent word that he no longer will appear for impresario Harry Zelzer. Tucker is burning because of Zelzer's alleged remarks that the

singer is suffering from a heart attack, which Tucker charges cost him a number of concert engagements...

I was astonished. I called Harry back and asked him whether I should speak to Sara Tucker. He thought that might be a good idea. He couldn't reach the singer. So I called Sara but she did not want to listen to anything I had to say. She insisted that Harry had told everybody that Richard's career was finished. I told her that was ridiculous; she couldn't believe that. I suggested that it was a rumor spread by someone who disliked Harry. "We're good friends," I said to her. "How can you think Harry would do anything to hurt Richard? And if Richard heard some rumor, don't you think he should have come to us to ask us if it was true?"

But all she would say was that anyone who spoke against her husband was her enemy. I told her I felt the same way about Harry, but it was a useless conversation. I told Harry about it; he felt sad but he was also resentful. He said that he was not going to attempt to bridge this gap any further. He said we should forget the Tuckers. He wrote a letter to CAMI saying that although he considered Tucker's statement to Kup to be ill-mannered and ill-advised, he did not intend to respond to Tucker's accusation in the press because he did not care to air the matter in public.

> I want you to know [he concluded]...that my livelihood does not depend on Richard Tucker, nor does his depend on me. He made an erroneous statement to the press and I expect him to retract it. I have always regarded Richard as a great tenor and a good friend, but I now no longer consider him a friend. He has more to lose than I have in Chicago.

I have several bookings pending for next year and I shall just have to give these organizations another artist. It is too bad when an adult...lets a friendship of such long years go by the wayside because of not verifying statements with the party concerned instead of listening to people who have an ax to grind.

Needless to say, Richard Tucker did not retract his statement and that ended our relationship with him for ten years, until he called unexpectedly around the time of the Jewish high holidays, saying that he was in Chicago and wanted us to have lunch with him and Sara. "It's time to forget hard feelings," he said. "It's the beginning of the new year. We should renew our friendship."

We had lunch with them. Harry had to go back to the office but the three of us went shopping. We tried, but we couldn't restore the feelings of close friendship we had had in the past.

I certainly understood Richard's desire for secrecy. In 1963 Harry himself had a heart attack at Pierpoint; we told everybody in the business that he had had a relapse of hepatitis. We didn't want people to wonder when he was going to retire; we wanted the public to believe that it was going to be business as usual, and it *was* business as usual until Harry finally decided to retire in 1978.

But the story does not quite end there. In March 1984 I was in Florida and I wanted something to read while I was sunbathing. I picked up a copy of a biography of Richard Tucker by James A. Drake. To my surprise, I read that in May of 1962, Richard Tucker was in the Long Island Jewish Hospital after a heart attack. His family stood around him; there were oxygen tubes in his nostrils and intravenous needles in his arms. He told his son Barry not to tell anyone: "Nobody must know about this, do you understand? Make up anything, but don't tell *anybody* that there's something wrong with my heart."

XXII. TRIBUTE DINNER

I N November, 1984, while I was suffering with my broken thigh bone, Keith Miller, who was still at Allied Arts—I left officially on December 13, 1984 and he stayed until 1985—told me that Noah Hoffman, the director of development for the American Conservatory, had asked him to approach me about a tribute dinner in honor of Harry and me. My first impulse was to refuse: Harry had never approved of testimonial dinners for fundraising. But Keith persuaded me to meet with Noah Hoffman. We talked and I agreed to be the honoree of a dinner set for Harry's birthday, April 15, 1985. I let myself be persuaded because Noah Hoffman said that the money raised by the dinner would go to establish a Zelzer Series dedicated to Harry's memory. Of course this was important to me. The Orchestral Association had omitted the standard line "Founded by Harry Zelzer" from the Allied Arts program; this was one of the things that had soured my relationship with them.

The American Conservatory had sold its building at 116 South Michigan Avenue and was in the process of purchasing a property at Monroe and Sangamon streets, which included a warehouse which the Conservatory planned to convert into a 400-seat theatre. I was told that if the dinner raised enough money to pay for the transformation of the warehouse, the resulting theatre would be called the Zelzer Concert Hall. I agreed to all this, on condition that I would control the use of the Zelzer name. The dinner evening was to be called "A Tribute to the Legend of the late Harry Zelzer and Sarah S. Zelzer."

Leonard Bernstein had become interested in the Conservatory through his friendship with Aaron Stern, who was on the staff there, and so he agreed to be chairman of the dinner. I was delighted, because our relationship with Lenny went back about forty years to the very beginning of his career when Harry engaged him to conduct the Women's Symphony Orchestra for a fee of $250. We had also booked him at Sinai Temple for lecture-recitals, a format he went on to develop into his brilliant television series with the New York Philharmonic and his Norton lectures. Whenever we got together over the years, he would always ask about that South Side temple on the lake where he had given his lecture and he would say, "I'll never forget how Harry booked me around when I was young. I'll always owe him for what he did for me."

He performed wonderfully as chairman. He gave a moving speech about Harry at the kickoff dinner on March 27, '85, in the Avenue One Room of the Drake Hotel; he said that every artist was welcomed by the impresario the instant he or she set foot in Chicago, and felt an immediate friendship with him.

Lenny and Harry had been so close that Lenny was one of the few people who had known about Harry's heart attack when it happened in the '60s. Lenny had been very concerned about Harry's health. He didn't want him to overtax himself and even suggested that we all skip a reception which was being held after one of Lenny's programs at the Opera House—that was about three weeks after Harry had left the hospital. I told Lenny we would go "just for ten minutes" and he gave me a moving lecture about how to care for my husband.

Mayor Harold Washington, who was at our table, also gave an excellent talk at the kickoff dinner. He and Lenny got on well together. Many pledges were made, the tributes to Harry were great and the press coverage was tremendous. We all felt we were on our way to producing a very successful event.

Four hundred people attended the elegant dinner in the Regency Ballroom of the Hyatt Regency Hotel on April 15. Victor Borge was the master of ceremonies. Noah Hoffman told me that Victor said he felt honored to be invited to take part in a tribute to his old friend "Alka-Seltzer"—a name he had given Harry years ago.

We went back a long way with Borge. We must have booked him for the first time in '46 in a straight concert with his own orchestra at Orchestra Hall. He didn't do the shtik then that he does now, but he was big box office even then. He always remembers a particularly wonderful performance at the Opera House where we had six hundred seats on the stage.

At the Tribute Dinner Borge played a piano medley that included "Happy Birthday". William Warfield sang. There were speeches and tributes. I couldn't hold back the tears. Donald Rumsfeld (politician, government official, Searle executive) was the general chairman, Senator Paul Simon was the honorary chairman. Our old friends Ralph Ergas and Bernard McKenna were co-chairmen. The Distinguished Artist Committee included Vladimir Ashkenazy, Lenny, of course; John Browning, Van Cliburn, James Dick, Malcolm Frager, Gary Graffman, Byron Janis, Edwin MacArthur, Robert Merrill, Carlos Montoya, Ruth Page, Roberta Peters and Pinchas Zukerman. There were certainly great possibilities in these names for a marvelous theatre season.

Then it was announced that the board of trustees, the faculty and the Administration of the American Conservatory had resolved to confer an honorary doctorate of musical arts upon me, "in recognition of distinguished service to the performing arts and the educational and cultural life of the city of Chicago. That ceremony to be performed at the commencement and concert program of the American Conservatory of Music to be held on the nineteenth day of May in the year of Our Lord one-thousand-nine-hundred and eighty-five." I was so proud. I prayed that somehow Harry knew about this and approved of it.

The morning after the dinner I went to look over the site with Lenny, Charles Moore, president of the American Conservatory, Aaron Stern, Noah Hoffman and a few students. We all thought it was great. I agreed on the spot to contribute $50,000 toward the development of the theatre if it was named for Harry. Lenny thought it was a good idea to do that.

Unfortunately the deal for the Conservatory's new building fell through. The building had a wood-beam construction; it was attractive but it violated the fire ordinance for educational institutions. It couldn't be used that way.

And that wasn't the only problem. I asked for an accounting of the dinner funds and gradually learned that the profits from the Tribute Dinner, which came to $34,000, were being used to pay the day-to-day expenses of the Conservatory, which was sliding into bankruptcy.

The Conservatory was not financially able to honor its commitment to a Zelzer Series.

Of course I was upset. Our name had always stood for honesty and now it had been used to raise money to set up a musical series and the series seemed to be an impossibility. We had always lived up to our commitments and kept our promises and I felt I must keep this one. I decided that a Zelzer Series had to take place and that I would assume financial responsibility for it, using the money I had set aside to put into the theatre. We would have a season dedicated to Harry. I owed that to the many people who had given money to create a memorial to him.

XXIII. THE ZELZER SERIES: GETTING STARTED AGAIN

IN November, 1986, I held a press conference at the Lake Point Tower Club to announce a Zelzer Season at the Auditorium Theatre for 1987-88. I had booked a modest calendar, just fifteen attractions for "Great Music at Affordable Prices" which I hoped would find a responsive audience. The Zelzer season included a Piano Series, a Concert Series and four Special Attractions. For the Piano Series I had Joaquin Achucarro, Mitsuko Uchida, Charles Rosen, Alicia de Larrocha, Philippe Bianconi, Susan Starr, Sergei Edelmann and David Bar-Illan, who cancelled at the last minute and was replaced by Santiago Rodriguez. The Concert Series featured Pinchas Zukerman, Paul Whiteman's Historic Aeolian Hall Concert and I Musici. The Special Attractions were the Warsaw Ballet; Mel Tormé, Peter Nero and Leslie Uggams in "A Tribute to George Gershwin"; the Bayanihan Philippine Dance Company and the Belgrade State Folk Ensemble.

I had very much wanted to include Leonard Bernstein in this first season. I wanted a mix of well-known and lesser-known names—the kind of mix we had introduced and implemented over the years. I thought that Lenny's involvement in the project would get it started

on the right track. So I wrote and asked him to open the
Piano Series with a lecture recital. I told him that I
certainly didn't expect him to donate his services, but I
was sure we could agree on a suitable fee. I reminded
him that he had been the guiding light for the Tribute
Dinner, and that it seemed to me that both he and I
were morally obligated to fulfill the promise of the
Zelzer Series.

Lenny turned my request over to Aaron Stern, who
was no longer with the Conservatory. And Aaron Stern
wrote to tell me that something had happened to sour
him and Lenny on the American Conservatory and
Lenny would not participate in anything that carried
the name of the school. (I was putting on the Zelzer
Concert Series in cooperation with the Auditorium Theatre Council and the American Conservatory which was
by then in Chapter 11. I did that for the first season, to
honor my connection with the Conservatory. But I
dropped their name the second season.)

It appeared that forty years of friendship counted
for nothing with Lenny.

Before deciding on the Auditorium, I had looked
into other halls. I tried to do something with the Chicago Theatre, which is conveniently located and was
being attractively renovated. I went to see the Chicago
Theatre people; they were interested, but plans never
materialized. They were having their own problems.
Henry Fogel, the executive director of the Chicago Symphony Orchestra, asked me why I didn't present my
Zelzer Series there. But I didn't think that was a serious
offer.

Some people thought I was starting my Zelzer Series in order to compete directly with the Orchestral Association. I have to be honest enough to admit that I may have been somewhat motivated by my feelings toward the Association. I had never made a secret of the fact that I thought their series had been poorly run. I felt then, and I feel today, that the people there have no idea about what their artists will draw at the box office.

Henry Fogel made a pleasant public statement: "There is room for both of us. Competition is healthy and I welcome whatever she will be doing. This is a pretty big city. There are audiences for both of us—look at all the music New York City can support." He talked about Allied Arts accounting procedures. "In 1983-84 the loss was $16,000. In 1984-85 there was a $6,000 surplus. During 1985-86, a season Zelzer booked before her retirement, there was a $140,000 loss. Income was up, but so were fees and expenses. This season, the first for which we had complete authority, fees are down $140,000, subscriptions are up 168 percent and management is anticipating a $60,000 surplus on the basis of our performance so far."

I heard that Fogel was privately predicting that we would fail. And he went back on our agreement about the box at Orchestra Hall which I was to keep for my lifetime. In April, '87, he wrote me:

> I received a copy of your Friday matinee renewal form for the Chicago Symphony concerts with your note to our subscription department. I am pleased to inform you that we do intend to continue to have you as our guest with these pairs of tickets to both Friday matinee series. I would, however, like to re-examine the box for all Allied Arts concerts that you have had on a

complimentary basis in the past. I have thought about this a great deal, and considered not only the demand we have for box seats and the value of the box for the entire Allied Arts series (about $3,500 worth of tickets), but I have also considered the fact that the situation has changed somewhat in view of your having a new series at the Auditorium Theatre.

In light of all of the above, and balancing that with my desire to continue to have you as our guest for all Allied Arts concerts, I would like to modify our offer to you, and we will make available to you a pair of main-floor tickets to each Allied Arts concert in the future. These tickets are, of course, with our compliments and they are in addition to the complimentary tickets for the Chicago Symphony Friday matinee concerts. I wish you the very best with your Auditorium series.

I answered him on April 5, 1987:

Thank you for your courtesy for the Chicago Symphony Orchestra Friday afternoon concerts.

Now, as to Box O for all Allied Arts concerts. I can understand your thoughts on the situation, and it does not surprise me any as I was expecting you to want to reconsider due to my presenting the Zelzer Series at the Auditorium Theatre. But I did think the Orchestral Association would keep its commitment as per Mr Staub's letter to me when I resigned from the Allied Arts Association. I, on the other hand, made no commitment to the Orchestral Association. I suppose, if I were in your position (the other side of the fence), I would take the same attitude. You mention $3,500 value in the tickets. In the *Tribune*, you mention you expect to be in the black this season. If so, my Box O does not exactly mean a deficit to you. I don't really think your decision is the best in terms of public relations, but if this means it will make you happier, I will, as a matter of good public relations, accept your offer of two main-floor tickets for all Allied Arts concerts for this next season. Thank you for your good wishes for the success of my series. I do hope you have a very successful Allied Arts 1987-88. I extend an open invitation to you and Mrs Fogel to attend any concert you wish to come to on my series as my guest.

I sincerely hope we will remain friends for the future.

On September 13, 1987, the Zelzer tradition was renewed with the opening concert of my Zelzer Piano Series. I planned to give a few words of welcome to the audience after the Miro Quartet played the Aria from Bach's Third Suite in Harry's memory; I was very nervous as I prepared this welcome because I was afraid that there would be no concert. The afternoon's artist, Joaquin Achucarro, was nowhere to be found. I was told that he had been practicing in the hall that morning. Noah Hoffman told me this; Noah was now my associate. He had become so fascinated with the concert world when, as director of development for the American Conservatory, he had worked on the Tribute Dinner, that he had come to work with me. He is a resourceful man, but even he did not know what to do about Achucarro, who had checked out of his hotel and wasn't to be found in any nearby coffee shop or restaurant.

At last, after forty minutes that seemed like a year to me, he walked in. I don't think I have ever been so happy to see anyone. What had happened? He had mistaken the hour of the concert; he thought it was supposed to begin at four, not at three, and he had gone for a walk because it was a lovely afternoon.

After that rocky beginning, everything went beautifully. Achucarro played a program of Schubert and

Chopin Sonatas—B Major and Minor respectively, Sy-
manowski *Preludes* and a De Falla group dedicated to
the memory of Arthur Rubinstein. His performance was
magnificent and the audience loved it. After the concert
invited guests stayed on for a champagne reception on
the stage—the food was prepared by Chef Hans, an old
friend of ours. He does a beautiful buffet.

The reviews the next day were almost better than I
could have written myself. I was back in business. The
only question was, for how long? Of course that would
depend on how well we could do financially and artistically. Each concert was an artistic success, but I must
admit that we were hurt by the large size of the hall,
especially for the Piano Series.

We had always intended to sell seats only on the
main floor, in the boxes and in the front rows of the first
balcony. But it was depressing to see a few hundred
people scattered through a hall that could hold more
than four thousand. One recital, of Russian pianist Sergei Edelmann, took place during the International Theatre Festival when, with a thrust stage and drapes, the
size of the theatre was reduced to accommodate about a
thousand patrons. Adler and Sullivan had designed the
theatre to adapt to a number of differently sized audiences: gallery seats, for instance, can be put up flush
against the wall, which vastly improves the sound and
the ambience.

But the cost of the hall was prohibitive on a per-
concert basis. And even more disappointing, some big-
name artists didn't begin to pull in large enough audiences to justify their fees. Pinchus Zukerman's receipts

were so-so, but Alicia de Larrocha was a financial disaster.

On the other hand, we had some successes. The Gershwin concert with Mel Tormé, Leslie Uggams and Peter Nero, did very well. Since Mel Tormé is a native Chicagoan, he has a large local following. Another special thing about that concert was that during intermission I was presented with a proclamation in my honor by Mayor Harold Washington.

The re-creation of the Paul Whiteman historic Aeolian Hall concert attracted a large and enthusiastic audience and brought back pleasant memories of the times "Pops" Whiteman had come to Chicago under Zelzer management. Noah Hoffman arranged a dance contest to be held during intermission and that got a lot of press. Luck was with us for that concert—it was very nearly a disaster. The clarinetist became violently ill during intermission—unfortunately the second half of the concert was set to open with *Rhapsody in Blue* with its famous clarinet part. We were frantic; then we learned that the road manager was a clarinet player. He suited up and started to prepare to go on. But at the last possible moment, the clarinetist recovered, at least enough to complete the second half of the concert. Then he went back to his hotel and went right to bed.

That reminds me of another tense incident involving Gershwin. Years ago we presented various orchestras and in 1953 we brought Thor Johnson and the Cincinnati Orchestra for two concerts. Oscar Levant was the soloist in the Gershwin concerto and the concert hall was rocked by his angry behavior. When he didn't get the tempo he wanted from the conductor, he began to conduct the tempo himself. Later he shouted at Johnson, "Diminuendo, diminuendo!" Some of the audience insisted he had shouted something else. When the concert ended, Levant took a quick bow and left the stage without shaking hands with the conductor. Then in response to prolonged applause, Levant came forward again, this time forcibly dragging Johnson with him to share the cheers. When the orchestra left the stage, Levant settled in to play some encores. He winked at the audience and said, "As you can see, the air is full of amiability."

After the concert I told Oscar that Harry was very angry with him for carrying on the way he had with Thor Johnson.

"He deserved it," Oscar said. "His tempi were all wrong and he didn't follow me."

I reminded him that we had another concert the following night.

"I lost my temper with him," Oscar said, "but I'll be good tomorrow night."

"You'd better be good," I told him, "or you're not coming back here again."

He behaved the next night. Oscar was neurotic as hell but it didn't show up in his playing. It showed up in the way he behaved otherwise.

To return to my Zelzer Series: the ethnic events we presented did fairly well in spite of their political ramifications. The Jugoslav community silently boycotted the Belgrade State Folk Ensemble; they considered it a traveling propaganda show. The Polish community did not rally behind Polish ballet, more especially since Chicago Poles were more comfortable with folk dancing than with ballet. Four or five dancers defected from the ballet after it left Chicago. If they had done it while the group was in Chicago, I imagine there would have been a strong response at the box office, because of publicity which, incidentally, can no longer be relied on as it was in the past. You can tell when you look at old newspapers that we used to get a lot of space, with both stories and pictures. If Harry needed help with something, he could call an editor and work something out. That doesn't happen nowadays.

And advertising is not as reliable as it was. You have to know where to advertise now and be flexible and realistic about how much you spend. If something isn't selling, it's not going to become a hot commodity just because you double the advertising budget. At Orchestra Hall I could never make them understand that. They would ask me to give them an advertising budget for the year and I would try to explain to them that if I gave them such a figure, it could only be a fantasy because there is no way of knowing what is going to happen a year ahead of time.

I had to make a decision about the future of my new Series. So I counted up pros and cons, wins and losses; I took into consideration our having started from scratch, without my subscriber lists, without experienced staff—and I decided to go a second season. Big names and big attractions hadn't paid off at the box office. I decided to go with just the Piano Series and with fine, lesser-known artists. The second season would open with Garrick Ohlsson in an all-Chopin program. He would be followed by Alexandre Toradze, Michel Block, Minoru Nojima, Alexander Slobodyanik,

Louis Lortie, Alexis Golovin and Ruth Slenczynska,
who had made her Chicago debut when she was a child
fifty years before on the original Zelzer Series. There
were no big draws on this list, but there were no possibilities of big losses there either.

Trouble started almost immediately. Dulcie Gilmore
had joined the Auditorium staff as a consultant shortly
after I had booked my first season. Now she had taken
over as manager and was trying to book a big show for
the theatre. She succeeded in getting *Les Misérables*,
which did very well when it eventually opened at the
Auditorium. But it caused a nightmare for me. Because
of the complicated preparations for staging that show, I
had to wait to the last minute to get dates when I could
use the theatre. There were many scheduling changes
and problems that cropped up at the last minute. And
worst of all, there would be no dates available for me
after January when *Les Misérables* began its run.

I had to decide what to do. I had gone from a
situation where I had total cooperation to one where I
could have no cooperation. It was a headache that
didn't look as if it could get better. True, I had brought
classical music back to the Auditorium. But there was
no question that the Piano Series had really been designed for a small hall that didn't exist.

I thought and thought about what to do. There were
many factors to consider: pride, reputation, commitment and courage were some of them. Then there was
my age and the fact that the money I was using was
mine and mine only. If I stayed a few more seasons,
would things begin to turn around financially or would
I be putting myself into jeopardy during my last years? I

had to ask myself these hard questions and take a hard look at myself and at the business. I decided that I would announce my decision at my eightieth birthday party. The envelopes that Noah handed to the people from the media contained that decision.

But before the envelopes were passed out, I had one happy announcement to make. I introduced Dean Grier, who had once worked for Orchestra Hall and was now in business for himself doing radio syndication. He announced that an agreement had been reached to broadcast the Zelzer Piano Series on WNIB-FM under the sponsorship of United Airlines. The Series was of course to be aired on tape.

The press release in the envelope was headed "Sarah Zelzer Announces the End of the Zelzer Series." It read:

Sunday afternoon, January 22nd, at 3 p.m., at the Auditorium Theatre the Alexis Golovin recital will be the final event on the Zelzer Piano Series, season 1988-89, as well as the end of the Zelzer Series in Chicago. I am honored to present the international pianist Alexis Golovin as my final event.

Monday, January 23, is my birthday and I feel it is now time to give up some of my responsibilities and enjoy the leisure and wonders of life.

When my husband, Harry Zelzer, retired in 1979, he did so with great acclaim and honor by giving our Allied Arts Corporation as a gift to the Orchestral Association. At that time Allied Arts...was a thriving business. The Zelzer Series at the present time is not a thriving business. I have been approached by a few individuals who would like to take over the Zelzer Series. I have turned down their requests. Why? I have tried for two seasons to build the Zelzer Series. Artistically it has been, according to the press, a great success. I chose artists that I

believed in and knew would give excellent performances. My training by one of the best teachers in the
field, Harry Zelzer, prepared me for this. Financially, in
spite of all my years of experience, the Series has not
been a success. Outstanding artists—great performances at affordable prices—have not been enough for
audience response. It would take at least five more
seasons to accomplish this. As my entire training in
presenting attractions has not been based on subsidy, I
find it not possible or feasible to go this route. I have
personally subsidized the Zelzer Series for the last two
seasons and now have come to the realization that I will
not continue.

The economic changes have taken a toll. Artists'
fees, theatre rentals, stagehands, insurance and marketing all have sky-rocketed. The independent concert
manager cannot function. Prices of tickets are sky-high.

The excitement of discovering new talent seems to
have diminished. The main objective now seems to be
able to have someone underwrite the cost of performances. But my question is, does this create audiences?
Until we can solve this situation, how can the music
industry continue? Marketing? The cost of that is so
tremendous that the deficits remain even greater than
before. Will more subsidy change this?

I am not willing to have any individual take over the
Zelzer name. I am retiring now, secure in the knowledge that the Zelzer name will remain in the history of
culture in Chicago with great respect and admiration.
Through the years we have discovered great talent,
helped them in their careers and presented the greatest
attractions in the world....

I gave the Auditorium Theatre special thanks and
wished continual success to the Orchestral Association.
And then I thanked everyone who had attended the
Allied Arts performances and the Zelzer Series.

And that would seem to be that. Except that it never
is. Alexis Golovin cancelled that final concert at the last

minute. We replaced him with Ivan Davis, a superb pianist who had appeared for us many times. He played a fine program, said a few words about Harry and gave a special encore. It brought tears to my eyes. The program book contained another farewell to the audience, my dearest friends for almost sixty years.

> The presentation of Ivan Davis marks a milestone in my life and perhaps in the cultural life of Chicago. This will be the last performance of the 1988-89 Zelzer Piano Series, as well as the last performance to be presented under the Zelzer name. For the last six decades I have dedicated my life along with my late husband, Harry Zelzer, to bringing to Chicago audiences, thousands of talented artists. Some of you in today's audience have been loyal to our presentations for many of those years. Others may have only been introduced to the Zelzer name more recently. But to each and every one who has attended our recitals, concerts, dance attractions, especially those subscribers, thank you for supporting quality culture....
> Please continue to support live performance with all the enthusiasm and joy that great art brings to the human spirit.

XXIV. RETIREMENT: FINAL THOUGHTS

WELL, that seems to be that for now. It still feels strange to go to a concert and realize it is not one of ours and that I can sit and listen without worrying about the million and one things that need to be taken care of.

People come up to me and tell me they miss our concerts and ask when we'll be back. I smile; I'm retired. For now.

When I look back, I wonder if people are crediting me with more than I deserve. I don't feel that I have accomplished enough when I compare it with what I had hoped to do. I had hoped to make a success of my Series: a lot of people, including the press, had great confidence in me when I started and although we had an artistic success, we did not, as I have said, succeed financially.

Maybe I was naive to think that the Zelzer name and reputation for good attractions at low prices would bring people in. There wasn't enough of an increase in the second season to make it pay. I can't blame that fact on the artists' fees, because I was able to keep those fees down. Of course advertising costs were very high and the Auditorium is expensive. But the bottom line is that we just didn't attract enough audience.

It's true that I started from zero, without my Allied Arts lists of 170,000 people who had bought tickets over the years, and without new marketing. If I had gone into subsidy, it might have helped, but I wasn't trained that way and I don't have the heart for it. I'm good at selling to organizations but I have never been good at asking people for money. Finally, and most importantly, I didn't have the time to build. We spent twenty to twenty-five years building Allied Arts; I had my Series for only two seasons. Maybe if I had been willing to stick it out for five years, I would have seen results. But I'm past eighty now, and I don't have that many years left. Besides, the music business in which I spent my life is a different business now. Mine were the days of the individual; today belongs to the corporation. I'm not convinced that art by committee can thrive. Time will tell.

I'd like to think that Harry would have been able to make the Series go because I have always believed that Harry could do anything. He had supreme self-confidence and if he lost money on something he would think of something else to do to make up for it. Yet, in my heart of hearts, I feel unsure. Harry was an impresario of the old school, the last of the old-time impresarios, and although he had a lasting effect on the music life of Chicago, the day of the impresario is done. It will not return.

Today because of fees and other expenses, a manager cannot operate on his own without government aid—federal, or state—or help from the community. Things have changed 180 degrees—in the old days the local manager got the first money; now the agent does.

Local managers therefore have to manage the theatres so that they can use the rental money to cover the deficits they incur from overpaying on attractions. It's not surprising that the fundraiser has become the most important person in today's musical organization, and that the manager's most important talent is fundraising. The first question an applicant for a job in concert management is asked is, "What is your fundraising background?" Look at the people who head today's organizations and that's what you see—fundraisers. Ravinia is the most striking example. While it's true that Zarin Mehta comes from a musical family, his most important credential has been his partnership in the international accounting firm of Coopers and Lybrand.

I remember when fees hit what we thought would be their maximum: $10,000. That was for Maria Callas. Harry and Roger Dettmer, music critic for the *Chicago American*, had lunch with her in New York to talk about a concert in Chicago. I had typed two different contracts for them to take with them: one for a percentage and the other for a $5,000 fee. During lunch Callas received a phone call from Mrs Walter Kirk, a Chicago socialite, offering to double any offer Harry made if Callas would do a benefit concert for the Alliance Française. You can guess what happened. But not surprisingly, two weeks before the concert Mrs Kirk called Harry for help: the concert was not drawing. Harry said he would do what he could and he did manage to help make the concert a success, but in doing that he helped to establish the $10,000 fee. Artists and managers went around quoting this fee and as a result managers began to lose control of their artists.

Now there's no longer a set fee for any artist. The agents push for whatever the traffic will bear—$40,000, $50,000, even $100,000. Recently the Vienna Philharmonic Orchestra received a fee of $125,000 and they will try for more. I've already mentioned Serkin's doubling his fee. The higher the fee the agent can get for his client, the longer the client will stay with him—and, of course, the higher the agent's commission.

But artists want more than fees. We were to present Zubin Mehta and the Israel Philharmonic Orchestra in Orchestra Hall as a benefit for the America-Israel Cultural Foundation. Unexpectedly, before the concert, the agent ICM, representing Mehta and the orchestra, announced that in addition to their enormous fee, they wanted a part of the benefit monies. We were outraged: we pointed out that we had presented that orchestra many times over the years and they could not attract a full house without participating organizations. We threatened to cancel the performance and tell the press why we were doing it. After many arguments, and with the assistance of Isaac Stern, we were able to put on the concert.

But I had words afterward with Mehta. And I informed ICM that Allied Arts would never again present the Israel Philharmonic with Mehta conducting.

Mehta isn't the only one who demands a percentage of a benefit over and above his fee. Everyone does it who thinks he can get away with it.

For a few years AT&T has sponsored American orchestra tours, covering the orchestras' deficits and purchasing some tickets for the concerts. But it would be helpful if they would also help cover local managers' deficits as well, because the box office cannot be counted on to cover high fees and other expenses. If AT&T would do this, the concerts could be put on in more cities.

Then too there is some bad business being done in the music field. The jet age has revolutionized the music industry the way the pill has revolutionized birth control. Some Fifty-seventh Street operators, those who are commonly known as "hi-jackers", have developed a new technique. They can travel about and find new customers in the organizations: men and women with no experience in the concert field. These "hi-jackers" find out what the budget is and then take it all. They are about as honest and have as much integrity as bawdy-house madames have true love.

Many of the new managers are ignorant; they have backgrounds as dilettantes or college arts management majors. But the important things about this business cannot be taught in school. A second group of managers are financially irresponsible; they expect fairy godmothers to cover their ever-increasing deficits. Instead of handling the money at their disposal as if it were their own, they seem to believe, along with the press, that "the bigger the deficit, the better the season." In this computer age, they seem to think they can just put the data into the machine and the machine will take over from there and make everything all right. Projections are substituted for perspiration and experience; no one pays attention to the artist's prior history of box-office receipts.

Or else they rely on modern marketing techniques, on radio and TV spot announcements and ads. As you will remember, I told them at Orchestra Hall that I could not give them an advertising budget for the year because I handled each attraction separately. If I put in an ad and saw that it wasn't pulling, then I didn't put in bigger ads in order to save the situation. You cannot just say you're going to spend so much on an attraction; you have to watch what that expenditure is bringing in, where to place ads and how many to run. Spot announcements are expensive. So is telemarketing. Some people are sold on the latter; they claim it brings in bodies. I say that by the time you pay for the telephones and the telephoners there's virtually nothing left.

So we come back to subsidy, which seems to be the only way in future. I'm against it not because it's something new in this country but because it's misunderstood and misapplied. Once the artist or manager knows that subsidy is available, fees escalate. Greed gobbles up the money and losses are greater than ever.

Certain concerts—lieder recitals, for example—never make money. The people who bring them book them into smaller theatres with limited audiences and look for subsidies rather than financing these kind of concerts themselves. We paid for Dietrich Fischer-Dieskau or other great artists who didn't draw by presenting Mantovani, Lawrence Welk, Johnny Cash, the Bolshoi Ballet, the Met or Marlene Dietrich.

My husband always told me that no matter whose money you're using to promote the arts, you should treat it as if it were your own. And that's the way I tried to run Allied Arts when I was at Orchestra Hall; I still thought of the business as ours and tried to keep to budgets and cut expenses. Why should sixty people in the office do the work of twenty? If you can go out and ask for $100,000 and get it—bingo!—and none of the money is yours, you don't worry about cuts.

The same amount of culture could be brought to Chicago for much less money. It might not be as glamorous an undertaking but it would be more honorable than making a name on other people's money. Not everyone who tries to run concerts is fit for it; some should remain part of the audience. And artists, especially the younger ones, go out for grants these days. But why should someone pay to support them just because they want to be artists? Either you have the talent and you can make a go of it or you don't and you can't. Does a stenographer ask for a grant to get a stenographer's job?

I'll tell you a secret: when I was in business I hated the responsibilities, the details, the payrolls. When I was in school, I was poorest in arithmetic. I skipped a year and a half in grammar school and that was the year and a half that fractions and decimals were being taught. I never felt secure about numbers. And suddenly I was in business and faced with payrolls, box-office statements and percentage contracts. Sometimes, working on a week's ballet run, I'd go home and have nightmares wondering if I had paid them the right amount.

But all that was balanced by things I loved. I could hear all the music and the great artists that I might have missed otherwise. I learned things that had not been included in my musical education, extensive as it was. Though I gave up the possibility of a concert career, I spent my life helping exciting new talent to succeed.

The artists who enriched our lives were many: Jan Kiepura, Marta Eggerth, Andres Segovia, Arthur Rubinstein, Artur Schnabel, Arturo Toscanini, Victor Borge, Leontyne Price, Leonard Bernstein, Sigmund Romberg, Paul Whiteman, Mantovani, Van Cliburn, Daniel Barenboim....And I was able to meet interesting and important people in fields outside music and we have been blessed throughout with marvelous friends. It hasn't been the life I planned when I was a girl in Wicker Park, but it has been wonderful.

This book presents only a part of the concert business. Everyone and everything cannot be included. I'm sorry for anyone I left out, and if anything I have said is offensive to anyone, I can only say that I have told the truth as I saw it.

List of Artists Presented by the Allied Arts Corporation, 1937-1977

by Marjorie Hassen

ACTORS/COMEDIANS (Male and Female)

Berman, Shelley, 10/18/60

Borge, Victor, 4/27/46; 5/28/46; 4/4/59; 3/26/60; 3/24/61; 12/2/61; 3/9/63; 4/11/64; 10/16/65; 2/26/67; 10/10/69; 11/29/70; 12/3/72; 2/8/76

Draper, Ruth, 1/24/43; 12/9-10/45

Gregory, Havard, 10/17/71

Kenneally, Philip, 1/27-2/1/58

King, Alan, 9/4-9/58; 6/1-7/59; 11/20/71

Korwin, Devra, 1/27-2/1/58

Kujath, Hannes, 12/5/72

Lowe, Ralph, 1/27-2/1/58

Picon, Molly, 3/24/46; 4/17-27/57

Ritchard, Cyril, 5/26/57

Russell, Anna, 11/14/54; 2/27/76; 3/27/77

Schell, Ronnie, 2/23/63

Sherman, Don, 7/19-20/63

Thomas, Aeronwy, 10/17/71

Westbrook, Paul, 3/23/58

Williams, Emlyn, 4/13-18/53; 2/14-15/59; 3/7/71; 12/14/75

BALLET COMPANIES *see* DANCE/BALLET COMPANIES

BANDS

Argyll and Sutherland Highlanders, 10/20/62

Guard Republican Band of Paris, 10/4/53

The Original Deutschmeister Band, 4/6/58; 2/28/60; 3/18/62

The Pipes and Drums, Regimental Band and Dancers of the Black Watch, 10/31-11/1/63

Royal Scots Greys, 10/20/62

The Scots Guards, 4/1-2/72

The Wiltener Stadtmusik Band of Innsbruck, Austria, 5/23/67

CHOIRS/VOCAL ENSEMBLES

All God's Children, 2/29/76

Arion Musical Club, 12/3/50

Berlin Mozart Choir, 11/19/67

The Blue Danube Choir of Vienna, 10/24/71

The Branko Krsmanovich Chorus of Yugoslavia, 10/29/60; 12/10/61; 2/14/65

The Camerata Singers, 10/27/68

Chanteurs de Paris, 3/6/60

Chicago Lithuanian Chorus, 11/7/37
Chicago Singing Academy, 5/16/48
Chicago Symphony Chorus, 12/15/68
Community Renewal Chorus, 2/29/76
Czech Singing Society Lyra, 3/21/71
de Cormier Singers *see* The Robert de Cormier Singers
De Paur's Infantry Chorus, 11/18/51; 2/15/53; 11/8/53;11/7/54;
    1/22/56
Don Cossack Russian Male Chorus *see* The Original Don Cossack
    Chorus and Dancers
Father Flanagan's Boys Town Choir, 10/5/46; 10/7/46
Federal Glee Club, 3/28/38
Feis Eireann *see* The Irish Festival Singers
The Filharmonia Chorus, 10/19/40
Gen. Platoff Don Cossack Chorus, 2/9/42; 11/21/43; 2/4/45;
    11/10/45; 3/2/47; 1/17/48; 11/7/48; 12/5/55; 9/30/56
Gordela, 11/17/74
Gumpoldskirchner Children's Choir, 4/6/58
The Harry Simeone Chorale, 11/12/67
The Heidelberg University Chorus, 3/6/59
The Helsinki University Chorus, 11/22/53; 11/7/65
The Irish Festival Singers, 1/21/56
Jaroff Male Chorus and Dancers *see* The Original Don Cossack
    Chorus and Dancers
KFUM *see* National Swedish Chorus
Krakow Choir and Orchestra, 2/5/66
Laredef Glee Club, 3/28/38
The Lira Polish Singers, 3/21/71
The Little Gaelic Singers of Country Derry, 11/3/56
The Little Singers of Paris, 3/7-8/57
Luboff Choir *see* The Norman Luboff Choir
The Mariners, 9/25/54
Mitrovich Sisters, 3/21/71
National Swedish Chorus, 11/4/56; 10/18/64
The New Wine Singers, 9/6/63
Ninos Cantores de Monterrey *see* Singing Boys of Monterrey
The Norman Luboff Choir, 10/17/65
North Park College Choir, 2/8/76
Obernkirchen Children's Choir, 10/15/54; 10/21-22/55; 5/12/57;
    2/12/61; 10/7/62; 10/25/64; 11/10/68
Olavs Guttene *see* Singing Boys of Norway
The Original Don Cossack Chorus and Dancers, 10/10/37; 10/24/37;
    10/23/38; 10/15/39; 10/29/39; 11/17/40; 11/16/41; 10/25/42;
    10/17/43; 12/12/43; 10/22/44; 2/25/45; 11/30/45; 12/2/45;
    2/16-17/46; 12/7/46; 12/13/46; 2/7/47; 2/7/48; 1/22/49; 2/27/49;
    10/1/49; 10/9/49; 11/14/49; 11/5/50; 10/5/52; 2/27/55; 2/19/56;

216

5/17/57; 5/19/57; 3/23/58; 3/27/60; 3/19/61; 3/11/62; 3/17/63; 3/8/64; 3/14/65; 4/9/67
Pendyrus Choir of Wales, 10/17/71
Les Petits Chanteurs a la Croix de Bois *see* The Little Singers of Paris
Poznan Choir, 3/24/63; 11/7/65
The RCA Victor Chorus, 10/31/48
Rhos Male Voice Choir, 4/16/67
The Robert de Cormier Singers, 4/20/69
The Robert Shaw Chorale, 3/16/52; 12/4/54; 11/20/55; 3/8/59; 2/13/60; 1/15/61; 2/25/62; 1/13/63; 2/23/64; 4/29/66; 4/30/67
The Roger Wagner Chorale, 10/16/66; 10/15/67; 10/13/68
The Royal Uppsala University Chorus of Sweden, 10/25/70
The St. Paul's Cathedral Choir of London, England, 10/31/53
The Sarmatia Male Chorus, 10/19/40
Schaumburger Maerchensaenger *see* Obernkirchen Children's Choir
Shaw Chorale *see* The Robert Shaw Chorale
Simeone Chorale *see* The Harry Simeone Chorale
Singing Boys of Monterrey, 10/30/66
Singing Boys of Norway, 4/26/52; 12/8/56
Sloboda Choir of Chicago, 6/26/76
Stevan Sijacki Choir of Milwaukee, 6/26/76
Stockholm Gosskör, 10/7/56
Stockholm University Chorus, 3/26/72
Surma, Ukrainian Male Chorus, 3/26/61
Tbilisi Polyphonic Choir, 11/17/74
Texas Boys Choir, 10/28/73
UCLA Men's Glee Club, 3/31/70
Ukrainian Choir Promotej, 3/21/71
Ukrainian Women's League Mixed Chorus, 3/26/61
The Vienna Academy Chorus, 12/6/53
The Vienna Boys Choir, 10/16/49; 1/27/51; 3/15/53; 1/22-24/55; 2/4-5/56; 1/26-28/57; 1/25-27/58; 1/25-26/59; 1/24/60; 2/5/51; 1/28/62; 3/2-3/63; 3/1/64; 1/24/65; 2/27/66; 2/25-26/67; 2/18/68; 2/25/68; 1/26/69; 2/28/70; 3/7/71; 3/5/72; 1/28/73; 2/24/74; 3/9/75; 11/23/75
Wagner Chorale *see* The Roger Wagner Chorale
The Westminster Choir, 2/23/40

CONDUCTORS/BAND LEADERS/MUSIC DIRECTORS
Abbado, Claudio, 4/7/76
Adler, Kurt, 5/20/54; 5/13-14/61; 5/30/62
Adler, Peter Herman, 10/11/57
Akos, Francis, 10/6/61; 12/3/63; 1/7/64; 2/4/64; 3/3/64
Algard, Erik, 10/7/56
Ancerl, Karel, 11/5/67

217

Anglberger, Albert, 2/28/70
Antonicelli, Giuseppe, 5/8/50; 5/13/50
Babich, Bogdan, 10/29/60; 12/10/61; 2/14/65
Bacharach, Burt, 12/1-2/61
Balatsch, Norbert, Dr., 4/6/58
Bamberger, Carl,10/13/47
Barbini, Ernesto, 10/20/40
Barbirolli, John, Sir, 2/28/65
Barenboim, Daniel, 5/29/71
Batiz, Enrique, 6/17/75
Beecham, Thomas, Sir, 11/25-26/50
Beinum, Eduard van, 10/30/54
Bernstein, Leonard, 2/10/51; 9/9-10/60; 9/7-8/63; 9/14-15/67; 7/1/76
Bertini, Gary, 2/16/69; 1/23/72; 2/9/75
Bjarne, Ragnvald, 4/26/52; 12/8/56
Boehm, Karl, 10/8/67
Bojanowski, Jerzy, 12/31/38; 4/7/40; 3/26/41; 5/18/41; 12/13/64
Boulez, Pierre, 12/10/71; 12/12/71
Bower, John Dykes, Dr., 10/31/53
Bragg, George, 10/28/73
Brandon, Henry, 3/21/71
Brun, Francois-Julien, Captain, 10/4/53
Brusilow, Anshel, 10/22/67
Caldwell, Sarah, 10/20/67; 10/22/67
Cantelli, Guido, 5/21/55
Caridis, Miltiades, 2/2/64
Case, Russ, 10/31/48
Caston, Saul, 4/4-5/53
Cimara, Pietro, 5/21-22/55
Cleva, Fausto, 5/21-23/54; 5/19/55; 5/21/55; 5/25-26/56; 1/15/57;
    5/23/57; 5/25/57; 5/24/58; 5/27/62
Cluytens, André, 11/18/56
Cooper, Emil, 5/13/50
Coppola, Anton, 12/27/64; 12/30/64; 1/3/65
Cortes, Amador, 10/30/66
Costa, Don, 7/19-20/63
Dankworth, John, 11/6/73; 3/30/74; 10/21/74
de Carvalho, Eleazar, 12/7/65
de Cormier, Robert, 4/20/69
de la Fuente, Louis Herrera, 11/9/58
De Paur, Leonard, 11/18/51; 2/15/53; 11/8/53; 11/7/54; 1/22/56;
    1/13/57; 3/23/58
de Stoutz, Edmond, 1/22/67
Dorati, Antal, 4/15/56; 4/20/58; 11/7/59; 3/10/68
Ellington, Duke, 4/28/66
Erede, Alberto, 5/22-23/54

Ericson, Eric, 10/25/70
Fasano, Renato, 3/3/52; 11/1/53; 3/10/56; 2/8/58; 4/14/62; 4/12/64; 4/23/67
Fedoseyev, Vladimir, 2/12-13/72
Fiedler, Arthur, 3/22/53; 2/27-28/54; 3/18/56; 2/17/57; 2/24/62; 4/12/64; 10/9/65; 3/18/72; 3/19/75
Foss, Lukas, 11/24/75
Frolich, Otto, 11/8/53
Froschauer, Helmuth, 2/4-5/56; 1/24/60
Furthmoser, Hermann, 2/5/61
Giulini, Carlo Maria, 11/26/60
Gnutov, Vitaly, 2/12-13/72
Goldberg, Szymon, 10/29/61
Goldschmidt, Walter, 10/14/73
Golschmann, Vladimir, 1/18/39; 2/2-3/52
Graziani, Y., 10/19/69
Greenberg, Noah, 1/17/59; 4/24/60; 4/15/61; 3/18/62
Grossmann, Ferdinand, Prof., 12/6/53
Guadagno, Anton, 3/25/66
Haitink, Bernard, 5/14/67; 11/7/76
Harrer, Uwe Christian, 3/7/71
Heath, Ted, 10/11/58
Hedding, Harald, 10/16/49; 3/15/53
Hemberg, Eskil, 3/26/72
Hendl, Walter, 3/24-25/51; 12/11/59
Hermelink, Siegfried, 3/6/59
Herrmann, Julius, Capt., 4/6/58; 2/28/60; 3/18/62
Hillis, Margaret, 12/15/68
Hilsberg, Alexander, 2/21/60
Hindemith, Paul, 12/15/45
Hoffman, Irwin, 12/10/65; 1/24-25/69
Ivanov, Konstantin, 1/31/60
Janigro, Antonio, 11/21/56; 10/30/60
Jaroff, Serge, 10/10/37; 10/24/37; 10/23/38; 10/15/39; 10/29/39; 11/17/40; 11/16/41; 10/25/42; 10/17/43; 12/12/43; 10/22/44; 2/25/45; 11/30/45; 12/2/45; 2/16-17/46; 12/7/46; 12/13/46; 2/7/47; 2/7/48; 1/22/49; 2/27/49; 10/1/49; 10/9/49; 11/14/49; 11/5/50; 10/5/52; 2/27/55; 2/19/56; 5/17/57; 5/19/57; 3/23/58; 3/27/60; 3/19/61; 3/11/62; 3/17/63; 3/8/64; 3/14/65; 4/9/67
Jenkins, Gordon, 6/1-7/59
Jensen, Thomas, 11/8-9/52
Jochum, Eugen, 4/30/61
Johnson, Thor, 3/7-8/53
Jones, Colin, 4/16/67
Jones, Glynne, 10/17/71
Kaplan, Abraham, 10/27/68

Karajan, Herbert von, 3/11-13/55; 11/5-6/55; 10/26-28/56; 11/14/59;
    11/5/61; 1/31-2/1/65; 11/4-5/74; 11/9-10/76
Kempe, Rudolf, 10/26/69
Kertesz, Istvan, 1/20/63
King, Wayne, 6/20/52
Kondrashin, Kiril, 1/30/60; 11/21/65
Kopp, Leo, 12/18/43
Kostelanetz, André, 4/28/40; 4/19/41; 4/5/44; 12/3/49; 2/22/58
Kostrukoff, Nicholas, 2/9/42; 11/21/43; 2/4/45; 11/10/45; 3/2/47;
    1/17/48; 11/7/48; 12/5/55; 9/30/56
Koussevitzky, Serge, 12/3/48; 2/11/51
Kozma, Tibor, 5/27/56
Kraft, Robert, 12/28/66; 1/1/67
Krips, Josef, 3/12/72
Kubelik, Rafael, 10/31/54; 11/3/68
Kurtz, Efrem, 3/5/50
Lacovich, Peter, 1/27/51
Lambrecht, Heinz, 9/20-23/67
Lang, Gerhard, 1/25-26/59; 3/2-3/63
Lehel, Gyorgy, 11/19/71
Leinsdorf, Erich, 3/4/50; 4/15/63; 3/28/68; 9/20/75
Lesko, John, 10/21-22/58
Lidstam, Martin, 11/4/56; 10/18/64
Lindsey, Mort, 5/6/61; 5/7/65
Lombardo, Guy, 5/3/69; 10/31/71
Luboff, Norman, 10/17/65
Maazel, Lorin, 5/9/53; 10/21/62
Maerzendorfer, Ernst, 4/8/56; 4/14/56
Maillet, Fernand, Msgr., 3/7-8/57
Malko, Nicolai, 11/9/52
Mander, Francesco, 10/27/57
Mantovani, 10/29-30/55; 10/13-14/56; 3/2/58; 3/22/59; 5/10/59;
    10/23/60; 10/15/61; 10/21/63; 10/11/64; 10/17/65; 10/15/66;
    10/22/67; 10/20/68; 10/12/69
Markowski, Andrzej, 2/5/66
Martin, Thomas P., 11/20/53; 11/22/53; 11/29/53
Martinon, Jean, 10/18/70
Matz, Peter, 11/7/62
Maurer, Wolfdieter, 2/27/66
Mauriat, Paul, 5/2/69; 10/16/70
Mazer, Henry, 5/11/72; 12/13/72; 12/4/73; 9/30/75
McCafferty, James, 11/3/56
McConathy, Osbourne, 10/19/67; 10/21/67
Mehta, Zubin, 11/8/70; 9/19/76
Melachrino, George, 11/15-16/58
Mitchell, Howard, 3/1-2/58

Mitropoulos, Dimitri, 1/23/49; 5/24/56; 5/25-26/57; 5/22/58; 5/24/58
Moeller, Edith, 10/15/54; 10/21-22/55; 5/12/57; 2/12/61; 10/7/62;
   10/25/64; 11/10/68
Monteux, Pierre, 5/16/53
Morel, Jean, 5/26/57; 5/25/58
Moresco, Carlo, 10/8-9/47; 10/11/47; 10/14/47; 10/18-19/47;
   10/24-25/47
Mravinsky, Eugen, 11/9/62
Muenchinger, Karl, 3/14/54
Munch, Charles, 10/30/48; 5/15/53; 5/17/53
Mund, Uwe, 3/1/64
Neyder, Anton, 1/24/65; 2/25-26/67; 1/26/69; 3/9/75
Nott, Hermann A., Dr., 12/3/50
Oberfrank, Geza, 11/4/73
Ormandy, Eugene, 1/5/38; 5/9/46; 6/6/46; 11/9/46; 11/8/47; 6/5/48;
   2/12/49; 2/6/50; 3/1/52; 2/20-21/54; 5/1/66; 5/3/69
Otterloo, Willem van, 5/5/63
Ozawa, Seiji, 9/8/63; 9/20/69
Paillard, Jean Francois, 11/5/67
Paray, Paul, 2/26/50; 2/27/55
Perlea, Jonel, 5/9-10/50; 5/12/50; 10/18/67; 10/21/67
Peroni, Carlo, 4/12-19/42
Piastro, Mishel, 10/22/50
Pohjola, Ensti, 11/7/65
Popper, Felix, 1/2/65
Puschacher, Walter, 2/28/71
Reentovich, Julius, 5/26/74
Reiner, Fritz, 5/11/50
Rescigno, Nicholas, 10/6-7/47; 10/9-12/47; 10/15-21/47; 10/23/47;
   10/25-26/47; 1/22/58
Rich, Martin, 5/20/55; 5/29/62
Riddle, Nelson, 9/4-9/58
Rohan, Jindrich, 3/4/72
Romberg, Sigmund, 4/29/45; 10/2/45; 1/26/46; 4/28/46; 5/17/47;
   5/8/48; 4/19/49; 4/29/50; 11/17/50
Rosenkranz, Raymond, 6/14/75; 2/29/76
Rosenstock, Joseph, 11/18-19/53; 11/22/53
Rowicki, Witold, 1/21/61; 10/18/64; 2/3/74
Rozhdestvensky, Gennady, 11/23/75
Rozsnyai, Zoltan, 11/8/59
Rudel, Julius, 11/21/53; 11/27-28/53; 11/29/64; 12/26-27/64; 12/29/64;
   12/31/64-1/1/65
Rudolf, Max, 5/22/55; 5/27/56; 5/24/57; 5/23/58; 5/25/58; 1/23/66
Savine, Alexander, 5/16/48
Sawallisch, Wolfgang, 2/23/64
Scheide, William H., 1/19/69

Schermerhorn, Kenneth, 4/14/74; 6/11/75; 11/8/75; 12/16/75; 6/20/76; 6/26/76
Schick, George, 5/28/62
Schippers, Thomas, 11/21/53; 11/25/53; 11/28/53
Schmitt, Francis, Rev., 10/5/46; 10/7/46
Serafin, Tullio, 12/31/52
Sevitzky, Fabien, 3/5/44; 3/4/45; 3/10/47; 5/28/53
Seyfert, Otto, 3/17/47
Shaw, Robert, 3/16/52; 12/4/54; 11/20/55; 3/8/59; 2/13/60; 1/15/61; 2/25/62; 1/13/63; 2/23/64; 4/29/66; 4/30/67
Silverstein, Joseph, 6/6/76
Simeone, Harry, 11/12/64
Skrowaczewski, Stanislaw, 4/1/62; 4/24/66
Slatkin, Leonard, 1/8/75
Stadlmair, Hans, 10/23/66
Steffen, Erich, 11/19/67
Steinberg, William, 8/7-8/67; 3/17/72
Stiedry, Fritz, 5/26/56
Stokowski, Leopold, 6/2/41; 9/23-24/48
Strauss, Eduard, 11/20/66; 11/26/66
Stravinsky, Igor, 12/28/66; 1/1/67
Stuligrosz, Stefan, 3/24/63; 11/7/65
Susskind, Walter, 11/28/71; 2/4/73
Svetlanov, Evgeni, 3/5/69
Szell, George, 11/15/53
Talmi, Yoav, 1/23/72
Temirkanov, Yuri, 2/13/77
Teutsch, Karol, 2/11/68
Theimer, Uwe, 3/5/72; 1/28/73
Thomas, Michael Tilson, 9/18/76
Toscanini, Arturo, 5/17/50
Trabesinger, Gerald, 2/24/74; 11/23/75
Track, Gerhard, 1/22-24/55; 1/25-27/58
Turunen, Martti, 11/22/53
Tuxen, Erik, 11/8-9/52
Verchi, Nino, 5/12-13/61
Vivanco, Moises, 12/10/54
Wagner, Roger, 10/16/66; 10/15/67; 10/13/68
Waring, Fred, 11/24/62; 11/1/64; 10/24/65
Weiss, Donn, 3/31/70
Weiss, Erwin, 10/24/71
Welk, Lawrence, 9/30/62; 3/29/63
Whiteman, Paul, 10/25/48; 4/26/58
Wich, Gunther, 11/12/72
Wichart, Pepi, 4/6/58
Williamson, John Finley, 2/23/40

Wilson, Charles, 1/2/65
Wislocki, Stanislaw, 1/22/61; 11/10/63
Wurthner, Rudolf, 1/21/61
Zeilinger, Roman, 1/28/62
Zessar, Walter, 2/18/68; 2/25/68

DANCERS/MIMES
Amala, 2/23-25/52
Amaya, Carmen, 10/16-17/56; 10/19-20/57
Ana Maria, 10/20/51; 11/30/52; 2/28/54
Antonio, 10/3-4/64; 12/4-5/65; 2/3-4/68
Argentinita, 1/28/45
Astor, Richard, 10/23/55
Beatty, Talley, 2/26/50
Camryn, Walter, 4/16/44
Danilova, Alexandra, 11/23-24/52; 10/10/54; 1/29/56
Deglin, Breandan, 11/3/56
Destine, Jean Leon, 10/9/55; 10/5/57
Devi-Dja, 11/18-19/39; 4/12/42; 1/3-4/43; 12/10/44
Draper, Paul, 12/22/40; 12/9/41; 12/6/42; 10/10/43; 3/18/45; 4/1/45;
  2/2/46; 2/1-2/47; 2/29/48; 10/9/55; 3/27/60
Enters, Angna, 3/1/41
Escudero, Vicente, 10/22-23/60
Fernandez, Paro, 1/2/50
Fonteyn, Margot, 1/27-30/64
Franklin, Frederic, 11/23-24/52
Graham, Martha, 3/18/39; 3/10/40; 3/20/49; 10/30/68
Greco, José, 1/28/45; 4/7-12/53; 1/19-23/55; 11/27/55; 2/9/58; 2/16/59;
  1/31/60; 3/19/61; 1/28/62; 1/26-27/63; 3/22/64; 2/7/65; 2/9/65;
  2/27/66; 3/3/67; 3/10/68; 2/9/69; 1/18/70; 1/31/71; 2/20/72; 2/25/73;
  2/16/75; 4/27/75
Halama, Loda, 12/14/37
Hari, Eugene, 3/15/52; 3/22/53
Holmes, Berenice, 5/16/43; 4/30/44; 3/11/45
Humphrey, Doris, 3/11/39
Hunter, Mary, 1/17/54
Iglesias, Roberto, 10/20/51; 11/2/58
James, Martha, 5/16/43
Jasinsky, Roman, 1/29/56
Jooss, Kurt, 2/11/40; 11/1-2/46
Kitchell, Iva, 11/10/51; 3/16/58
Koner, Pauline, 3/20/55
Kovach, Nora, 4/18/62; 11/3/63
Kreutzberg, Harald, 11/14/37; 2/26/39; 11/30/47; 10/17/48; 3/1/53
Larkin, Moscelyne, 1/29/56
Limon, Jose, 3/20/55; 2/20/66
Lopez, Pilar, 1/28/45

223

Lorca, Nana, 1/18/70; 1/31/71; 2/20/72; 2/25/73; 2/16/75; 4/27/75
Maracci, Carmalita, 12/1/40
Marceau, Marcel, 2/18-3/8/58
Mariemma, 1/2/50
Martin, Clarita, 11/29/38
Martin, Ellen, 3/27/60
Martinez, Rosita, 1/25-26/61
Mata, Ruth, 3/15/52; 3/22/53
Maule, Michael, 1/29/56
McBride, Patricia, 10/31/71
Molina, Jose, 10/13/63; 2/5/67; 11/12/67
Mordkin, Mikhail, 10/24-25/38
Moreno, Yolanda, 12/1/68; 2/13/77
Nureyev, Rudolf, 1/27-30/64; 1/15-17/71; 4/5-8/73; 3/19-24/74
Page, Ruth, 4/16/44
Rabovsky, Istvan, 4/8/62; 11/3/63
Rao, Shanta, 11/1-5/57
Sai, Shoki, 2/22/40
Sanders, Dirk, 10/21-22/58
Schoop, Trudi, 2/5/39
Segal, Gilles, 2/18-3/8/58
Shankar, Uday, 2/19-20/50; 2/23-25/52; 11/2-4/62; 10/28/68
Shearer, Sybil, 1/16/72
Slavenska, Mia, 1/23/44; 3/15/48; 2/26/49; 11/23-24/52
Valentino, Charro, 11/5/67
Vargas, Manolo, 1/28/45
Veloz, 10/30/41
Verry, Pierre, 2/18-3/8/58
Villa, Joaquin, 1/2/50
Villella, Edward, 4/19/70; 2/21/71; 10/31/71; 2/3/74
Weidman, Charles, 3/11/39
Xochitl, Princess Teo, 10/28/66; 11/5/67
Yolanda, 10/30/41

DANCE/BALLET COMPANIES
Agnes de Mille's Heritage Dance Theatre, 11/18/73
America Dances, 3/10/63
American Ballet Theatre, 2/22-27/57; 2/14-16/58; 2/2-5/61;
    11/11-12/61; 12/25-31/62; 3/26-27/66; 2/16-19/67; 4/4-7/68; 4/2-7/74
American Folk Ballet see Burch Mann's American Folk Ballet
Ana Maria's Spanish Ballet, 10/20/51; 11/30/52; 2/28/54
The Australian Ballet, 1/15-17/71
Bali-Java Dancers, 11/18-19/39; 4/12/42; 1/3-4/43; 12/10/44
Ballet Aztlan de Mexico see National Dance Company of Mexico
Ballet Caravan, 10/16/38
Ballet Espanol, 10/14/51; 2/23/54
Ballet Espanol Roberto Iglesias, 11/2/58; 2/14/60; 10/7/61; 2/10/63

Ballet Espanol Ximenez-Vargas, 3/11/62

Ballet Folklorico of Mexico, 9/7-9/62; 12/26-31/63; 3/18-21/65; 3/31-4/2/67; 2/21-23/69; 10/2-4/70; 2/19-20/72; 1/18-20/74; 2/1-2/75; 10/23-24/76

The Ballet of Sybil Shearer, 1/16/72

Ballet Repertory Company, 11/29-12/1/43

Ballet Russe de Monte Carlo, 12/25-29/54; 12/15/55; 12/20/55; 12/24/55-1/2/56; 12/15-16/56; 12/22/56; 12/25/56-1/6/57; 4/7-13/58; 12/24/58-1/4/59; 12/25/59-1/3/60; 3/6-8/61; 12/24-31/61

Ballet Theatre, 10/26/52; 2/27-3/2/55; 2/22-27/57; 2/14-16/58

Ballet West, 5/6/73

Les Ballets Africains, 4/13-15/73; 4/27/59

Ballets Basques de Biarritz, 3/24/57

Ballets de Madrid, 10/3-4/64; 12/4-5/65; 2/3-4/68

Bayanihan Philippine Dance Company, 11/20-22/59; 10/22/61; 4/4-5/64; 11/15/70; 3/6/77

Bernice Holmes Ballet, 4/30/44; 3/11/45

Beryozka Russian Dance Company, 1/9-11/59; 1/16/59

The Bolshoi Ballet, 10/26-11/3/62; 10/18-20/63; 6/14-19/66; 4/29-5/2/68; 2/12-13/72; 8/6-11/73; 8/24-27/74; 7/8-10/75

Burch Mann's American Folk Ballet, 3/24/68

Canada's Royal Winnipeg Ballet *see* The Royal Winnipeg Ballet

Chicago Ballet, 5/12-14/72

Chilean National Ballet, 12/6/64

Ciocirlia *see* The Rumanian Folk Ballet

City Center Joffrey Ballet *see* The Robert Joffrey Ballet

Compagnie Nationale de Danses Francaises *see* French National Dance Company

Dance Theatre—Berlin, 10/16/55

Dance Theatre of Harlem, 5/12-14/72

Dancers of Bali, 11/16/52

Dancers of Mali, 10/22/72

Danzas Venezuela, 12/1/68; 2/13/77

De Leon's (Javier) Carnival de Mexico, 2/24/74

De Leon's (Javier) Fiesta Mexicana, 10/28/66; 11/5/67; 11/10/68; 11/23/69; 3/26/72

de Mille's Heritage Dance Theatre *see* Agnes de Mille's Heritage Dance Theatre

The Dukla *see* Ukrainian Dance Company

First Chamber Dance Company of New York, 3/1/70

Flakara!, 3/24/74

French National Dance Company, 3/3/68

Frula, 3/3/68; 6/23/68; 10/24/71; 1/21/73

Georgian State Dance Company, 4/14-17/60

Grand Ballet Classique de France, 11/25/65

Les Grands Ballets Canadiens, 10/15/67

Harkness Ballet of New York, 3/3/74
Heritage Dance Theatre *see* Agnes de Mille's Heritage Dance
   Theatre
Holmes Ballet *see* Bernice Holmes Ballet
Holmes Palette Ballet, 5/16/43
Hungarian Ballets "Bihari," 11/3/63
The Hungarian National Ballet and Folk Ensemble, 2/13/66
Inbal, 3/18-23/58; 11/15-19/59
Javier De Leon's Carnival de Mexico *see* De Leon's Carnival de
   Mexico
Javier De Leon's Fiesta Mexicana *see* De Leon's Fiesta Mexicana
Joffrey Ballet *see* Robert Joffrey Ballet
Jooss Ballet, 11/21/37; 2/11/40; 11/1-2/46
Jose Limon Dance Company, 2/20/66
Jose Molina Bailes Espanoles, 10/13/63; 2/5/67; 11/12/67
Karmon Israeli Dancers and Singers, 2/18-22/59
"Kolo" from Belgrade *see* The Yugoslav State Company
Krasnayarsk Dance Company of Siberia, 11/18/73
Leningrad Kirov Ballet, 12/7-10/61; 10/15-21/64
Limon Dance Company *see* Jose Limon Dance Company
The Littlefield Ballet, 2/1/41
Lorca's Flamenco Dance Theatre *see* Nana Lorca's Flamenco Dance
   Theatre
Lucnica, Czechoslovakian Folk Ballet, 4/4/76
Mann's American Folk Ballet *see* Burch Mann's American Folk
   Ballet
Massine's Ballet Russe, 7/6/45; 7/8/45; 7/10/45
Mazowsze, 10/27-29/61; 1/24-26/64; 2/26-3/1/71; 3/11/73; 3/16-18/73;
   3/20/73; 2/13-15/76
Moiseyev Dance Company, 5/16-21/58; 4/29-5/2/65; 5/6/65;
   8/26-30/70; 9/4-8/74
Molina Bailes Espanoles *see* Jose Molina Bailes Espanoles
Mordkin Ballet, 10/24-25/38
Nana Lorca's Flamenco Dance Theatre, 1/18/70; 1/31/71; 2/20/72
The National Ballet, 1/25/70
National Ballet of Canada, 2/14-19/55; 5/7/61; 4/5-8/73; 3/19-24/74
National Dance Company of Mexico, 11/7/71; 11/26/72; 11/25/73;
   10/27/74; 10/5/75
National Folk Ballet of Yugoslavia, 3/20/77
New York City Ballet, 9/7-15/55; 4/3-15/56; 4/23-5/12/57
Original Ballet Russe, 10/20-23/41; 10/25/41; 10/30-11/1/41
Page Ballet *see* Ruth Page Ballet
The Pennsylvania Ballet, 12/17-21/69
Pittsburgh Ballet Theatre, 12/21/75
The Polish Ballet, 10/19/40; 2/22/42
The Polish Mime Ballet Theater, 3/7/76

Polish State Folk Ballet, 12/1-6/59; 11/15-17/74; 11/19/74
The Robert Joffrey Ballet, 3/5/61; 3/25/62; 3/1/64; 5/28-6/1/68; 1/27-2/1/69
The Royal Ballet, 12/16-22/57; 12/24-29/57; 12/31/57-1/15/58; 12/18/60-1/1/61; 6/11-16/63; 6/17-20/65; 6/22-27/67; 6/12-15/69
The Royal Danish Ballet, 9/22-10/2/60; 10/29-30/65
The Royal Swedish Ballet, 10/12-13/74
The Royal Tahitian Dance Company, 3/6/76
The Royal Winnipeg Ballet, 3/27/54; 1/29/67; 1/28/68; 2/16/69; 3/22/70; 2/14/71; 11/7/71; 3/16/75; 1/16/77
The Rumanian Folk Ballet, 2/26/66; 10/27/68
Ruth Page Chicago Opera Ballet, 3/17/63
Ruth Page's International Ballet, 2/2/69
The San Francisco Ballet, 1/27-30/64
San Francisco Opera Ballet, 2/21/40
The Sierra Leone National Dance Troupe, 1/5/72
SLASK *see* Polish State Folk Ballet
Slavenska-Franklin Ballet, 11/8/53
Soviet Georgian Dancers, 11/17/74
The Stuttgart Ballet, 10/27-29/69; 6/7-12/71
Sumac Dancers *see* Yma Sumac Dancers
Takarazuka Dance Theatre, 9/10-13/59
TANEC *see* The Yugoslav National Folk Ballet
Ukrainian Dance Company, 11/19/72
The Ukrainian Dance Company from Kiev, 6/2-7/62; 12/25/66; 12/29/66-1/1/67
Yma Sumac Dancers, 12/10/54
Yugoslav National Folk Ballet, 2/4-5/56; 3/20/77
The Yugoslav State Company, 12/7-9/56

ENSEMBLES and GROUPS
  Chamber Music
    Chamber Ensembles (Here are listed ensembles of 10 or more instruments)
    Bach Aria Group, 12/4/55; 1/19/69
    The Brandon Ensemble, 1/13/71
    The Chamber Symphony of Philadelphia, 10/22/67
    The Chicago Strings, 10/6/61; 12/3/63; 1/7/64; 2/4/64; 3/3/64
    Collegium Musicum Italicum di Roma *see* Virtuosi di Roma
    Grinzing Schrammel Ensemble, 4/6/58
    The Hohner Accordion Symphony Orchestra, 1/21/61
    The Israel Chamber Orchestra, 2/16/69; 1/23/72; 2/9/75
    The Munich Chamber Orchestra, 10/23/66
    I Musici, 1/15/55; 2/21/56; 1/24/59; 4/18/76
    The Netherlands Chamber Orchestra, 10/29/61
    New York Pro Musica, 1/17/59; 4/24/60; 4/15/61; 3/18/62
    Prague Chamber Orchestra, 3/7/65

I Solisti di Zagreb, 11/21/56; 10/30/60; 2/27/77
The String Ensemble of the Bolshoi Theatre, 5/26/74
The Stuttgart Chamber Orchestra, 3/14/54
Virtuosi di Roma, 3/3/52; 11/1/53; 3/10/56; 2/8/58; 4/14/62;
    4/12/64; 4/23/67
The Warsaw Chamber Orchestra, 2/11/68
The Wienerwald Ensemble, 10/24/71
The Zürich Chamber Orchestra, 1/22/67

Duos
Schoen Duo, 1/17/73

Trios
The Chicago Contemporary Trio, 11/26/74
The Japan Trio, 12/4/73
Manalan String Trio, 3/5/39
Mel Dokich Trio, 3/21/71
Musical Arts Trio, 12/24/44
Pacific String Trio, 4/24/68
Pro Musica Trio, 2/13/54
Trio di Belgrade, 4/15/70
The Yuval Trio, 11/9/71; 11/9/76

Quartets (Various instrumental combinations)
The Festival Quartet, 1/20/57
The First Piano Quartet, 11/11/51; 11/13/51; 11/11/55

String Quartets
The American String Quartet, 1/10/68
Berkshire String Quartet, 2/1/63
Berlin String Quartet, 3/24/76
Chicago Symphony String Quartet, 2/7/68; 4/25/75
The Composers String Quartet, 3/13/74
The Contemporary Arts Quartet, 10/30/73
The Copenhagen String Quartet, 11/9/66
The Dvorak String Quartet, 10/31/72
The Fine Arts Quartet, 10/17/56; 11/21/56; 1/23/57; 2/27/57;
    4/3/57; 5/1/57
Iowa String Quartet, 12/6/67
Julliard String Quartet, 1/23/76; 2/6/76; 3/5/76; 4/30/76; 5/7/76
The New Cleveland Quartet, 12/8/70
The Paganini Quartet, 1/11/53
Panocha String Quartet, 11/11/75
The Purcell String Quartet, 10/29/74
The Severance String Quartet, 3/8/72
Talich String Quartet, 5/6/77
Tokyo String Quartet, 3/14/73

The Vághy String Quartet, 12/9/69; 1/14/70; 5/17/74
The Vienna on Parade String Quartet, 2/28/60
The Walden String Quartet, 12/7/76

Quintets
The Richards Quintet, 11/10/70

Country/Jazz/Pop
Allen Brothers, 5/7/65
The Athenians, 11/22/69; 3/19/72; 3/25/73
The Brothers Four, 9/6/63
The Dave Brubeck Quartet, 10/1/61
The Don Shirley Trio, 2/7/69
Homer and Jethro, 9/6/63
The Kingston Trio, 5/11/62; 2/23/63; 4/18/64
The Lennon Sisters, 3/29/63
The Limeliters, 10/12/62; 5/31/63
The Modern Jazz Quartet, 10/14/62
The Pennsylvanians, 11/24/62; 11/1/64; 10/24/65
Royal Canadians, 5/3/69; 10/31/71
Shirley (Don) Trio *see* The Don Shirley Trio
The Vocal Four, 12/5-11/60

FOLK COMPANIES
Ambakaila, Trinidad Carnival Ballet and Steel Band, 3/10/74
Arirang Dance and Song Spectacular, 10/11/64
The Azuma Kabuki Dancers and Musicians, 2/13-19/56
Barbu Lautaru Orchestra, 11/11/62
Broln-Moravian Folk Ensemble, 12/5/71
Chinese Acrobats of Taiwan, 11/6/75; 10/20/76
Foo Hsing Theatre, 12/2/62
Kathakali Dancers and Musicians, 11/1-5/57
Kitzbühel Singers and Dancers *see* Toni Praxmair's Kitzbühel
    Singers and Dancers
Koutev Bulgarian National Ensemble, 10/27/63
Kyogen, National Comic Theatre of Japan, 3/30/70
Lado, 11/1/70; 2/11/73
Moscow Balalaika Orchestra, 3/2/75
The Osipov Balalaika Orchestra, 11/7/69; 11/9/69; 2/12-13/72;
    3/20/77
Praxmair's Kitzbühel Singers and Dancers *see* Toni Praxmair's
    Kitzbühel Singers and Dancers
Rajko, 10/29/72; 11/10/74; 2/13/77
Roumanian National Folk Ensemble, 11/11/62
Siberian Dancers and Singers of Omsk, 3/13-14/71
Toni Praxmair's Kitzbühel Singers and Dancers, 11/7/71

FOLK and ETHNIC MUSICIANS
Bikel, Theodore, 5/12/73
Douai, Jacques, 3/3/68
Dyer-Bennet, Richard, 6/22/51
Ghosh, Shankar, 9/11/65
Gill, Geula, 5/12/73
Gornish, Jean *see* Sheindele the Chazente
Ives, Burl, 2/22/48; 1/15/50
Khan, Ali Akbar, 9/11/65; 11/17/66
Khan, Rajdulari, 11/17/66
Lifschitz, Nehama, 10/19/69
Maciel, Antonio, 11/5/67
Makeba, Miriam, 12/5-11/60
Marais, Josef, 1/4/67
Marais, Miranda, 1/4/67
Misra, Mahapurush, 11/17/66
Mookerjee, Sheela, 9/11/65
Premice, Josephine, 11/11/46
Reyes, José, 11/18/66
Sheindele the Chazente, 12/24/44
Sumac, Yma, 12/10/54
White, Josh, 12/3/44; 11/11/46; 1/31/48; 12/31/48; 6/19/49; 5/27/50
White, Josh, Jr., 12/31/48

FOLK FESTIVALS *see* REVUES/FOLK FESTIVALS

INSTRUMENTALISTS
Accordion
Tollefsen, Toralf, 1/25-26/61

Bass
Calhoun, Edward, 10/12/58; 3/19/60; 2/25/61; 3/10/62; 4/7/63

Cello
Bolognini, Ennio, 11/12/50
Chung, Myung-Wha, 11/15/76
Drinkall, Roger, 11/4/69; 1/8/75
Du Pré, Jacqueline, 5/29/71
Flachot, Reini, 3/16/63
Fournier, Pierre, 3/21/71
Janigro, Antonio, 10/30/60
Magen, Shmuel, 1/23/72
Miller, Frank, 9/25/68
Nelsova, Zara, 3/3/64
Piatigorsky, Gregor, 3/5/49; 12/10/50; 12/1/51; 2/24/57
Rose, Leonard, 11/27/66; 5/5/68; 4/27/69; 5/17/70; 12/13/72

Rostropovich, Mstislav, 5/7/56; 3/23/75; 11/8/75

Clarinet
De Caprio, Domenico, 11/6/38
Goodman, Benny, 2/1/63
Lindemann, Robert, 2/16/47

Flute
Bove, Henry, 10/28/45
Callimahos, Lambros Demetrios, 1/14/38
Covone, Fortunato, 4/2/38; 5/7/45; 4/14/46; 3/16/47
Knauss, Roy, 3/12/39
Pratt, Samuel, 3/21/64
Rampal, Jean-Pierre, 1/21/72; 3/18/73; 1/20/74; 3/16/75; 3/14/76; 1/16/77
Versaci, Frank, 1/11/47; 12/3/49

French Horn
Tarjani, Ferenc, 11/4/73

Guitar
Atkins, Chet, 3/19/75
Bonfa, Luiz, 10/21-22/58
de la Isla, Paco, 1/2/50
de Lucia, Paco, 11/30/75
De Plata, Manitas, 11/18/66
Diaz, Alirio, 12/19/65; 10/21/73; 10/27/74
Ghiglia, Oscar, 3/9/75; 2/15/76
Lorimer, Michael, 5/19/74; 5/18/75
Montoya, Carlos, 1/28/45; 10/20/51; 9/25/71; 12/3/72; 4/21/74; 4/6/75; 10/16/76
Niedt, Douglas, 12/14/75
Parkening, Christopher, 4/28/74
Ramos, Manuel Lopez, 10/26/75
Romero, Angel, 10/15/61; 3/20/66; 12/15/74
Romero, Celedonio, 10/15/61; 3/20/66
Romero, Celin, 10/15/61; 3/20/66
Romero, Pepe, 10/15/61; 3/20/66
Sabicas, 10/16-17/56; 10/19-20/57; 4/3/66; 10/9/66; 5/2/76
Segovia, Andres, 3/13/38; 1/19/44; 3/11/45; 2/4/51; 2/10/52; 3/12/53; 3/21/54; 3/6/55; 4/1/56; 4/14/57; 1/12/58; 3/29/59; 3/13/60; 2/26/61; 1/14/62; 3/31/63; 1/19/64; 1/10/65; 1/9/66; 3/19/67; 2/4/68; 2/9/69; 2/8/70; 1/24/71; 2/13/72; 2/11/73; 2/17/74; 2/23/75; 2/22/76; 1/23/77
Yepes, Narcisco, 10/31/65

Harmonica
Adler, Larry, 12/22/40; 12/9/41; 12/6/42; 10/10/43; 3/18/45; 4/1/45; 2/2/46; 4/12/46; 2/1/47; 2/2/47; 2/29/48; 5/10/52

Harp
Pfeil, Walter, 11/15-16/58

Harpsichord
Braatz, Thomas, 12/5/72
Conant, Robert, 4/11/73
Edwards, Ryan, 3/18/73
Ritter, John Steele, 3/16/75; 3/14/76; 1/16/77

Lute
de Zayas, Rodrigo, 12/14/71

Oboe
Lardrot, Andre, 1/22/67
Still, Ray, 12/3/63

Organ
Bower, John Dykes, Dr., 10/31/53

Percussion
Bellson, Louis, 2/11/67
Macurije, Indio, 11/11/46
Martin, Kelly, 10/12/58; 3/19/60; 2/25/61; 3/10/62; 4/7/63

Piano
Aldvik, Sune, 11/4/56
Allison, Herman, 11/21/48
Alwin, Carl, 3/5/39
Amato, Albert Carlo, 10/25/62
Anda, Geza, 11/14/65; 2/23/69
Anderson, Jane, 10/25/48
Andrews, Mitchell, 1/12/69
Angerman, Hans, 1/29/56
Anievas, Agustin, 11/24/74; 12/21/75; 6/20/76; 6/27/76
Arminski, Herman, 11/15-16/58
Arrau, Claudio, 1/5/58; 2/1/59; 1/17/60; 12/18/60; 1/30/66; 8/7/67; 2/1/76; 1/16/77
Arshanskaja, Janna, 5/6/62
Artymiw, Lydia, 4/6/75; 5/9/76
Arzruni, Sahan, 11/29/70; 12/3/72
Ashkenazy, Vladimir, 10/19/58; 11/18/62; 3/15/71; 5/16/71; 2/17/74; 4/4/76; 3/20/77
Aster, Alexander, 3/19/44; 4/1/45; 5/7/49; 6/7/58
Ax, Emanuel, 2/10/74

Aybar, Francisco, 5/30/76; 5/22/77
Babin, Stanley, 2/7/60
Babin, Victor, 2/12/50; 4/6/52; 1/15/56; 11/11/56; 11/22/59; 4/1/62; 11/9/63; 2/20/66
Bachauer, Gina, 1/10/54; 5/14/72; 5/12/74
Backhaus, Wilhelm, 2/19/55; 4/8/56
Badura-Skoda, Paul, 1/11/59; 11/12/61
Bakst, Ryszard, 10/31/64
Baldwin, Dalton, 12/7/57
Baller, Adolph, 2/1/53
Balsam, Artur, 3/23/47; 3/23/52; 10/19/52; 3/1/53; 4/3/54; 2/6/55; 2/25/56; 3/2/57; 12/8/57
Bamboschek, Giuseppe, 3/29/40; 9/11/42
Bar-Illan, David, 4/23/61; 12/12/61; 2/4/62; 4/28/68; 1/28/73
Barbosa, Antonio, 2/6/72;/ 12/19/76
Barenboim, Daniel, 1/19/58; 11/2/58; 4/15/62; 10/13/63; 1/30/65; 12/12/65; 11/30/66; 2/20/72; 5/16/76
Barer, Simon, 12/6/37; 1/18/39
Barr, Howard, 1/29/56
Bartholomew, Frank, 2/27/76; 3/27/77
Bashkirov, Dimitri, 4/6/69
Basilevsky, Ivan, 1/14/46
Bass, Warner, 4/16/50; 4/15/51; 4/19/53; 2/5/55; 3/10/57; 3/30/57; 1/9/60
Bauer, Frieda, 11/12/63; 12/24/67; 1/25/70
Bay, Emanuel, 10/24/37; 4/24/38; 12/4/38; 2/15/42; 2/14/43; 2/27/44; 1/19/46; 2/8/47; 4/17/49; 1/22/50; 3/12/50; 3/17/51; 10/21/51; 10/23/51; 3/9/52; 1/23/54
Bazala, Borislav, 4/23/50
Beane, Reginald, 1/25-26/61
Bechterev, Boris, 2/16/75; 10/26/75
Becker, Helga, 3/4/75
Beecham, Lady see Humby, Betty
Behr, Jan, 12/10/49; 4/29/51; 4/5/52
Bell, Beatrice, 11/20/38
Benditzky, Leon, 2/11/46
Benner, James, 10/21-22/55; 5/12/57; 2/12/61; 10/7/62; 10/25/64; 11/10/68
Bergmann, Ludwig, 2/16/47; 12/11/48; 10/29/50; 1/27/52; 11/30/52; 2/20/55; 11/3/57; 11/5/57
Berkowitz, Ralph, 3/5/49; 12/10/50; 12/1/51; 2/24/57
Berl, Paul, 10/7/51; 1/24/53; 1/28/55; 12/10/55; 2/14/60; 4/8/61; 3/3/64; 3/15/64; 11/22/64
Bernstein, Leonard, 9/10/60; 7/1/76
Bibl, Rudolf, 2/28/60
Biegon, Bernard, 11/7/65

Biltcliffe, Edwin, 1/7/56
Block, Michel, 4/4/65; 3/26/67; 3/19/78
Bodfors, Franz, 11/27/38
Bogas, Roy, 1/17/54
Bolet, Jorge, 3/31/57; 4/13/58; 4/26/58; 12/4/73
Borge, Victor *see under* Actors/Comedians
Bos, Coenraad V., 3/9/46; 4/3/48
Bossart, Eugene, 10/18/49; 12/6/59; 11/7/61; 3/24/63
Boszormenyi-Nagy, Bela, 10/22/49
Braggiotti, Mario, 6/17/55
Brailowsky, Alexander, 3/18/51; 12/13/52; 3/24/57; 4/20/58;
    2/10/63
Brendel, Alfred, 3/15/70; 2/7/71; 4/2/72; 3/11/73; 3/31/74; 3/16/75;
    5/10/76; 5/12/77
Brice, Jonathan, 1/30/49; 12/4/49; 10/18/53
Brown, Harold, 1/29/56
Brown, Harvey, 11/10/51; 3/16/58
Brown, Tom, 6/13/76; 5/21/78
Browning, John, 4/10/60; 9/30/75; 9/18/76
Browning, William, 4/26/59; 3/25/62
Butler, Marion, 11/7/37
Callinicos, Constantine, 4/7/51; 5/9/54
Carlson, Jane, 12/15/45
Casadesus, Jean, 2/8/59; 1/8/67
Casadesus, Robert, 2/20/49; 2/5/50; 2/18/51; 12/13/53
Cellini, Renato, 4/2/50
Chadaillat, Patrick, 10/17/71
Cherkassky, Shura, 11/11/62
Chung, Myung-Whun, 11/15/76
Ciccolini, Aldo, 11/19/50; 1/13/52
Cliburn, Van, 3/7/60; 3/18/61; 3/14/65; 12/10/65; 4/18/66; 4/16/67;
    3/5/69; 4/28/71; 5/1/72
Cobb, John, 6/16/68
Collup, Donald, 10/28/73
Colman, John, 12/6/42; 2/1-2/47; 10/9/55
Corbett, Richard, 11/4/69
Crochet, Evelyne, 5/26/68
Crooks, Barbara, 5/24/70
Curzon, Clifford, 2/13/55
Czerny-Stefanska, Halina, 12/9/55
D'Attili, Glauco, 5/7/45; 10/28/45; 4/14/46; 11/11/51; 11/13/51
Davis, Ivan, 2/11/62; 5/28/67
Davis, Laurence, 1/14/70; 3/11/70
Day, Charlotte, 1/8/75
Dedukhin, Alexandre, 5/7/56
de Gaetano, Robert, 6/1/75

234

de Larrocha, Alicia, 4/26/67
Dell'Anno, Lee, 5/10/52
Demus, Joerg, 1/11/59; 11/12/61; 1/27/63
de Oliveira, Jocy, 12/7/65
Dichter, Misha, 2/15/70; 4/11/71; 12/9/73; 4/13/75; 1/4/76; 5/1/77
Dick, James, 12/1/74
Dickerson, Carroll, 11/6/60
Dodds, Ralph, 10/2/60
Dorfmann, Ania, 3/4/45
Duval, Cele, 4/27/58
Ebert, Harry, 11/27/38; 1/21/40; 2/16/41
Eden, Bracha, 11/6/66; 2/2/69
Edson, Edward, 11/11/51; 11/13/51
Edwards, Ryan, 1/21/72; 1/20/74
Eisberg, Harold, 3/1/58
Ellis, Richard, 10/10/54
Endt, Hendrik, 2/19/39
Entremont, Philippe, 1/20/63
Erokhin, Mikhail, 2/22/76
Eschenbach, Christoph, 2/22/70
Evans, Ethel, 1/29/49; 2/18/50
Farr, Lowell, 5/29/54
Favaretto, Giorgio, 2/15/59
Fedri, Dino, 5/8/55
Fenster, Laura, 5/25/69
Ferrante, Arthur, 10/10/43; 3/18/45; 4/1/45; 2/2/46; 4/12/46;
    11/11/62
Fialkowska, Janina, 12/12/76
Fidler, Genya, 3/16/47
Firkušný, Rudolf, 2/13/49; 3/5/50; 1/28/51; 5/2/53; 4/29/56; 3/5/61;
    3/12/67
Fleisher, Leon, 1/16/55
Fliere, Jakov, 10/27/63
Flissler, Eileen, 11/27/55
Foley, John, 10/5/46; 10/7/46
Frager, Malcolm, 6/11/61; 5/26/74; 1/5/75
François, Samson, 12/20/59; 11/27/60
Frank, Bernard, 9/28/47
Freed, Fred, 5/10/68
Freeman, Mildred, 12/10/44
Freire, Nelson, 10/26/69
Fuschi, Olegna, 3/28/65
Gale, Richmond, 4/11/48
Garbulinska, Teresa, 4/11/65
Garner, Adam, 11/11/51; 11/13/51
Garner, Erroll, 10/12/58; 3/19/60; 2/25/61; 3/10/62; 4/7/63

Garvey, David, 4/11/55; 5/6/56; 4/7/57; 12/6/58; 2/3/63; 2/1/70; 2/27/72; 4/4/76; 2/6/77
Gieseking, Walter, 1/17/54; 3/20/55; 5/20/56
Gilels, Emil, 10/21/55; 2/2/58; 1/30/60; 2/18/62; 11/29/64; 3/23/69
Glass, Beaumont, 1/17/65
Goffen, Linda, 9/22/57
Gordon, Daniel, 1/29/56
Gordon, Eddy, 5/29/54; 5/6/56
Gorobetz, Ray, 2/29/48
Gould, Glenn, 5/21/61; 4/22/62; 3/29/64
Graffman, Gary, 11/25/56; 4/1/73; 4/27/75; 5/23/76; 1/2/77
Gulda, Friedrich, 3/9/58
Gutierrez, Horacio, 10/8/72
Hambro, Leonid, 2/26/67; 10/10/69
Hammond, Harriette, 4/24/38
Hammond, Margaret Dee, 1/17/38
Hansen, Jack, 5/5/57
Harbison, Janice, 4/17/60
Harris, Edward, 11/29/47
Haynes, Owen, 11/29/38
Hebert, Bliss, 2/17/63
Heidsieck, Eric, 1/29/61
Herbst, Erwin, 4/20/52
Herz, Herman, 5/6/50
Herz, Otto, 11/24/40; 3/2/41; 5/16/43; 5/4/52; 4/26/53; 6/19/53; 4/11/54
Hill, Gilbert, 11/25/55
Hilsley, William, 11/1-2/46
Hinshaw, Harvey, 1/9/55
Hirsh, Albert, 3/4/56; 3/13/56
Hokanson, Leonard, 5/2/76
Hollander, Lorin, 12/8/68
Hollister, Carroll, 3/12/49
Horowitz, Norman, 5/6/73; 4/14/74; 1/26/75
Horowitz, Vladimir, 5/12/68; 5/19/68; 10/27/74; 11/3/74; 11/2/75
Horszowski, Mieczyslaw, 4/22/51
Hughes, William, 4/30/50
Humby, Betty, 11/25/50
Isepp, Martin, 3/5/67
Istomin, Eugene, 11/27/66; 5/5/68; 4/27/69; 5/17/70; 5/23/71; 4/9/72; 12/13/72; 12/23/73
Iturbi, Jose, 4/22/45
Jablonski, Marek, 3/16/63
Jackson, J. Calvin, 12/9/41
Jalbert, Jean, 4/21/56
Janis, Byron, 3/25/56; 3/15/58; 4/9/61; 4/29/62; 1/16/66; 1/29/67;

12/1/68; 5/5/74; 12/16/75; 2/8/76
Johannsen, Grant, 11/10/57; 2/21/60
Jonas, Maryla, 12/1/46
Jospe, Erwin, 12/24/49; 3/14/53; 4/2/55; 3/3/56; 9/23/56;12/4/56;
    3/25/58; 11/20/62
Kalichstein, Joseph, 12/10/72; 2/9/75
Kapell, William, 12/12/48
Kaplan, Herbert, 4/8/62
Kaufman, Robert, 3/27/60
Kempff, Wilhelm, 4/17/66; 4/9/67
Kentner, Louis, 12/2/56
Kilburn, Weldon, 4/21/57; 4/18/71
Kim, Jung Kyu, 5/17/64
Kirsch, Florence, 1/4/53
Kiss, Gyula, 11/4/73
Klass, Edward, 2/16/57
Klein, Jacques, 11/13/60; 1/26/64
Kocsis, Zoltan, 11/19/71; 4/29/73
Kohnop, Louis, 6/18/50; 11/12/50; 6/19/56
Konatkowska, Gertruda, 3/24/63
Kopp, Leo, 1/22/41
Krainev, Vladimir, 11/29/70
Kraus, Lili, 12/11/49; 4/7/68
Kubick, Howard, 11/7/37
Kuerti, Anton, 4/21/68
Kunc, Božidar, 2/7/54
La Forge, Frank, 4/2/38; 1/11/47
Lamport, Brian, 11/15/70
Lamson, Carl, 12/3/45; 11/28/48
Laredo, Ruth, 3/28/71
Laszlo, Ervin, 10/7/50; 11/16/52; 10/25/53; 6/14/57
Lateiner, Jacob, 1/14/51; 4/28/57; 1/5/64
Lavilla, Felix, 2/12/67
Lettvin, Theodore, 11/25/51; 11/15/53; 10/8/61
Levant, Oscar, 3/4/50; 3/7-8/53
Levine, Donald, 1/4/58
Levine, Joseph, 2/3/50
Lewenthal, Raymond, 1/30/72
Linsley, Ralph, 10/31/59
List, Eugene, 4/1/50; 2/22/58; 4/21/63
Longas, Federico, 2/20/38
Louwenaar, Karyl, 6/11/67
Lowe, Jack, 5/23/47; 10/18/59
Lowenthal, Jerome, 4/14/63; 1/9/72
Luboshutz, Pierre, 2/8/53; 1/23/60; 1/6/63
Luvisi, Lee, 1/7/62; 10/20/63; 12/5/65

237

Luzuriaga, Enrique, 1/2/50
Lympany, Moura, 2/12/56
MacDonald, Robert, 1/4/46
Malcuzynski, Witold, 3/21/43; 1/16/49; 12/9/49; 11/2/52; 3/28/54;
    4/17/55; 3/17/57; 11/30/58; 1/31/60; 1/21/62; 11/10/63
Malloy, George, 4/21/56
Markova, Juliana, 12/2/73; 3/13/77
Marsh, Ozan, 2/24/62; 4/12/64; 10/9/65
Martin, Thomas, 12/22/40
Maximovych, Boris, 3/26/61
Mayer, Herbert, 3/6/49
Mayer, Thomas, 1/16/54
McArthur, Edwin, 4/11/47; 1/12/48; 1/9/49; 11/13/49; 12/3/50;
    3/4/51; 4/13/52
McNeil, Marjorie, 4/18/65
Menuhin, Hephzibah, 10/25/59; 12/2/61; 3/17/74; 3/7/76
Merrill, Marion, 4/29/62
Meyer, Paul, 11/13/56
Michelangeli, Arturo Benedetti, 11/9/66
Miller, Mayne, 11/20/62
Miquel, Pablo, 1/28/45; 11/6/48
Mitnick, Andre, 2/14/58; 10/16/60
Mittler, Frank, 11/11/51; 11/13/51
Mittman, Leopold, 10/1/39
Moiseiwitsch, Benno, 4/24/49; 10/23/49; 2/10/57
Molivani, Marina, 11/24/63
Moltke, Veronica Jochum von, 10/23/66
Moravec, Ivan, 4/25/65
Mosbacher, K. E., 11/1-2/46
Mueller, Leo, 10/8/44
Munar, Alfredo, 10/20/51; 11/30/52; 2/28/54
Nemenoff, Genia, 2/8/53; 1/23/60; 1/6/63
Newmark, John, 12/9/56; 4/27/57; 11/15/64
Niwa, Eloise, 2/23/58
Nojima, Minoru, 2/25/73
Novaes, Guiomar, 11/29/59; 11/25/62
Novak, Alvin, 2/17/65
Nowak, Lionel, 3/11/39
Oborin, Lev, 11/17/63
O'Callaghan, Kitty, 1/21/56
Odom, Spencer, 9/25/54
Ohlsson, Garrick, 12/30/73
Padwa, Vladimir, 1/29/39; 4/21/40
Parham, Percival, 12/12/37
Parsons, Geoffrey, 1/21/68; 3/2/69; 3/8/70; 2/3/74; 2/10/74; 2/9/75
Pavlovsky, Valentin, 12/17/44

Paxson, Theodore, 2/21/38; 3/4/39; 3/3/40; 3/29/41; 3/21/42;
    3/14/43; 4/9/44; 4/20/48; 10/31/49
Pennario, Leonard, 10/9/60; 4/29/62; 5/10/64
Perl, Lothar, 3/15/52; 3/22/53
Pludermacher, George, 11/21/76
Pollack, Daniel, 10/24/65; 4/24/66
Pommers, Leon, 4/3/49; 5/5/51; 1/8/52; 1/12/52; 1/4/59; 3/5/60;
    11/19/60; 11/19/61; 3/10/63; 6/25/64; 2/21/65; 3/17/68; 3/21/71
Ponti, Michael, 1/23/77
Pope, David, 5/12/63
Postnikova, Viktoria, 11/23/75
Pressler, Menahem, 4/26/70; 12/24/72
Preyss, Adelina, 12/14/37
Rabinof, Sylvia, 6/30/67
Rankin, Eugene, 11/14/54
Reed, Paul, 5/15/66
Reeves, George, 1/15/49; 11/27/49; 10/21/56; 11/25/57
Richardson, Diane, 6/4/67
Richter, Sviatoslav, 11/5/60; 11/27/60; 5/15/65; 5/23/65; 3/29/70
Richter-Haaser, Hans, 11/15/59; 11/20/60; 2/7/65; 2/18/73
Ridgway, Paul, 5/15/77
Ritter, John Steele, 3/16/75; 3/14/76; 1/16/77
Rogers, Allen, 4/21/57; 3/4/62; 1/5/63; 5/4/69; 12/25/69; 5/13/73
Rosé, Wolfgang, 9/22/46; 12/6/47; 1/8/50; 11/5/50; 1/6/51; 1/29/52
Rosen, Charles, 12/9/62; 1/11/70; 12/6/70; 4/16/72; 2/4/73; 10/7/73;
    11/16/75; 10/24/76
Ross, Stuart, 10/14/51; 4/4/54
Roubakine, Boris, 3/19/44
Rubinstein, Aida, 6/19/56
Rubinstein, Arthur, 2/4/49; 10/8/49; 11/6/49; 1/20/51; 3/11/51;
    3/30/52; 4/12/52; 1/25/53; 2/21/53; 3/7/54; 12/19/54; 3/11/56;
    2/3/57; 4/20/57; 1/18/59; 12/10/60; 2/24/63; 12/15/63; 3/21/65;
    2/6/66; 2/5/67; 3/31/68; 1/24/69; 3/30/69; 3/7/70; 1/17/71;
    11/28/71; 11/15/72; 3/21/76
Rupp, Franz, 1/15/46; 10/24/48; 1/21/50; 1/29/50; 1/21/51; 4/8/51;
    2/29/52; 5/3/52; 1/31/53; 3/29/53; 1/30/54; 12/5/54; 1/8/56;
    2/23/57; 1/24/58; 4/5/59; 2/28/60; 2/19/61; 12/16/62; 5/11/63;
    2/9/64; 12/6/64; 2/19/67
Ruskin, Abbott, 1/7/73
Ryce, Joel, 5/13/62
Sammel, Goodwin, 1/8/39
Sanders, Samuel, 4/2/67; 12/19/71; 1/14/73; 3/23/75
Sandor, Arpad, 12/5/48; 11/21/54
Sanromá, Jesús Maria, 5/9/53
Sauer, Angelica Morales von, 11/9/58
Scalin, Burton H., 1/16/65

Schauwecker, Frederick, 3/29/47; 3/6/48; 2/6/49; 2/25/51; 12/9/51; 2/26/56; 3/16/58
Scheja, Staffan, 5/11/75
Schenly, Paul, 4/21/74; 5/8/77
Schick, George, 2/9/46; 10/30/49
Schmidt, Kimberly, 12/17/72
Schnabel, Artur, 4/6/46; 3/28/48
Schumacher, Thomas, 5/18/75
Scott, Hazel, 11/9/47; 3/27/49
Segall, Bernardo, 3/6/66
Seiger, Joseph, 1/10/53; 11/29/53; 11/27/54; 12/18/55; 2/17/57; 1/18/58
Sektberg, Willard, 4/30/49; 10/10/53; 2/26/55; 2/16/58
Serkin, Rudolf, 11/20/49; 12/2/51; 1/31/54; 1/30/55; 10/16/55; 3/10/57; 12/1/57; 12/7/58; 12/12/59; 5/1/60; 12/3/61; 12/2/62; 12/8/63; 12/13/64; 3/13/66; 11/13/66; 12/3/67; 3/9/69; 10/4/70; 2/27/72; 3/4/73; 3/10/74; 12/8/74; 3/6/77
Sevidov, Arkadii, 10/20/74; 1/25/76
Seyfert, Otto, 2/18/45; 12/1/45
Shelters, Rhea, 12/7/41; 11/5/51; 4/12/53
Sherman, Russell, 9/12/76
Shkolnik, Sheldon, 5/7/61
Shomate, James, 11/12/50; 1/20/52; 2/2/57
Siebach, Fritzi, 12/24/44
Siegel, Clara, 2/20/38
Siegal, Jeffrey, 9/25/68; 1/5/69; 1/16/72; 3/18/72
Silsbee, Nancy, 12/3/44
Silverman, Robert, 1/2/72
Simon, Abbey, 4/12/70; 4/17/77
Simonsen, Melvyn, 12/8/56
Singer, Werner, 10/15/50; 11/3/50; 3/3/51; 2/22/53; 1/28/54; 4/12/58; 11/23/58
Skolovsky, Zadel, 10/28/51; 5/2/54
Slenczynska, Ruth, 2/27-28/54; 3/18/56; 2/17/57
Slobodyanik, Alexander, 11/2/69; 11/19/72; 3/28/76
Smendzianka, Regina, 1/22/61
Smith, Brooks, 2/15/51; 2/17/51; 11/4/51; 2/20/55; 3/24/56; 1/10/69; 12/6/69
Smith, Collins, 12/12/43; 9/28/52
Sokolov, Grigory, 1/19/75
Solomon, 4/3/55
Somer, Hilde, 3/22/53
Spielman, Louis, 12/22/40
Stamer, Fred, 9/24-25/62; 9/27-29/62; 5/31/64
Starr, Susan, 1/16/66; 5/21/67
Stecher, Melvin, 5/6/73; 4/14/74; 1/26/75

Stepan, Russell, 11/8/64
Straight, Willard, 3/16/57; 4/11/59
Sukman, Harry, 1/28/46
Sunnegardh, Arne, 4/30/49
Sutherland, Robert, 3/2/74
Svetlanova, Nina, 10/16/74
Tamir, Alexander, 11/6/66; 2/2/69
Tarnowsky, Sergei, 11/6/38; 3/12/39
Taubman, Leo, 4/17/39; 2/14/43; 1/18/53; 11/7/53
Tazaki, Etsuko, 5/4/75
Tchaikowsky, Andre, 11/24/57; 4/19/59
Tcherepnin, Alexander, 5/28/53
Teicher, Louis, 11/11/62
Templeton, Alec, 4/11/46; 4/28-29/46; 2/10/47
Trochman, Rosalia, 2/13/70
Trovillo, George, 4/28/51; 2/13/54; 3/21/64
Ts'ong, Fou, 11/26/61; 2/3/63; 1/22/67
Tureck, Rosalyn, 4/10/49; 11/4/62; 12/1/63; 1/3/65; 12/11/66;
    12/10/67; 11/25/73
Turini, Ronald, 10/22/61; 4/28/63; 6/9/68; 4/15/73; 1/8/75
Ulanowsky, Paul, 1/14/38; 3/13/49; 2/25/50; 4/9/50; 10/11/53;
    10/17/54; 11/13/55; 3/17/56; 4/13/57; 10/26/58; 2/7/59; 11/1/59;
    1/8/61; 3/12/61
Uninsky, Alexander, 3/26/50; 2/17/52; 10/24/54
Vakman, Sofia, 3/1/59
Vasary, Tamas, 10/28/62
Viardo, Vladimir, 10/10/76
Votapek, Ralph, 2/22/59; 1/3/71; 1/6/74
Vronsky, Vitya, 2/12/50; 4/6/52; 1/15/56; 11/11/56; 11/22/59;
    4/1/62; 11/9/63
Wadsworth, Charles, 12/4/66; 11/24/68
Walter, Naum, 3/20/60
Wasowski, Andrzej, 3/27/66
Watts, Andre, 9/8/63; 8/8/67; 2/18/68; 3/16/69; 9/20/69; 3/1/70;
    4/25/71; 3/26/72; 4/8/73; 3/24/74; 2/23/75; 2/15/76; 4/24/77
Weiderhirn, John, 4/17/39
Weissenberg, Alexis, 11/14/71; 3/17/72; 12/16/73
Whitaker, William, 5/13/62
Whittemore, Arthur, 5/23/47; 10/18/59
Wikstrom, Inger, 2/13/66
Wilckens, Friedrich, 11/14/37; 2/26/39; 11/30/47; 10/17/48; 3/1/53
Wolf, Kenneth, 11/11/49
Wolff, Ernst Victor, 4/8/45
Wustman, John, 11/17/68; 12/13/70; 10/31/76
Wyatt, Kelley, 11/28/65
Yampolsky, Vladimir, 11/28-29/55

241

Yerokhin, Alexander, 3/15/59; 2/16/62
Yost, Kenneth, 3/1/41
Zaitseva, Irina, 5/26/74
Zakin, Alexander, 11/14/48; 10/8/50; 1/6/57; 1/17/61; 6/1/63;
    12/7/63; 4/5/64; 11/18/69; 2/14/71
Zamboni, Rainaldo, 1/8/39
Zaremba, Sylvia, 4/22/50
Zybtsev, Alexei, 4/8/62

Saxophone
Desmond, Paul, 10/1/61
Gallodoro, Al, 10/25/48

Trumpet
Hackett, Bobby, 2/1/63

Viola
Preves, Milton, 9/25/68

Violin
Aitay, Victor, 9/25/68
Bacon, John, 1/22/67
Becker, Mary, 10/2/45; 4/28/46; 11/17/50
Besrodni, Igor, 3/1/59
Chung, Kyung-Wha, 11/15/76
David, Lukas, 10/23/66
Davis, David, 4/11/55
Deane, Derry, 11/4/69
Donenberg, Elaine, 6/18/50
Elman, Mischa, 1/29/39; 4/21/40; 9/22/46; 12/6/47; 1/8/50; 11/5/50;
    1/6/51; 3/24-25/51; 4/20/52; 1/10/53; 11/29/53; 11/27/54;
    12/18/55; 2/17/57; 1/18/58
Francescatti, Zino, 3/23/47; 2/6/55
Gampel, Lilit, 3/12/72
Goldberg, Szymon, 2/26/50; 12/27/54; 10/29/61; 2/4/64; 2/20/66
Golub, Elliott, 4/11/73
Grosz, Mikulas, 6/25/64
Heifetz, Jascha, 10/24/37; 4/24/38; 12/4/38; 2/15/42; 2/14/43;
    2/27/44; 1/19/46; 2/8/47; 4/17/49; 1/22/50; 3/12/50; 3/17/51;
    10/21/51; 10/23/51; 3/9/52; 1/23/54; 2/20/55; 3/24/56
Huberman, Bronislaw, 3/19/44
Ilmer, Irving, 4/17/39
Kiss, Andras, 11/4/73
Klimov, Valerii, 1/31/60
Kogan, Leonid, 2/14/58; 10/16/60
Kohon, Harold, 10/22/50
Kreisler, Fritz, 12/3/45; 11/28/48

Kulka, Konstanty, 2/3/74
Lustgarten, Alfred, 10/1/39
Menuhin, Yehudi, 2/19/39; 10/22/49; 1/8/52; 1/12/52; 10/19/52;
 2/1/53; 1/16/54; 3/4/56; 3/13/56; 10/25/53; 12/2/61; 3/17/74;
 3/7/76
Milstein, Nathan, 12/17/44; 5/5/51; 3/23/52; 3/1/53; 4/3/54;
 2/25/56; 3/2/57; 12/8/57; 1/4/59; 3/5/60; 11/19/60; 11/19/61;
 3/10/63; 2/21/65; 1/23/66; 3/17/68; 11/15/70; 2/10/74; 11/21/76
Morini, Erica, 4/3/49
Novelo, Hermilo, 6/17/75
Odnoposoff, Ricardo, 3/14/54
Oistrakh, David, 11/28-29/55; 12/11/59; 11/9/62; 1/12/64; 11/21/65;
 12/24/67; 1/25/70
Oistrakh, Igor, 4/8/62; 11/12/63; 1/12/64; 11/21/65
Olevsky, Julian, 1/29/52
Perlman, Itzhak, 12/28/66; 1/1/67; 4/2/67; 1/12/69
Příhoda, Váša, 3/6/49
Rabin, Michael, 1/10/60
Rabinof, Benno, 6/30/67
Ricci, Ruggiero, 9/28/47; 1/25/69
Rosand, Aaron, 11/27/55; 10/11/70; 3/4/72; 6/14/75
Sacher, Hazay, 4/19/49
Schneiderhan, Wolfgang, 10/26/56
Senofsky, Berl, 5/5/63
Silverstein, Joseph, 3/28/68; 6/6/76
Skorodin, Elaine, 2/23/58
Spivakov, Vladimir, 2/16/75; 10/26/75
Spivakovsky, Tossy, 2/2-3/52; 4/15/56
Stanic, Jelka, 10/30/60
Stern, Isaac, 11/14/48; 10/8/50; 1/6/57; 3/2/58; 1/17/61; 6/1/63;
 12/7/63; 4/5/64; 11/27/66; 5/5/68; 4/27/69; 11/18/69; 5/17/70;
 2/14/71
Szigeti, Joseph, 2/3/50; 4/22/51
Thaviu, Samuel, 1/14/70; 3/11/70
Tretyakov, Viktor, 2/22/76; 2/13/77
Ushioda, Masuko, 6/11/75
Wilkomirska, Wanda, 1/21/61; 10/18/64; 2/11/68; 12/6/69; 2/6/72;
 2/10/74; 2/6/77
Wilkomirski, Michael, 2/20/38
Zeitlin, Zvi, 11/20/62
Zukerman, Pinchas, 2/20/72

Unidentified Instruments
Briggs, Bunny, 2/11/67
The Cumberland Three, 10/18/60
Drake, Alan, 11/10/62

Harold Harris Trio, 11/10/62

OPERA COMPANIES
The American National Opera Company, 10/18-22/67
Bolshoi Opera, 2/12-13/72
De Paur's Opera Gala, 1/13/57
D'Oyly Carte Opera Company, 12/18-22/62; 12/16-18/66;
    11/30-12/1/68
The Metropolitan Opera, 5/8-13/50; 5/20-23/54; 5/19-23/55;
    5/24-27/56; 5/23-26/57; 5/22-25/58; 5/12-14/61; 5/27-30/62
The NBC Opera Company, 10/11/57
New York City Opera, 11/18-29/53; 11/29/64; 12/26/64-1/3/65
The Opera Theatre, 10/20/40
San Carlo Opera Company, 4/12-19/42; 10/6-26/47
Theater an der Wien, 9/20-23/67

ORCHESTRAS
All American Youth Orchestra, 6/2/41
The Baroque Orchestra of the West German Radio of Cologne,
    11/12/72
The Bavarian Symphony Orchestra of Munich, 11/3/68
The Berlin Philharmonic Orchestra, 3/11-13/55; 10/26-28/56; 11/5/61;
    1/31-2/1/65; 11/4-5/74; 11/9-10/76
The Boston Pops, 3/22/53; 2/27-28/54; 3/18/56; 2/17/57; 2/24/62;
    4/12/64; 3/18/72; 3/19/75
Boston Symphony Orchestra, 12/3/48; 5/15-17/53; 4/15/63; 3/28/68;
    3/17/72
Budapest Symphony Orchestra, 11/19/71; 11/4/73
The Buffalo Philharmonic Orchestra, 10/9/65; 9/18/76
Chicago Pops Concert Orchestra, 3/21/71
Chicago Symphony Orchestra, 1/15/57; 1/22/58; 2/22/58; 12/11/59;
    11/10/63; 1/12/64; 12/10/65; 12/15/68; 1/24-25/69; 11/18/69;
    12/4/73; 1/8/75; 9/20/75; 9/30/75
The Cincinnati Symphony Orchestra, 3/7-8/53; 1/23/66
The Cleveland Orchestra, 11/15/53; 12/10/71; 12/12/71
Concertgebow Orchestra of Amsterdam, 10/30-31/54; 4/30/61;
    5/14/67
Czech Philharmonic, 11/5/67
The Dallas Symphony Orchestra, 3/24-25/51
The Danish National Orchestra of the State Radio, 11/8-9/52
The Denver Symphony Orchestra, 4/4-5/53
The Detroit Symphony Orchestra, 2/27/55
The Gershwin Concert Orchestra, 5/9/53
The Hague Philharmonic, 5/5/63
The Houston Symphony Orchestra, 3/5/50; 2/28/65
Indianapolis Symphony Orchestra, 3/5/44; 3/4/45; 3/10/47; 12/3/49

244

Israel Philharmonic Orchestra, 2/10-11/51; 11/26/60; 8/7-8/67; 9/19/76

The Jerusalem Symphony Orchestra, 11/24/75

Johann Strauss Ensemble of the Vienna Symphony Orchestra, 2/28/71

The Leningrad Philharmonic Orchestra, 11/9/62; 2/13/77

London Philharmonic Orchestra, 11/7/76

Longines Symphonette, 10/22/50

Los Angeles Philharmonic Orchestra, 11/8/70

Milwaukee Symphony Orchestra, 4/14/74; 6/11/75; 12/16/75; 6/20/76

The Minneapolis Symphony Orchestra, 1/23/49; 4/15/56; 4/20/58; 4/1/62; 4/24/66

The Moscow Philharmonic, 11/21/65

Moscow State Symphony, 1/30-31/60; 3/5/69

The Mozarteum Orchestra of Salzburg, 4/8/56; 4/14/56

National Symphony Orchestra, 3/1-2/58

The National Symphony Orchestra of Mexico, 11/9/58

The NBC Symphony Orchestra, 5/17/50

NDR Symphony Orchestra of Hamburg, 1/20/63

The New Orleans Philharmonic Symphony Orchestra, 2/21/60

The New York Philharmonic, 9/23-24/48; 5/21/55; 9/9-10/60; 9/7-8/63; 9/14-15/67; 9/20/69; 7/1/76

North Side Symphony Orchestra of Chicago, 6/14/75; 2/8/76; 2/29/76; 6/6/76

Orchestre Jean-Francois Paillard, 11/8/67

L'Orchestre National de la Radiodiffusion-Television Francaise, 10/30/48; 10/21/62; 10/18/70

Philadelphia Orchestra, 1/5/38; 5/9/46; 6/6/46; 11/9/46; 11/8/47; 6/5/48; 2/12/49; 2/6/50; 3/1/52; 2/20-21/54; 5/1/66; 5/3/69; 5/29/71

Philharmonia Hungarica, 11/7-8/59; 2/2/64

Philharmonia Orchestra of London, 11/5-6/55

The Pittsburgh Symphony Orchestra, 2/26/50

Prague Symphony, 3/4/72

The RCA Victor Orchestra, 10/31/48

The Royal Philharmonic Orchestra of London, 11/25-26/50; 10/26/69

St. Louis Symphony Orchestra, 1/18/39; 2/2-3/52; 12/7/65; 11/28/71; 2/4/73

State of Mexico Symphony Orchestra, 6/17/75

The Stockholm Philharmonic Orchestra, 3/10/68; 11/23/75

Symphonie Orchester des Bayerischen Rundfunks Munchen *see* The Bavarian Symphony Orchestra of Munich

Symphony Orchestra of the Florence Festival, 10/27/57

U.S.S.R. State Symphony *see* Moscow State Symphony

Vienna Johann Strauss Orchestra, 11/20/66; 11/26/66; 10/14/73

Vienna Philharmonic, 11/18/56; 11/14/59; 10/8/67; 4/7/76

The Vienna Symphony Orchestra, 2/23/64; 3/12/72

The Warsaw Philharmonic Orchestra, 1/21-22/61; 10/18/64; 2/3/74

REVUES/FOLK FESTIVALS, etc.
American Dances, 3/10/63
Carib Creole Carnival, 10/5/57
Fiesta Folklorico, 11/7/71; 11/26/72; 11/25/73; 10/27/74; 10/5/75
International Ice Revue, 3/18-20/71
Ireland on Parade, 10/23-25/64
The Israeli Folk Festival '74, 11/3/74
Mary Hunter's Musical Americana, 1/17/54
The National Israeli Song Festival 1972, 10/14-15/72
The 1965 Fred Waring Show, 11/1/64
Odori Festival of Japan, 7/19-20/67
Panhellenion Folk Festival of Greece, 10/20/62
Pomp and Ceremony, 9/27/64
Rapsodia Romina, 11/11/62
Russian Festival of Music and Dance, 7/21-26/59; 8/5-7/76
The Traveling Hootenanny, 10/6/63
Tyrolerfest!, 11/7/71
Vienna on Parade, 4/6/58; 2/28/60; 3/18/62
The World of Music, 1/25-26/61

THEATRE COMPANIES
Foo Hsing Theatre *see under* Folk Companies
Greek Tragedy Theatre, 9/16-17/61; 10/12/64; 10/14/64
Kukla, Fran and Ollie, 2/27-28/54
The Old Vic Company, 11/4-9/58; 4/2-7/62; 4/17-22/67
Piraikon Theatron *see* Greek Tragedy Theatre
The Salzburg Marionette Theatre, 1/30-31/54; 11/7/54
The Stratford Festival Company, 11/6/64
Theatre an der Wien *see under* Opera Companies
Yiddish Art Theatre, 5/9-12/40

VOCAL ENSEMBLES *see* **CHOIRS/VOCAL ENSEMBLES**

VOCALISTS
  Popular
  Aznavour, Charles, 10/17/71; 10/22/72
  Bagheera, 12/28/62
  Bailey, Pearl, 2/11/67
  Baird, Eugenie, 10/25/48
  Belafonte, Harry, 12/5-11/60
  The Black Panther *see* Bagheera
  Bubbles, John W., 6/1-7/59
  Chevalier, Maurice, 9/24-25/62; 9/27-29/62; 5/31/64; 5/10/68
  Dietrich, Marlene, 12/1-2/61
  Garland, Judy, 9/4-9/58; 6/6-7/59; 5/6/61; 11/7/62; 5/7/65

Holman, Libby, 12/3/44
Laine, Cleo, 11/6/73; 3/30/74; 10/21/74
Martin, Mary, 10/21-22/58
Mathis, Johnny, 11/10/62; 7/19-20/63
McIntyre, Russell, 10/25/48
Mouskouri, Nana, 11/22/69; 3/19/72; 3/25/73
Nero, Peter, 11/20/71
Pingatore, Mike, 10/25/48

Operatic (Here are listed vocalists who performed operatic roles)
Sopranos
Albanese, Licia, 5/10/50; 5/23/54; 5/21/55; 5/25/57
Amara, Lucine, 5/22/54; 5/22/55; 5/26/56; 5/23/57; 5/26/57; 5/22/58; 5/13/61
Ayars, Ann, 11/25/53
Arroyo, Martina, 12/27/64; 12/30/64
Belle, Mary, 4/13/42; 4/18/42
Bergey, Carol, 1/1/65
Bishop, Adelaide, 11/29/53
Bogard, Carole, 10/20/67
Bower, Beverly, 10/20/67; 10/22/67
Brooks, Patricia, 1/1/65
Carron, Elisabeth, 10/8/47
Collier, Marie, 10/18/67; 10/21/67
Conner, Nadine, 5/9/50; 5/20/54; 5/27/56
Cravi, Mina, 10/17/43; 10/6/47; 10/9/47; 10/19-21/47; 10/23/47
Cullen, Patricia, 10/19/67; 10/21/67
Cundari, Emilia, 5/24/56; 5/25/57
della Chiesa, Vivian, 10/8/47; 10/11/47
de los Angeles, Victoria, 5/13/61
Di Gerlando, Maria, 11/21/53; 11/29/53
Di Nicola, Esterina, 10/15/47; 10/25/47
Elgar, Anne, 11/29/64; 12/31/64; 1/2/65
Evangelista, Lucia, 10/25/47
Farrell, Eileen, 5/28/62
Fenn, Jean, 11/29/53; 5/22/54
Fletcher, Lola, 4/16/42
Gannon, Teresa, 11/21/53
Glowacki, Valerie, 4/7/40; 3/26/41; 5/18/41
Goapere, Berte, 10/11/57
Goodall, Valorie, 9/20-23/67
Graf, Uta, 12/31/52
Haskins, Virginia, 10/20/40
Hunt, Lois, 5/13/50
Hurley, Laurel, 11/18/53; 11/21-22/53; 11/28/53; 5/21/55; 5/23/57

Kampo, Mary, 12/18/43
Kaye, Selma, 10/12/47; 10/16/47; 10/19/47; 10/26/47
Kirsten, Dorothy, 5/13/50; 5/20/55; 5/22/55; 5/27/62
Koller, Dagmar, 9/20-23/67
Koyke, Hizi, 10/7/47; /10/15/47; 10/25/47
Krall, Heidi, 5/23/54; 5/22/55
Kurenko, Maria, 12/31/38; 4/17/42
Lamont, Eunice Steen, 12/18/43
Landia, Basel, 10/7/47; 10/10-11/47; 10/21/47; 10/25-26/47;
    10/23/55
Le Sawyer, Mary, 11/20-22/53; 11/28-29/53
Likova, Eva, 11/20/53; 11/28/53
Lynn, Jackie, 12/18/43
MacNeil, Dorothy, 11/19/53; /11/25/53
Manski, Dorothee, 12/18/43
McKnight, Anne, 11/27/53
Meusel, Lucille, 4/13/42; 4/18/42
Milanov, Zinka, 5/21/54; 5/19/55; 5/25/56; 5/24/57
Moffo, Anna, 5/14/61; 5/29/62
Munsel, Patrice, 5/12/50; 5/26/57
Nilsson, Birgit, 5/13/61
Norton, Marybelle, 10/20/47
Ordassy, Carlotta, 5/29/62
Panvini, Grace, 4/15/42
Peters, Roberta, 5/23/54; 5/21/55; 5/27/56; 5/23/58; 5/25/58
Pobbe, Marcella, 5/25/58
Pons, Lily, 5/22/54; 5/26/56
Price, Leontyne, 5/30/62
Rivera, Graciela, 10/10/47; 10/18/47; 10/22/47
Roggero, Margaret, 5/20/54; 5/23/54; 5/24/58
Roman, Stella, 5/13/50
Roselle, Anne, 4/12/42; 4/18/42
Rysanek, Leonie, 5/12/61
Saroya, Bianca, 4/19/42
Sills, Beverly, 12/26/64; 11/29/64; 12/31/64; 1/2/65
Silvan, Monica, 12/13/64
Sloniowska, Halina, 12/13/64
Smith, Carol, 12/31/52
Smith, Doras, 12/31/52
Sokil, Maria, 5/18/41
Sorrelle, Shirley, 10/20/40
Steber, Eleanor, 5/26-27/56; 5/23/58
Stella, Antonietta, 5/24/58
Stewart, Willa, 10/9/47; 10/11/47; 10/18/47; 10/24/47
Stratas, Teresa, 5/14/61
Sunahara, Michiko, 11/22/53

Symons, Charlotte, 10/14/47
Tebaldi, Renata, 5/25/57
Troyanos, Tatiana, 12/27/64; 1/3/65
Turner, Leola, 4/14/42; 4/16/42; 4/18-19/42
Valente, Benita, 10/22/67
Vanni, Helen, 5/24-25/57; 5/24/58; 5/14/61
Varnay, Astrid, 10/13/47; 5/11/50
Votipka, Thelma, 5/20/54; 5/22-23/54; 5/26/56; 5/23/58; 5/25/58
Welitch, Ljuba, 5/8/50
Wilson, Dolores, 10/11/57
Witkowska, Nadja, 10/23/55; 11/29/64; 12/27/64; 1/3/65
Zambrana, Margarita, 11/21/53

Mezzo Sopranos/Contraltos
Alberts, Eunice, 10/22/67
Allen, Betty, 10/20/67; 11/28/85
Altman, Thelma, 5/10/50; 5/12/50
Bayle, Ilma, 12/18/43
Bible, Frances, 11/18/53; 11/21-22/53; 1/1/65
Blair, Lynn, 5/27/62
Bradford, Mona, 10/10/47
Brown, Elizabeth, 12/18/43
Bruno, Charlotte, 4/15/42; 4/17-19/42
Chambers, Madelaine, 5/25/57
Dalis, Irene, 5/12/61
Data, Maria, 10/20/40
Dixon, Dorothy, 10/8-11/47; 10/19/47; 10/22/47; 10/25/47
Dunn, Mignon, 5/28/62
Elias, Rosalind, 5/26/56; 5/25/57; 5/22/58; 5/25/58; 5/13/61;
    5/27/62
Evans, Beverly, 12/26-27/64; 12/30/64
Gentile, Lois, 10/19/47
Glade, Coe, 4/12/42; 4/14/42; 4/18/42
Glaz, Herta, 5/26/56
Greenspan, Muriel, 12/27/64; 1/1/65
Guile, Helen, 1/3/65
Hallberg, Ingrid, 10/21/47
Harshaw, Margaret, 5/11/50; 5/13/50
Heckman, Winifred, 10/7/47; 10/9/47; 10/11/47; 10/15/47;
    10/25/47; 11/18/53; 11/21/53; 11/28/53
Heidt, Winifred, 10/6/47; 10/17/47; 10/23/47
Kaskas, Anna, 10/11/47; 10/18/47
Kleinman, Marlena, 12/26-27/64; 12/30/64
Knapp, Eleanor, 10/23/55
Kreste, Mary, 11/20-22/53; 11/28-29/53
Lane, Gloria, 11/19/53; 11/28/53
Larrimore, Martha, 10/12/47; 10/24/47; 10/26/47

Leone, Maria, 5/23/54; 5/22/55; 5/26/56
Lipton, Martha, 5/24/56; 5/22-23/58
Madeira, Jean, 5/12/50; 5/24/57
Manski, Inge, 5/10/50; 5/12/50
Matsuchi, Kazuko, 11/22/53
Miller, Mildred, 5/24/56; 5/23/58
Povia, Charlotte, 1/3/65
Powers, Marie, 10/23/55
Przybylinski, Loretta, 4/7/40; 3/26/41
Repp, Ellen, 10/13/47
Simon, Joanna, 10/19-22/67
Snow, Helen Clare, 12/31/52
Stevens, Risë, 5/9/50; 5/22/55; 5/27/56; 5/26/57; 5/24/58
Thebom, Blanche, 5/21/54; 5/25/56; 5/27/56
Ward, Cecilia, 10/11/57
Warren, Louise, 4/13/42; 4/15/42; 4/17/42; 4/19/42
Wolff, Beverly, 12/29/64; 1/2/65

Tenors
Anthony, Charles, 5/24/57; 5/13/61; 5/29/62
Arbizu, Ray, 10/18/67; 10/20-22/67
Barioni, Daniele, 5/23/57; 5/25/57
Baum, Kurt, 5/13/50; 5/21/54; 5/25/56; 5/24/57; 5/26/57
Bentonelli, Joseph, 12/31/38
Bergonzi, Carlo, 5/24/58; 5/28/62
Berini, Mario, 10/14/47; 10/16/47; 10/25/47
Billings, James, 10/18-22/67
Bjoerling, Jussi, 5/8/50; 5/12/50
Campora, Giuseppe, 5/20/55; 5/25/57
Carelli, Gabor, 5/23/54; 5/22/55; 5/26-27/56; 5/25/57; 5/14/61
Cassilly, Richard, 12/29/64; 1/2/65
Conley, Eugene, 4/13/42; 4/15/42; 4/18/42; 5/23/54; 5/21/55
Corelli, Franco, 5/13/61
Craig, John, 12/26/64
Crain, Jon, 11/21/53; 11/27/53; 11/29/53; 11/29/64; 12/27/64;
    12/30-31/64
Cranston, Albert, 10/22/47
Curci, Francesco, 4/13/42; 4/15/42; 4/18-19/42
Da Costa, Albert, 5/26/56
Del Monaco, Mario, 5/24/58
De Paolis, Alessio, 5/8/50; 5/12/50; 5/23/58; 5/13/61
Di Stefano, Giuseppe, 5/10/50; 9/20-23/67
Duval, Pierre, 12/27/64
Fernandi, Eugenio, 5/12/61; 5/27/62
Franke, Paul, 5/10/50; 5/22-23/54; 5/30/62
Fredericks, Walter, 12/31/52; 11/21/53; 11/28/53
Gari, Giulio, 10/11/47; 10/15/47; 10/19/47; 5/24/56

Gedda, Nicolai, 5/23/58; 5/25/58
Grabinski, Edward, 4/7/40; 3/26/41
Grobe, Donald, 12/31/52
Hayward, Thomas, 10/10/47; 10/20/47; 5/22/54; 5/27/56
Jagel, Frederick, 10/26/47
Jamerson, Thomas, 10/18/67; 10/21/67
Kiepura, Jan, 5/18/41
Kiepura, Ladis, 4/7/40; 3/26/41; 10/21/47
Krause, Richard, 12/26/64; 1/1/65
Kullman, Charles, 5/24/56; 5/27/56
La Chance, Adrien, 10/8-11/47; 10/16/47; 10/19/47; 10/22/47;
    10/25-26/47
Laufkoetter, Karl, 5/11/50
Lindi, Aroldo, 4/12/42; 4/18-19/42
Lloyd, David, 11/18/53
Luporini, Joseph R., 10/20/40
Mackenzie, Tandy, 10/11/47; 10/17/47
Martinelli, Giovanni, 10/9/47; 10/19/47
McCracken, James, 5/24-25/56; 5/24-25/57
Miller, Kellis, 1/3/65
Morrell, Barry, 5/30/62
Nagy, Robert, 5/13/61
Oreste, Kirk, 10/11/57
Palermo, Mario, 10/7/47; 10/9/47; 10/18/47; 10/25/47
Paprocki, Bogdan, 12/13/64
Peerce, Jan, 5/22-23/54; 5/21-22/55; 5/26/56; 5/14/61; 5/29/62
Petrak, Rudolf, 11/20/53; 11/22/53; 11/25/53; 11/29/53
Poleri, David, 11/19/53; 11/25/53; 11/28/53
Pollock, Michael, 11/21/53; 11/28/53
Pravadelli, Alfonso, 10/12/47; 10/18/47; 10/24/47
Ralf, Torsten, 10/13/47
Rall, Thomas, 10/19/67; 10/21/67
Rayner, Sydney, 4/14/42; 4/16-17/42; 4/19/42
Shirley, George, 1/3/65
Stamford, John, 11/29/64; 12/31/64
Svanholm, Set, 5/11/50
Tagliavini, Ferruccio, 5/13/50
Tucker, Richard, 10/8/47; 10/22/47; 5/20/54; 5/22/54; 5/19/55;
    5/22/55; 5/27/56; 5/22/58; 5/13/61
Valletti, Cesare, 5/25/58
Velis, Andrea, 5/29/62
Vellucci, Luigi, 11/20-22/53; 11/27/53; 11/29/53; 10/11/57
Vinay, Ramon, 10/6/47; 10/23/47; 5/9/50
Vrenios, Anastasios, 10/19-22/67

Baritones/Basses
Aiken, David, 10/23/55

251

Alvary, Lorenzo, 5/8-9/50; 5/24/56
Baker, John, 5/12/50
Ballarini, Stefan, 10/9/47; 10/11/47; 10/13-14/47; 10/17/47;
    10/19-21/47; 10/23/47; 10/26/47
Bayle, Theo, 9/20-23/67
Bottcher, Ron, 12/27/64; 12/30/64; 1/3/65
Bozza, Fausto, 4/13/42; 4/15/42; 10/8/47; 10/10/47; 10/25/47
Brazis, Algerd, 10/16/47; 5/23/54
Brownlee, John, 5/27/56
Budney, Arthur, 5/24/50
Carell, Victor, 10/20/40
Cass, Lee, 12/26/64; 12/29/64; 1/2-3/65
Cassel, Walter, 11/22/53; 11/28-29/53
Cehanovsky, George, 5/10/50; 5/12-13/50; 5/23/54; 5/26/56;
    5/25/57; 5/14/61
Colzani, Anselmo, 5/30/62
Corena, Fernando, 5/20-21/55; 5/25/58
Cossa, Dominic, 12/26/64
Cranston, Albert, 10/10/47
Czaplicki, George, 12/31/38; 4/7/40; 3/26/41; 5/18/41
Davidson, Lawrence, 5/10/50; 5/20/54; 5/23/54; 5/22/55
De Cesare, Louis, 4/13/42; 4/15/42
Edelmann, Otto, 5/26/56; 5/23/58
Elyn, Mark, 10/11/57
Ernster, Dezso, 5/11/50
Flagello, Ezio, 5/12/61; 5/30/62
Foldi, Andrew, 10/19/67; 10/22/67
Fourié, George, 10/18/67; 10/20/67
Giaiotti, Bonaldo, 5/13/61; 5/29/62
Glossop, Peter, 10/21/67
Gramm, Donald, 11/29/53; 10/19/67
Green, Eugene, 10/11/57
Gorin, Igor, 10/11/57
Guarrera, Frank, 5/22/54; 5/21-22/55; 5/27/56; 5/23/57; 5/25/58;
    5/13/61; 5/29/62
Harris, Lloyd, 12/31/52
Harvuot, Clifford, 5/22-23/54; 5/21/55; 5/24/56; 5/23/57;
    5/25/57; 5/14/61
Hawkins, Osie, 5/10/50; 5/22/55
Hedlund, Ronald, 10/22/67
Herbert, Ralph, 11/21-22/53; 5/23/58
Hines, Jerome, 5/12-13/50; 5/22/54; 5/21/55; 5/25/56; 5/25/58;
    5/12/61; 5/28/62
Hurshell, Edmund, 10/21/67
Janssen, Herbert, 5/11/50
Kinsman, Philip, 5/13/50

Koehn, Charles, 10/20-22/67
Kossakowski, Zygmunt, 12/13/64
Kozakevich, Stefan, 4/16/42; 4/18-19/42; 12/18/43
Kravitt, Harold, 4/12/42; 4/14-17/42
Ledbetter, William, 11/29/64; 12/26-27/64; 12/31/64; 1/3/65
Lishner, Leon, 11/20/53; 11/28-29/53
London, George, 5/26/57; 5/22/58
Luca, Milo, 4/7/40; 3/26/41
Ludgin, Chester, 1/3/65
MacNeil, Cornell, 11/20/53; 5/12/61
Malas, Spiro, 1/1/65
Marsh, Calvin, 5/22/55; 5/26/56; 5/25/57; 5/25/58; 5/14/61
Merrill, Robert, 5/9/50; 5/13/50; 5/20/54; 5/23/54; 5/21/55;
    5/25/56; 5/25/57; 5/25/58; 5/14/61; 5/28/62
Milnes, Sherrill, 12/27/64
Morelli, Carlo, 10/9/47; 10/12/47; 10/14-15/47; 10/18/47;
    10/20/47; 10/22/47; 10/25/47
Moscona, Nicola, 5/21/54; 5/26/56
Newman, Arthur, 11/20/53; 11/25/53; 11/28-29/53
Pasterczyk, Narcy, 12/31/52
Pechner, Gerhard, 5/8/50; 5/11/50; 5/26/56; 5/13/61
Petersen, Robert, 10/21/67
Petroff, Ivan, 4/13/42; 4/15/42; 4/17/42
Reardon, John, 11/29/64; 1/1-2/65
Redding, Earl, 11/29/53
Renan, Emile, 11/20/53; 11/29/53; 10/11/57; 11/29/64; 1/2/65
Rickert, Lawrence, 12/31/52
Rimini, Giacomo, 10/20/40
Ruisi, Nino, 12/31/38
Russell, Jack, 11/29/53
Schon, Kenneth, 5/12/50
Scott, Norman, 5/22-23/54; 5/21-22/55; 5/26-27/56; 5/26/57;
    5/24/58; 5/30/62
Sereni, Mario, 5/27/62
Sgarro, Louis, 5/25/56; 5/25/57; 5/28/62
Siepi, Cesare, 5/20/54; 5/24/56
Singher, Martial, 5/24/58
Smith, David, 11/29/64; 12/26/64; 12/31/64
Sudler, Louis, 10/7/47
Sved, Alexander, 10/6/47; 10/16/47; 5/8/50
Tajo, Italo, 5/13/50
Tatozzi, Victor, 10/8/47; 10/10-12/47; 10/18/47; 10/21-22/47;
    10/24-26/47
Telasko, Ralph, 10/8/47; 10/13/47; 10/16/47; 10/25/47
Thomas, Mostyn, 4/12/42; 4/14/42; 4/18-19/42
Torigi, Richard, 11/21-22/53; 11/25/53; 11/28/53

Tozzi, Giorgio, 5/24/56; 5/26/56; 5/23-24/57; 5/22/58; 5/25/58; 5/13/61

Treigle, Norman, 11/19/53; 11/25/53; 11/27-28/53; 12/27/64; 12/29/64; 1/1-3/65

Trevisan, Vittorio, 12/31/38

Uppman, Theodore, 5/26/57

Valentino, Frank, 5/22/54

Valle, Mario, 4/16/42; 10/18/47

Vichegonov, Lubomir, 12/31/52; 5/21/54; 5/23/54

Walters, Jess, 10/8/47; 10/10-11/47; 10/19/47; 10/24-25/47

Warren, Leonard, 5/10/50; 5/12/50; 5/21/54; 5/23/54; 5/19/55; 5/22/55; 5/26/56; 5/24/57

Weber, Karl, 9/20-23/67

Weede, Robert, 12/31/52

Wentworth, Richard, 4/12-13/42; 4/15/42; 4/17-18/42; 11/18/53; 11/21-22/53; 11/27-28/53

Wilderman, William, 10/6/47; 10/10-14/47; 10/17-18/47; 10/20-21/47; 10/23-24/47

Winters, Lawrence, 11/19/53; 11/21/53; 11/27/53

Yarnell, Bruce, 10/18-19/67; 10/21/67

Zaichenko, Nicholas, 4/19/42

Zanasi, Mario, 5/24/58

Vocal Soloists
Sopranos

Arroyo, Martina, 3/25/62

Beck, Irmgard, 10/24/71

Beems, Patricia, 5/9/54

Berger, Erna, 3/4/51

Bollinger, Anne, 2/22/53

Brancato, Rosemarie, 1/26/46

Brown, Anne, 2/18/45

Callas, Maria, 1/15/57; 1/22/58; 3/2/74

Crowley, Mary Frances, 1/29/56

Davrath, Netania, 11/20/62

de los Angeles, Victoria, 10/7/51; 1/24/53; 2/14/60; 4/8/61; 3/3/64; 3/15/64; 11/22/64

Dobbs, Mattiwilda, 1/28/55; 12/10/55

Eggerth, Martha, 5/16/43; 6/19/53; 6/7/58

Farr, Naomi, 5/29/54

Flagstad, Kirsten, 4/11/47; 1/12/48; 1/9/49; 11/13/49; 12/3/50; 4/13/52

Groth-Braatz, Barbara, 12/5/72

Gueden, Hilde, 2/7/59

Hall, Bernice, 1/13/57; 3/23/58

Hunt, Lois, 11/17/50

Ilitsch, Daniza, 5/16/48

James, Olga, 1/25-26/61
Kaye, Selma, 4/1/45
Kiszely, Itza, 3/5/39
Kojelis, Valentina, 5/4/69
Koller, Dagmar, 11/20/66; 11/26/66
Korjus, Miliza, 5/7/45; 10/28/45; 4/14/46; 3/16/47
Kurenko, Maria, 11/6/38; 3/12/39; 3/5/44
Lee, Alyne Dumas, 10/2/60
Lehmann, Lotte, 3/13/49; 2/25/50
Long, Carolyn, 5/9/53
Loose, Emmy, 4/8/56; 4/14/56
MacDonald, Jeanette, 3/29/40; 9/11/42; 12/12/43; 9/28/52
Manners, Gail, 5/17/47; 4/29/50
Marshall, Lois, 4/21/57; 4/18/71
Matthews, Inez, 1/13/57; 3/23/58
Maynor, Dorothy, 4/8/45; 2/9/46; 2/16/47; 12/11/48; 10/30/49;
    10/29/50; 1/27/52; 11/30/52; 2/20/55; 11/3/57; 11/5/57;
    12/6/59
Milanov, Zinka, 2/7/54
Moore, Grace, 4/17/39
Mulvey, Marylyn, 10/10/69; 11/29/70; 12/3/72; 2/8/76
Munsel, Patrice, 10/14/51
Nash, Marie, 10/2/45; 1/26/46; 4/28/46
Neblett, Carol, 10/16/66; 10/15/67; 4/14/74
Nilsson, Birgit, 11/17/68; 12/13/70
Novotna, Jarmila, 4/19/49
Ordassy-Baransky, Charlotte, 3/26/61
Panvini, Grace, 10/2/45
Pemberton, Virginia, 1/22/41
Peters, Roberta, 3/21/64
Pons, Lily, 4/2/38; 4/28/40; 4/19/41; 4/5/44; 1/11/47; 12/3/49
Price, Leontyne, 5/6/56; 4/7/57; 12/6/58; 2/3/63; 2/1/70;
    2/27/72; 4/4/76
Reale, Marcella, 5/9/54
Resnik, Regina, 3/25/58
Rudenko, Bella, 2/13/70; 10/16/74
Sack, Erna, 11/25/55
Sarata-Pitsch, Birgit, 10/14/73
Schwarzkopf, Elisabeth, 11/21/54; 11/13/55; 10/21/56;
    11/25/57; 3/5/67; 1/21/68; 3/2/69; 3/8/70; 2/3/74; 2/9/75
Seefried, Irmgard, 10/11/53; 10/17/54; 3/17/56;12/9/56; 11/1/59;
    3/12/61
Shoshan, Shoshana, 1/16/65
Sorokina, Tamara, 5/26/74
Steber, Eleanor, 1/7/56
Stratas, Teresa, 11/24/68

Sumac, Yma *see under* Folk and Ethnic Musicians
Tassinari, Pia, 2/18/50
Tebaldi, Renata, 3/25/66; 2/15/69
Tennyson, Jean, 11/24/40
Teyte, Maggie, 1/4/46; 3/10/47
Tourel, Jennie, 11/27/49
Traubel, Helen, 3/9/46; 4/3/48
Tyler, Veronica, 6/4/67
Vishnevskaya, Galina, 1/31/60
Warner, Eleanor, 4/26/58
Welitch, Ljuba, 4/9/50; 4/4-5/53
Widmann, Christine von, 2/28/60
Williams, Camilla, 4/23/50; 4/21/56
Woytowicz, Stefania, 2/3/74
Yeend, Frances, 3/3/51
Zarou, Jeanette, 9/14/67

Mezzo Sopranos/Contraltos
Allen, Betty, 11/28/65
Anderson, Marian, 1/15/46; 10/24/48; 1/21/50; 1/29/50;
    1/21/51; 4/8/51; 2/29/52; 5/3/52; 1/31/53; 3/29/53; 1/30/54;
    12/5/54; 1/8/56; 2/23/57; 1/24/58; 4/5/59; 2/28/60; 2/19/61;
    5/11/63; 12/6/64; 2/29/76
Ayer, Anne, 2/17/65
Berganza, Teresa, 2/12/67
Bonazzi, Elaine, 2/17/63
Brice, Carol, 1/30/49; 12/4/49; 10/18/53; 3/12/55
Bumbry, Grace, 12/16/62; 2/9/64; 1/24/65; 2/19/67
Doloukhanova, Zara, 3/15/59; 2/16/62
Elmo, Cloe, 12/5/48
Finnila, Birgit, 12/19/71; 1/14/73
Kaskas, Anna, 11/7/37
Mayer, Margery, 12/15/45
Merriman, Nan, 10/31/59
Nikolaidi, Elena, 12/10/49; 4/29/51; 4/5/52; 4/4/54; 4/26/59
Obraztsova, Elena, 10/31/76
Perret, Anne, 12/14/71
Smith, Carol, 11/5/51
Stevens, Risë, 2/15/51; 2/17/51; 11/4/51; 2/2/57
Swarthout, Gladys, 2/13/54
Thebom, Blanche, 4/30/50
Thorborg, Kerstin, 10/8/44
Tourel, Jennie, 1/15/49
Verrett, Shirley, 12/4/66

Tenors
Bachleda, Andrzej, 2/5/66

Berini, Mario, 4/1/45
Bjoerling, Jussi, 11/27/38; 1/21/40; 2/16/41; 2/14/43; 3/29/47;
    3/6/48; 2/6/49; 2/25/51; 12/9/51; 2/24-26/56; 3/16/58
Bjoerling, Rolf, 11/8/64
Cary, Gerhard, 10/24/71
Di Stefano, Giuseppe, 3/2/74
Ferguson, Lester, 1/25-26/61
Gedda, Nicolai, 4/27/57; 4/12/58; 11/23/58
Gigli, Beniamino, 1/8/39; 5/8/55
Gross, Erwin von, 2/28/60
Hayes, Roland, 12/12/37
Johansson, Karl-Olof, 11/4/56
Johnson, Robert, 12/15/68
Jones, Dai, 10/17/71
Kiepura, Jan, 3/5/39; 3/2/41; 2/14/43; 5/16/43; 6/19/53; 6/7/58
Kraeutler, Walter, 11/20/66; 11/26/66
Kusevitsky, Moishe, 5/7/49; 12/24/49; 9/23/56; 12/4/56
Lanza, Mario, 4/7/51
Lynch, Christopher, 10/18/49
Marvey, Gene, 10/2/45; 4/28/46; 5/17/47; 4/19/49; 4/29/50
Melchior, Lauritz, 12/1/45; 3/17/47; 5/9/54
Melton, James, 3/12/49; 4/28/51
Pane-Gasser, John, 3/5/39
Peerce, Jan, 4/16/50; 4/15/51; 4/19/53; 2/5/55; 11/13/56; 3/10/57;
    3/30/57; 1/9/60; 1/8/61; 3/4/62; 1/5/63; 1/7/64; 12/25/69;
    5/13/73
Saxon, Luther, 1/13/57
Schipa, Tito, 2/20/38; 11/6/48; 10/25/62
Siesz, Wolfgang, 10/14/73
Simoneau, Leopold, 4/21/57
Stewart, Melvin, 3/23/58
Svanholm, Set, 4/30/49
Tagliavini, Ferruccio, 1/29/49; 2/18/50; 10/15/50; 11/3/50;
    2/22/53; 11/28/54; 3/24/63
Tokatyan, Armand, 1/22/41
Tucker, Richard, 2/11/46; 3/14/53; 4/2/55; 3/3/56
Valletti, Cesare, 2/16/58
Wicik, Stefan, 5/13/62

Baritones/Basses
Baransky, Wolodymyr, 3/26/61
Belarsky, Sidor, 3/19/44; 1/14/46
Boatwright, McHenry, 3/23/58
Bottcher, Ron, 12/27/64; 12/30/64
Chapman, William, 5/9/54
Del Val, Antonio, 11/29/38
Dresslar, Len, 4/26/58

Duncan, Todd, 4/21/56
Eddy, Nelson, 2/21/38; 3/4/39; 3/3/40; 3/29/41; 3/21/42; 3/14/43; 4/9/44; 4/20/48; 10/31/49
Fardulli, Jean, 1/17/38
Fischer-Dieskau, Dietrich, 10/26/58
Gilbert, J. Charles, 12/7/41
Gorin, Igor, 5/6/50; 1/9/55; 3/16/57; 4/11/59
Herbert, Ralph, 4/8/56; 4/14/56
Lisitsian, Pavel, 3/20/60
Lloyd, Ifor, 10/17/71
London, George, 3/3/51; 11/15/64
Marshall, George, 1/13/57; 3/23/58
Mazurok, Yuri, 5/26/74
McWilliams, Michael, 11/3/56
Merrill, Robert, 10/3/48; 11/7/61; 4/29/62
Nekolny, Miles, 3/1/58
Pierson, Don, 4/24/38
Pinza, Ezio, 11/21/48
Prey, Herman, 5/2/76
Rosenau, Willy, 3/4/75
Rossi-Lemeni, Nicola, 7/16/54
Siepi, Cesare, 1/18/53; 11/7/53
Souzay, Gerard, 11/12/50; 1/20/52; 12/7/57
Sudler, Louis, 4/12/53
Sved, Alexander, 11/24/40
Sze, Yi-Kwei, 4/13/57
Tajo, Italo, 4/2/50
Thomas, John Charles, 4/11/48
Tibbett, Lawrence, 11/29/47
Uppman, Theodore, 5/9/53
Warfield, William, 5/4/52; 4/26/53; 4/11/54
Warren, Leonard, 4/30/49; 10/10/53; 2/26/55
Winters, Lawrence, 1/13/57

ZELZER
MEMORABILIA

Impresario

1938

by Sienkiewicz
Sarmatia Male Chorus

SOLDIER FIELD

STATEMENT

AIDA – JULY 24, 1943   and   CARMEN – JULY 31, 1943

*   *   *   *   *   *   *   *   *   *   *   *   *   *   *

RECEIPTS (Gross)

Aida	$ 15059.30	
Carmen	14252.95	
		29312.25

EXPENSES

Mailing and Postage	$ 297.64	
Newspaper Advertising	2197.16	
Publicity Salary & Expenses	246.91	
Billposting	31.50	
Car Advertising	228.64	
Auto Advertising	84.00	
Car and Window Cards	249.37	
Circulars	91.00	
Printing Signs	11.05	
Express Charges	12.08	
Commissions	326.80	
Transportation of Scenery	605.67	
Cartage of Scenery	313.41	
Rental of Scenery	700.00	
Rental of Mirrors	17.25	
Rental of Lights	281.15	
Rental of Chairs	278.32	
Telephone	221.42	
Office Salaries	491.05	
Miscellaneous Office Expense	91.58	
Admission Tickets	178.51	
Costumes & Property Expense	156.75	
Music – Costumes	378.10	
Cast – Aida	3452.50	
Cast – Carmen	2365.00	
Musicians – Aida	1060.00	
Musicians – Carmen	1618.00	
Stage Band – Aida	265.00	
Stage Band – Carmen	60.00	
Ballet – Aida	390.00	
Ballet – Carmen	460.00	
Chorus – Aida	723.00	
Chorus – Carmen	609.00	
Stage Hands – Aida	724.92	
Stage Hands – Carmen	701.90	
Wardrobe – Aida	80.00	
Wardrobe – Carmen	80.00	
Ushers – Aida	453.00	
Ushers – Carmen	410.00	
Wigs – Aida	25.00	
Wigs – Carmen	15.00	
Supers	65.00	
Box Office – Hub	320.00	
Box Office – Aida	141.00	
Box Office – Carmen	123.00	
Decorations – Aida	75.00	
Decorations – Carmen	75.00	
Canvas	45.00	
Marking Chairs	10.00	
Horses	30.00	
Rental of Soldier Field	3021.15	
Labor at Soldier Field	1252.61	
Soldier Field Electricians	200.38	
Insurance	394.48	
Programs	34.00	
U. S. Tax	3046.15	
Artists Travel	137.07	
Bank Charges & Check NSF	3.05	
Social Security	72.35	
Gallo Expense	100.00	
Zelzer Expense	25.00	
Cain Salary & Expenses	125.00	29653.95

	LOSS $	341.70

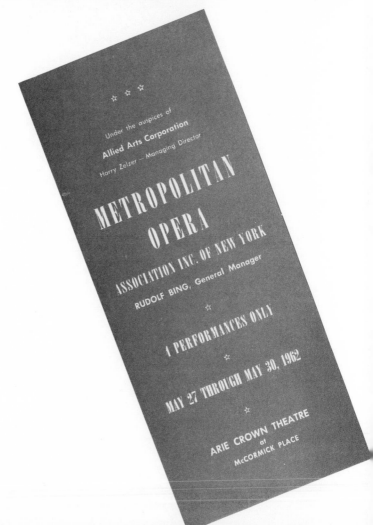

ELEANOR ROOSEVELT LECTURE

MRS. ELEANOR ROOSEVELT lectured here last Saturday night at the Civic Opera House as part of a nation-wide tour. Earlier Mrs. Roosevelt was honored at a dinner held at the Covenant Club. L. to r. Judge Harry Fischer, who acted as Moderator and Chairman of the lecture; Mrs. Roosevelt, Mayor Martin Kennelly and Harry Zelzer, of Allied Arts Corp. who sponsored the lecture.

COVENANT CLUB News

Vol. 30, No. 4

COVENANT CLUB NEWS — CHICAGO, ILL.

January, 1959

ROOSEVELT BALL JANUARY 31

● **Dinner at Seven . . .**
Outstanding Floor Show

The midwinter social scene will be brightened on Saturday evening, January 31 when the annual Roosevelt Ball is held in the ballroom. The informal ball which starts 1959 gaiety has become a tradition in the Club calendar.

Dinner at seven o'clock, a floor show which will round up a number of outstanding entertainers, dancing and general merriment will comprise the evening schedule.

Early reservations are indicated for the popular event.

Champagne Dinner Dance
By Popular Request

Last spring a Champagne Dinner Dance was held and it proved such a success that by request a second party is being arranged by I. J. Silverman and the Entertainment Committee.

Saturday, March 7

Saturday evening, March 7, has been set for it.

Photo by Lawrence Philip

After Dinner Party Honors Ballet

Mrs. Harry Zelzer, Mr. Zelzer, Mr. and Mrs. Philip H. Mitchel were among those present at the recent After-Theatre Party which honored Alicia Alonso and Igor Youskevitch and other members of the Ballet Russe de Monte Carlo troupe.

ALLIED ARTS CORPORATION

HARRY ZELZER, Managing Director

PRESENTS

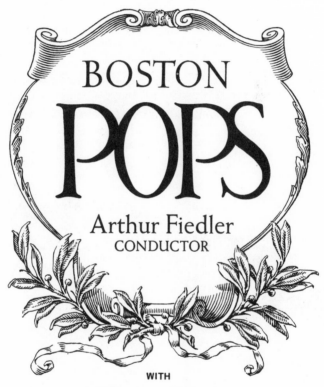

BOSTON

POPS

Arthur Fiedler

CONDUCTOR

WITH

Chet Atkins

WEDNESDAY EVENING, MARCH 19, 1975

AT 8:00 P.M.

ARIE CROWN THEATRE   CHICAGO

ALLIED ARTS
AND HARRY ZELZER

"Incorporated" has been replaced by "Association." That's another way of saying that Allied Arts, Inc., Chicago's fabled concert attraction agency for nearly half a century, now is a part of The Orchestral Association and is called the Allied Arts Association.

Allied Arts is now associated with The Orchestral Association because Harry Zelzer wanted it that way. After forty-eight years as the premier concert and dance impresario in Chicago and the Midwest, Mr. Zelzer called it quits and turned over his operation to The Orchestral Association.

Not that Mr. Zelzer is out of the picture. While the diminutive living legend in the music firmament officially is retired, he is serving as an "advisor" to The Orchestral Association. In fact, on his desk in the Allied Arts office is a nameplate that proclaims him as "Honorary Impresario."

Allied Arts has been a part of the Chicagoland culture scene since 1930 when Harry Zelzer, tired of his job in a bank, promoted his first concert attraction and lost money on it. In the thirties the organization was known as Zelzer Concerts, but in the early forties he absorbed another concert organization and its title, Allied Arts.

Through the years, Allied Arts has brought to Chicago the famous and the about-to-be famous. The Allied Arts piano series introduced to Chicago audiences young artists on their way up the ladder to fame and fortune. The ethnic music and dance groups Harry Zelzer brought to Chicago under the banner of Allied Arts were eagerly awaited by thousands of people continuing to savor the culture of their origins. And there have been the great orchestras of the world and the great dancers of the world — all here under the auspices of Allied Arts.

In the lifetime of Zelzer Concerts and Allied Arts, Harry Zelzer, the president, and Sarah Zelzer, his wife and vice president, cultivated enviable personal relationships with the great artists of the world. For years the great Sol Hurok booked his attractions into Chicago under the auspices of Mr. Zelzer and his Allied Arts. Horowitz, Serkin, Elman ... the list of greats is endless ... have been here countless times in Allied Arts series. Segovia, for example, has been coming to Chicago for forty-three years to perform for Mr. Zelzer, and he'll be back again this season as a special attraction on the Allied Arts schedule.

Harry Zelzer is a tough act to follow, but The Orchestral Association is committed to keeping the Allied Arts philosophy of presenting the most outstanding performers in the world to Orchestra Hall audiences in a number of attractive series. And while "incorporated" has given way to "Association," the product — Allied Arts, forty-eight years old this season — remains the same. ∎

Allied Arts: A New Era

The 1978-79 season marks the beginning of a new era for Allied Arts presentations in Orchestra Hall. Active management of the cultural events given under Allied Arts auspices has been transferred to The Orchestral Association, parent organization of the Chicago Symphony Orchestra.

Harry Zelzer founded the Allied Arts Series in Chicago 48 years ago and made it a unique force in the musical and cultural life of the city. Now over 80 years old, the impresario launched his career in the 1920s when most major cities had local concert managers who presented outstanding musical personalities in recital and concert.

"Quality has always been a part of the series of events offered by Allied Arts," Mr. Zelzer commented, "and patrons have been generous in their support. We know that under the direction of The Orchestral Association, the consistently high standards of these series will be assured."

In accepting the gift, Paul R. Judy, president and chief executive officer of The Orchestral Association, said: "We are aware of the significant contribution Harry Zelzer has made over the years to the prestige of Orchestra Hall by bringing recitals of virtually every world famous singer and instrumentalist. It is in this spirit that we hope to continue and enhance the work that Mr. Zelzer has done so effectively." ■

ALLIED ARTS ASSOCIATION

Harry Zelzer, *Honorary Impresario and Consultant*

Carolyn Bean, *Office Manager* Robert L. Meissner, *Publicity and Promotion*
Shirley K. Silver, *Subscriptions* Michelle F. Cucchiaro, *Special Services*
116 South Michigan Avenue, Suite 1201, Chicago, Illinois 60603
(312) 782-6094

Brenda Starr
wishes SSZ
a Happy 70th
Birthday.

ALLIED
ARTS
CORPORATION

presents

The
75th BIRTHDAY
of

HARRY ZELZER

OFFICE OF THE MAYOR

CITY OF CHICAGO

HAROLD WASHINGTON
MAYOR

P R O C L A M A T I O N

WHEREAS, on Sunday, November 15, 1987, Mel Torme, Peter Nero, and Leslie Uggams will appear at the Auditorium Theatre in "The Great Gershwin Concert;" and

WHEREAS, this concert is part of a season of international attractions being presented and underwritten by Sarah S. Zelzer and the Sarah S. Zelzer Foundation, in cooperation with The American Conservatory of Music and the Auditorium Theatre Council; and

WHEREAS, in February of 1985, a tribute dinner was held in honor of Sarah and the late Harry Zelzer (Chicago's legendary impresario) for their more than 50 years of dedication to presenting top name performers to Chicago audiences at reasonable prices; and

WHEREAS, in recent years Sarah Zelzer has emerged as an impresario in her own right and still continues the effort of keeping culture affordable; and

WHEREAS, Mel Torme, a native Chicagoan, Peter Nero and Leslie Uggams have given their time and talents to the citizens of this city through their many contributions in the entertainment industry, and through Mrs. Uggams' participation in the recent Chicago Aids benefit:

NOW, THEREFORE, I, Harold Washington, Mayor of the City of Chicago, do hereby proclaim November 15, 1987, to be GREAT GERSHWIN CONCERT DAY IN CHICAGO in recognition of Sarah S. Zelzer's continued effort to bring top entertainers to Chicago audiences at popular prices, and in honor of Mel Torme, Peter Nero and Leslie Uggams for their significant accomplishments in the entertainment world and contributions to the residents of Chicago as well as this nation as a whole.

Dated this 9th day of November, 1987.

Harold Washington
Mayor

San Carlo Opera Company

1697 Broadway

New York 19

August 20, 1952

Mr. Harry Zelzer
Civic Opera House,
20 North Wacker Dr.,
Chicago, Ill.

Dear Harry:

Congratulations on the Allied Arts brochure. I
know that ballet are the ones that are bringing
in the cash all over the U.S. and particularly
in a big way in Chicago; maybe it is the management that lures the ticket buyers.

Haven't heard from you for a long time - where
are you? Is it possible that you and Sarah spend
all the time at the Zelzer estate? I wonder if
it is true what I heard, that one carries the
sack of gold, and the other one digs the earth
to bury it. Maybe on my next trip, I can find the
spot, and can do a little digging and lifting.
After the business we did in a partner-like, I
deserve a few drops of that hidden gold, to fall
on my head.

How about you giving me advance notice of your
next arrival in the big city? I am willing to meet
you at the depot and escort you at your hotel.

With all best wishes to you and Sarah.

Sincerely,

Fortune Gallo

Andrés Segovia
Av. Concha Espina. 61
. Madrid - 16

PARA HARRY ZELZER.

CUARENTA AÑOS DE TRABAJO, EN ESTE GIGANTESCO CHICAGO, EN ESTRECHA UNIÓN CON HARRY ZELZER : ÉL, COMO EXPERTO ORGANIZADOR DE MI ACTIVIDAD PÚBLICA. YO, COMO ARTISTA, SIEMPRE ATENTO A SUS DISCRETOS CONSEJOS Y FELICES INICIATIVAS. CUARENTA AÑOS SIN QUE, RECIPROCAMENTE, NINGUN DESCONTENTO Ó QUEJA HAYAN PUESTO NOTAS AGRIAS EN EL ACORDE PERFECTO DE NUESTRA FIRME AMISTAD.

— 16—Febr.—1972.

A.S.
etc...

Forty years of work - in this gigantic Chicago - in close union with Harry Zelzer - he being the expert organizer of my public activity - I, as an artist, always attentive to his discreet advice & happy initiatives. Forty years without - reciprocally - any discontent or complaint having put any bitter notes in the perfect accord of our firm friendship.

Andres Segovia
16 Febr. 1972 -

METROPOLITAN OPERA

METROPOLITAN OPERA ASSOCIATION, INC.
LINCOLN CENTER PLAZA

FRANCIS ROBINSON
ASSISTANT MANAGER

NEW YORK, N. Y. 10023

6 March 1972

Mr. Harry Zelzer
President
Allied Arts Corporation
20 North Wacker Drive
Chicago, Illinois   60606

Dear Harry,

Seventy-five years!

I have known you more than a third of them and you have never
bored me. Thank you for that and for many other things about
which I do not have to be specific at this point having made
myself explicitly clear previously. You see I don't want to
bore you either.

Seriously, it is a privilege as well as a pleasure to salute
you on this important birthday, to congratulate you on your great
accomplishments, to thank you for what you have done for music,
the Metropolitan, and me and to wish you many more years of good
health and good fortune.

The foregoing applies to Sarah too and love to you both.

Ever,

Franci

FR:mpl
AREA CODE 212
TELEPHONE 799-3100

CABLE ADDRESS: METOPERA NEW YO

KURT WEINHOLD

My dear Harry,

Congratulations!

I'm happy to have this opportunity to congratulate
you on this special day. It's a day for sentiment
and pride -- pride in the work you've done and the
many moments of joy those labors have given to others
and sentiments to be shared with family and friends.

Having known you for half of the years you celebrate,
my expressions are not only those from a business
acquaintance but from a friend who appreciates and
values friendship.

Harry, Liz and I send our best wishes for health
and happiness with your dear Sarah and many more
special days full of celebration.

Most sincerely,

Kurt

March 14, 1972

161 West 54th Street
New York, N. Y. 10019

272

The Carnegie Hall Corporation

154 WEST 57TH STREET, NEW YORK, N. Y. 10019 • (212) 247-1350

JULIUS BLOOM
Executive Director

15 April 1972

Mr. Harry Zelzer
Impresario Extraordinary
Chicago
U.S.A.

Dear Harry:

Every warmest wish to you on your birthday. If you insist,
I shall have to believe you are 75 years old today, but you
certainly do not act your age. If we could all have your
zest, your elan, the obvious relish with which you participate in all your projects, the concert field in the United
States would not be taking aspirins.

As always, my deepest affection to you on this joyous day.
I wish I could be present in person to help celebrate it.

                    Cordially,

                    Julius Bloom

HUROK CONCERTS INC.

S. HUROK, PRESIDENT

1370 AVENUE OF THE AMERICAS, NEW YORK, N. Y. 10019
TELEPHONE: (212) 245-0500   CABLE: HURAT, N. Y.

SHELDON GOLD
VICE PRESIDENT

April 15, 1972

Mr. Harry Zelzer, President
Allied Arts Corporation
20 North Wacker Drive
Chicago, Illinois 60606

Dear Harry:

Mikki and I want to send you our most heartfelt personal wishes
for a very happy 75th birthday.

I must personally thank you as friend and advisor for what has
become a number of years, and will rely on you for many more
years to come.

Our thoughts are with you today as always.

Fondly,

Sheldon Gold

SG:kk

JUDD CONCERT ARTIST BUREAU

127 WEST 69th STREET
(POB 874, Ansonia Station)
NEW YORK, N. Y. 10023
(212) 877-8810
Cable Address:
JUDARTBURO NEWYORK

WILLIAM M. JUDD

April 15, 1972

Mr. Harry Zelzer
Allied Arts Corporation
20 North Wacker Drive
Chicago, Illinois 60606

Dear Harry:

On this 75th, or Diamond Anniversary, of your birth, please
let me congratulate you on what you have done for music in Chicago
and throughout America.

You have exhibited the wisdom of Solomon, the patience of Job,
the editorial thrust of Ochs, and the success of the "All-American Boy".

To all of this I can only hope that you will add all the years of
Methuselah.

Affectionate greetings to you and Sarah on this shining occasion.

Yours,

William M. Judd

●LMAR-LUTH ENTERTAINMENT, INC. 1776 Broadway, New York, N.Y. 10019 • (212) 581-5833 • Cable: Kolutent N.Y.

March 22, 1972

Mr. Harry Zelzer
Allied Arts Corporation
20 North Wacker Drive
Chicago, Illinois 60606

Dear Harry:

I am delighted to have the opportunity to write this "manifesto" upon the auspicious occasion of your 75th birthday.

You have diligently devoted the major part of your busy life to the cultural enrichment of your city and deserve every accolade ever bestowed upon you. I consider it a privilege to have known you for 25 years, in business as a man of great integrity, a tough bargainer and a thorough professional; and personally as a true friend and counselor.

Here is wishing you many more years of health and success. The concert field needs you, Chicago needs you, Sarah needs you and we New York managers certainly need you.

Happy birthday!

Very sincerely yours,

KOLMAR-LUTH ENTERTAINMENT, INC.

Klaus W. Kolmar

KWK:cs

Walter Foy Prude
25 East Ninth Street
New York 3

Dear Harry,

It makes me very happy to send greetings to
you on your 75th birthday. The Bible says
"three score and ten" is enough, but there
will never be enough Zelzer for me and your
other devoted friends. What a dull world
it would be without those thundering denunci-
ations, those blistering philippics, and the
genial philosophizing on milder occasions.
May you live a hundred years, Harry, in
good health and happiness.

                    Always affectionately,

                         Walter

March 8, 1972
Mr. Harry Zelzer
Chicago, Illinois

277

From F C Schang 45 Sutton Place South NYC 10022

On Michigan's shores resides a sage
To whom we dedicate this page.
On national affairs or local
This character waxes vocal:
If the problem is economic
He can name the curing tonic;
If the matter is political
He sounds off stern and critical.
He is able to settle things ad lib
Or by writing a letter to the Trib.

Now in business this fellow is quite a showman,
An able, tireless on-the-go man.
But he turns real pale at the demands
Of musicians' union or those stage hands.
Soprano fees are higher than ever
Removing profit on honest endeavor,
So why spend money to advertise
A would-be star who can't draw flies?

In spite of this continual holler
Sometime or other he made a dollar.
And now at the age of 75
He still is very much alive.
His stout old heart is in there ticking,
Yes, he's alive --- ALIVE AND KICKING!

Woes of the world he has to carry
But they don't faze our dear pal Harry.
He bubbles with wit like Alka Seltzer,
So here's a toast to Harry Zelter!

J C Schang
Apr 7, 1972

220 S. MICHIGAN AVENUE, CHICAGO, ILLINOIS · 60604 · TELEPHONE: 427-0362 · CABLE ADDRESS: CHICAG

GEORG
MUSIC DI
JOHN S. EDW
GENERAL M

April 7, 1972.

Mr. Harry Zelzer,
Allied Arts Corporation,
20 N. Wacker Drive,
Chicago, Illinois.

Dear Harry:

On the occasion of your 75th birthday, words which usually come readily to mind fail me. For weeks, I have struggled to find the right words to mark this auspicious occasion.

Only those of us who have been in the day to day grind of the "presenting" business can understand and marvel at the way you have furnished the performing musical arts to Chicago audiences for so many years. How you could have done this without having lost all of your shirts is one of the miracles of our time. Nobody else, from sandy San Diego to the rockbound coast of Maine, has accomplished such a feat.

In your house there are many mansions - symphony, opera, ballet, recitals, chamber music, Liederabend, travelogues, ice shows, and every other form of artistic habitation known to man. Age hath not withered nor custom staled your infinite variety and all of us who have been privileged to be in Chicago for any period of time are deeply indebted to you for making available so many unforgettable experiences.

On this memorable day I salute you as a bon vivant, a raconteur, a gourmet, a host, a counsellor and a friend par excellence. I hope for all our sakes that there will be many more such anniversaries to be celebrated with you.

Sincerely yours,

John S. Edwards.

MAURICE H. COTTLE

April 15, 1972

Harry Zelzer
Chicago

Dear Harry,

On the occasion of this noble birthday we
send you our most affectionate best wishes and
sincere congratulations.

You are a unique person and a rare friend to
your community, to your dedication to music and
making its beneficence available to everybody and to
your many devoted friends. What you have done for
music is now a legend.

Your sensitive sympathetic and empathetic
feeling for the great and lesser artists whom you have
carefully chosen and ofttimes prepared for presentation to your audiences have enhanced their performances
and their effectiveness in reaching the many thousands
you have brought into the halls of music. The artists
themselves, Chicagoans and other publics, owe you an
eternal debt of gratitude.

In the life of people who find themselves in a
leading role in the midst of critical civic exigencies,
it is of crucial importance whether 'these elite remain
loyal to their duty to society, establishing a relationship
to it rather than to themselves and whether they have the
power to replenish and renew themselves in a manner
conformable to their task." All this you have eminently
accomplished and continue to do.

With the loving help and cooperation of
your dear Sarah, you will, we know, carry on
your prestigious and beautiful contribution to our
lives and to the lives of all in our community for
many many years to come.

Our fondest love to Sarah and to you and
again congratulations and all best wishes.

Maurice

CHICAGO SUN-TIMES   CHICAGO DAILY NEWS

401 NORTH WABASH AVENUE • CHICAGO, ILLINOIS 60611

EMMETT DEDMON
Vice President
and Editorial Director

March 16, 1972

Dear Harry:

What kind of a billing can we give the man who is already the greatest Impresario of them all?

That at 75 he has –

The vigor of Youskevitch?

The eloquence of FDR?

The palate of a Caesar?

The mind of a banker?

The soul of a poet?

The vocabulary of Pushkin?

The zest of Rubenstein?

The ability as a critic of (censored)?

All of these are true, of course. But there is one billing that tops them all for Claire and me. It is just this:

A warm and witty friend.

Harry, you have enriched our lives with your friendship. You have dined us well.

You have let us share some great evenings in the theater and concert hall (in the best seats yet!)

Happy Birthday, then, to a man for whom every day is a celebration of the excitement of life and art.

Affectionately,

Emmett
(and Claire!)

(and Hey Boy, too)

L

OFFICE OF THE MAYOR

CITY OF CHICAGO

RICHARD J. DALEY
MAYOR

March 15, 1972

Dear Harry:

As you may know, I have had the opportunity
to send birthday greetings to many of our citizens,
but rarely has such an opportunity given me as
much pleasure as now.

Today marks an important and exciting mile-
stone in your long and well-spent life, and I am
delighted to join your many friends in wishing you
a Happy Birthday. I hope that this - your 75th
year - will be marked by many happy and good times,
and that you will continue to enjoy those rewards
in life which you so richly deserve.

With warmest regards and again, my best wishes
for a Happy Birthday.

Sincerely,

Mayor

Mr. Harry Zelzer
Allied Art Corp.
20 N. Wacker Drive
Chicago, Illinois 60606

United States District Court

For the Northern District of Illinois

Chicago, Illinois 60604

Chambers of
Abraham Lincoln Marovitz
Judge

March 13, 1972

My dear, dear friend "Uncle Harry":

April 15, 1972 marks your 75th birthday and in the language
of our beloved parents of blessed memory "Biz A. Hoondred
Un Tzwadek". "Auf Mir Gezacht" at 75.

I have learned a lot from you about life, people and human
nature and a good deal about Jewish history. I have truly
looked forward to our frequent dinner sessions with your
beloved Sarah and my own dear Mickey.

I don't know whether I was the first to give you the
appellation of "Mr. Culture" but whether I originated it
or someone else, - you truly are "Mr. Musical Culture"
here in Chicago. You are an "institution" for Chicago
music lovers.

Chicago owes you a debt of gratitude for bringing outstanding ballets and International Orchestras here. I
believe too that the public appreciates your efforts.

One thing I know for sure - you have a grateful, devoted,
appreciative and admiring friend in 'yours truly' and
I am looking forward to enjoying at least another "Chai"
of our friendship with Sarah and Mickey enjoying it with
us.

On this, your 75th birthday, please count me among those
who feel they know you best and love you the most.

Good luck, God Bless and enjoy many more fruitful, useful
and happy years with Sarah and all of your beloved family
and admiring friends.

Affectionately,

your admiring friend
Abe Marovitz

Harry Zelzer, Esq.
Chicago, Illinois

APPELLATE COURT OF ILLINOIS

CHICAGO CIVIC CENTER

60602

April 15, 1972

CHAMBERS OF
JUSTICE HENRY L. BURMAN

321·8422

My dear Harry,

Florence joins me in wishing you a very happy
75th birthday!

Nature has been kind to you my dear friend. She
gave you the blessed gift of presenting to all people,
of every economic circumstance, for more than four
decades, the opportunity to see and hear the great
artists of our nation and of the entire world.

Your devotion, throughout your life, to the uplift-
ing of the cultural pleasure of so many, is the work of
a genius and will always be remembered with love and appreciation. You have endeared yourself to hundreds of
thousands of people in every walk of life.

In this short letter, it is impossible to adequately
convey and express the depth of our gratitude for your
kind friendship and warm generosity. If I were to attempt
to name but five very close friends, your name would in-
delibly be at the top. For every kindness shown you, I
have been repaid ten times over. I know of no other friend
I hold in higher esteem.

Again, many, many happy birthdays to come and may
they all bring you and Sarah contentment and good health.

Affectionately,

Your friend and admirer

Hy L Burman

HLB/z

THE UNIVERSITY OF CHICAGO HOSPITALS AND CLINICS

BOX 439 · 950 EAST 59TH STREET · CHICAGO, ILLINOIS 60637

JOSEPH B. KIRSNER, M.D., PH.D.
Chief of Staff
and
Deputy Dean for Medical Affairs
The Division of the Biological Sciences
and The Pritzker School of Medicine;
Louis Block Professor of Medicine

Telephone: 312—947-6676

Dear Harry,

If there were not a Harry Zelzer in our lives, and I mean the whole Chicagoland community as well as Minnie and myself, God would have to create you. As Minnie and I look back on the highlights of our 39 years in Chicago, and indeed of our entire lives, we count you, Harry and Sarah, as among our very special friends. Apart from all the great things you have done for the cultural nourishment of ourselves and Chicago, you have been a truly good friend in every sense of the word. We wish you many more years of productive activity, and we look forward to these years of continuing mutual stimulation and genuine friendship. Our very best to you, Harry, on your 75th birthday.

Cordially,

Joe

Joseph B. Kirsner, M.D.

ALFRED C. STEPAN, JR.

PRESIDENT
STEPAN CHEMICAL COMPANY

EDENS & WINNETKA
NORTHFIELD, ILLINOIS 600

April 15, 1972

Dear Music Guru:

Mary Lou joins me in congratulations to you -- on this, your 75th birthday!

It has been a delight to know you and your wonderful wife, Sara. I have enjoyed your friendship for 14 years -- I wish I had known you since your first presentation in 1931.

Harry, you have a great knowledge of music, politics, history, and you respect tradition. You are an impresario with real style -- a fine judge of talent, with the proper striped trousers -- expert and gracious host at your soirees after the performances -- wonderful "joie de vivre".

All music lovers know what you have done for us. Chicago --- and your friends -- are very fortunate that you came here.

With affection,

Your friend,

Mr. Harry Zelzer
President
Allied Arts Corporation
20 North Wacker Drive
Chicago, Illinois 60606

Isaac Stern

211 CENTRAL PARK WEST, APT. 19F
NEW YORK, N. Y. 10024

January 21, 1985

Mr. Charles Moore
President
American Conservatory of Music
116 South Michigan Avenue
Chicago, IL 60603

Dear Mr. Moore,

Thank you very much for your letter of January 15th asking
me to join the distinguished artists committee for the
tribute to Sarah and Harry Zelzer on Monday, April 15th,
1985. Nothing would have given me more pleasure, nor
indeed would I have felt more honored, than to take part
in this special event. Particularly as my close friend
Leonard Bernstein is equally concerned and involved.
Unhappily, I am in France at that time in the middle of
a European concert tour and there is no way that I can
change that at this point, as you will well understand.

Harry and Sarah were both very much a part of my career
in its early days and he was a particularly close friend
in the years we worked together. Even when I was not
performing on the series we would meet, either in New
York or Chicago and have worthwhile discussions on the
state of music. These have always remained warm memories
because he was a caring and thoughtful man with a marvellous
sense of humor. We all miss him. Heaven knows, we need
more people like him today.

Please accept my good wishes for every success on the
April 15th event. With warmest personal greetings,

Sincerely yours,

Isaac Stern

IS:nms

Robert Merrill

79 OXFORD ROAD
NEW ROCHELLE, NY 10804
FEBRUARY 1, 1985

CHARLES MOORE, PRESIDENT
AMERICAN CONSERVATORY OF MUSIC
116 SOUTH MICHIGAN AVENUE
CHICAGO, ILLINOIS 60603

DEAR PRESIDENT MOORE:

I AM IN RECEIPT OF YOUR JANUARY 15, 1985 LETTER AS WELL AS A LETTER FROM RALPH ERGAS OF DECEMBER 5, 1984 RE THE APRIL 15, 1985 TRIBUTE TO SARAH AND THE LATE HARRY ZELZER.

IT WOULD GIVE ME GREAT PLEASURE TO ADD MY NAME TO THE HONORARY COMMITTEE FOR THE EVENT. REGRETFULLY, MY SCHEDULE DOES NOT PERMIT ME TO BE WITH YOU IN PERSON ON THAT DATE, HOWEVER, I DO SEND MY WARMEST REGARDS TO MRS. ZELZER. I ALSO CONGRATULATE THE AMERICAN CONSERVATORY OF MUSIC FOR ARRANGING THIS TRIBUTE TO TWO WONDERFUL PEOPLE WHO GAVE SO MANY OF US THE SUPPORT AND OPPORTUNITY WE NEEDED AT THE BEGINNING OF OUR CAREERS. BLESS THEM BOTH!

MAY I ALSO AT THIS TIME SEND MY HEARTIEST CONGRAT-ULATIONS TO THE AMERICAN CONSERVATORY OF MUSIC ON THE CELEBRATION OF ITS CENTENNIAL IN 1986. LONG MAY YOU CONTINUE TO FLOURISH!

WITH ALL GOOD WISHES FOR A MOST SUCCESSFUL APRIL 15TH CELEBRATION,

SINCERELY YOURS,

ROBERT MERRILL

A T·R·I·B·U·T·E

to SARAH and the Legend of the Late HARRY ZELZER

SONNETS FOR SARAH

Chairman
Leonard Bernstein

General Chairman
1985 Annual Campaign
Donald Rumsfeld

Honorary Chairman
The Honorable Paul Simon

Co-chairmen
Ralph Ergas
Bernard McKenna

Master of Ceremonies
Victor Borge

Distinguished Artists
Committee In Formation
Vladimir Ashkenazy
Leonard Bernstein
John Browning
Van Cliburn
James Dick
Malcolm Frager
Gary Graffman
Byron Janis
Edwin McArthur
Robert Merrill
Carlos Montoya
Ruth Page
Roberta Peters
Pinchas Zukerman

Chicago Committee
In Formation
Dorothy D. Avedisian
Marcelle Bear
Henry Brandon
Mr. and Mrs. Ralph Ergas
Mr. and Mrs. Milton Faber
Maxim Gershunoff
Martin Janis
Dr. Joseph Kirsner
Ardis Krainik
The Honorable
Abraham Lincoln Marovitz
Bernard McKenna
Charles Moore
Danny Newman
Mr. and Mrs.
Bernard Verin
Mr. and Mrs.
Julian Wineberg

Chairman
Alumni Committee
Keith Miller

Hail, Music Lovers, all 'round me here,

Tonight we have gathered for applause and good cheer,

To recall Harry with respect, and to honor his spouse.

Would that I played like their pianist, Lili Kraus,

For Kraus they brought, with her talent galore,

And Warfield and Price, and Charles Aznavour.

Their spice of life was always variety,

Witness Maria Callas, the talk of society.

And McArthur and Flagstad, Heifetz and Stern,

For the good old days all memories burn.

To Merrill, Borge, and Nelson Eddy,

We raise our glasses with champagne heady,

To tenors two, with voices sterling,

Rolf and his father, Jussi Bjoerling.

To Cliburn, Bernstein, and Alex Brailowsky,

Toscanini, Leinsdorf, Leo Stokowski,

To Horowitz, Templeton, and Art Rubinstein,

All of them great, all one of a kind.

To orchestras splendid, a musical tonic,

Berlin, Boston, the Hague Philharmonic.

Opera and ballet drew Zelzer attention,

Let's Danilova, Ruth Page, and Slavenska mention.

Toast Gigli, Toast Schipa, Toast the great Lawrence Tibbett,

To listen much more will your powers inhibit,

So ceasing beforehand, in affection rare we,

Toast the Zelzers, Sarah and Harry

AMERICAN CONSERVATORY OF MUSIC
116 South Michigan Avenue – Chicago, Illinois   60603 – 312 / 263 - 4161

Written by Charles Moore, former President of the American Conservatory of Music, on the occasion of the Tribute Dinner, April 15, 1985.

OFFICE OF THE MAYOR

CITY OF CHICAGO

HAROLD WASHINGTON
MAYOR

P R O C L A M A T I O N

WHEREAS, Harry and Sarah Zelzer presented the very highest caliber concerts in Chicago for over half a century; and

WHEREAS, Harry and Sarah Zelzer presented opera, ballet, recitals, folk groups, and popular artists in their series, bringing Chicago audiences a rich variety of the finest international entertainment; and

WHEREAS, Harry and Sarah Zelzer often gave opportunities for young performers from Chicago to appear professionally before large audiences; and

WHEREAS, April 15th is the 88th birthday of Harry Zelzer; and

WHEREAS, the respected American Conservatory of Music has chosen April 15th to pay tribute to the legend of the late Harry Zelzer and to Sarah Zelzer:

NOW, THEREFORE, I, Harold Washington, Mayor of the City of Chicago, proclaim April 15, 1985 to be HARRY AND SARAH ZELZER DAY IN CHICAGO.

Dated this 8th day of April, 1985.

Harold Washington
Mayor

HONORS

May 2, 1978

Impresario Harry Zelzer feted for his cultural contributions by The Artists Advisory Council at the Drake Hotel.

June 4, 1978

America-Israel Cultural Foundation honors Harry and Sarah Zelzer at the Arts Club. A scholarship fund endowed by and named for the Zelzers will be established at the event. Through the years they have helped the careers of many Israeli and other Jewish artists, including the Israel Philharmonic Orchestra, the Israel Chamber Orchestra, Daniel Barenboim, Itzhak Perlman, Pinchas Zukerman, and others.

Harry Zelzer has long been known in Chicago as "Mr. Culture" and was recently cited by Mayor Bilandic in the City Council for his contribution...

May 5, 1979

FRIENDS OF LITERATURE

is honored to present this

citation

to

HARRY ZELZER

who for forty-eight star-filled years served Chicago
and its citizens with distinction as the city's "Impresario of the Arts." Through his Allied Arts Corporation and his own unflagging appreciation of the musical and performing arts, he brought to the stages and
concert halls of Chicago all of the great international
names in music, theatre and dance. Not only did he
present the very best in cultural entertainment, but
also has had a flair for discovering young talent and
helping it grow. For all this we offer now this grateful
"Bravo!"

♩♩♩

WASHINGTON CROSSES THE DELAWARE

Written by Sarah Schectman at age fourteen

Floating ice. A frost bitten and snowy night. Men fatigued, bravely fighting their way across the river. Boats tipping almost constantly. Oars dropping out of the frozen hands of the men. Horses plodding, slowly feeling their way.

Onward! Onward! Onward!

Washington and his men are crossing the Delaware.

"Foolish move," said many.

Washington, however, said, "Cross the river we must." Before leaving he prayed to God to guide his men safely across.

A foolish move. Yet not one backed out when Washington gave the command to go. They left. Most of them felt that this was the last they would see of each other. Some, perhaps, thought of the women and children left behind and felt that they must go on and free themselves from England's clutches. They must fight for the Declaration of Independence. For the new country.

Onward! Onward! Onward!

Onward into the dim hours of the night. Slowly plodding, and plodding, and plodding.

Their destination is reached. The men were frozen and unable to take a step. Fires are lighted and they are somewhat warmed. Many of them are now warmed by a spark of hope. They have crossed the Delaware. God would not foresake them now. They mount their horses and they take the Hessians by surprise. The Hessians are astonished. It seems to them as if the impossible has happened. Washington has crossed the Delaware.

To me, also, it seems as if the impossible has happened. Was luck with us, or was it the patriotic feeling of our men to plod onward and onward and onward, in order to live up to the Declaration of Independence?

Patriotism. Nothing is nobler, finer. Nothing can require more patience, more patriotism, than Washington's Crossing of the Delaware.

ʄʄʄ

I attended a concert of the People's Symphony at the Eighth St. Theatre, and you were in the lobby watching the people enter and keeping an eye on the box office. My music teacher later told me you were the "ANGEL" of the Orchestra and that some day in the near future I would play the Tchaikowsky Concerto for you, and you might let me perform with the Orchestra. I never did audition for you.

Our first supper date after a performance of the San Carlo Opera Company.

Our Wedding Day.

Your decision to go into the concert business.

Our excitement when we bought our house "Pierpoint".

The things we planned—each friendly little chat when we were together and just talked.

Your contribution to the cultural life of Chicago, of which I am so proud to be a part.

Your helping hand and guidance to those who needed it.

Our great hearted partnership that gives for the joy of giving without bargaining or recrimination.

The happy occasions spent with the children and family.

I recall these memories as I go along life's way, and I find they grow more precious with each passing day. I thank God for all the wonderful years we have shared.

And now my dear, may you have continued years of good health and happiness.

Enjoy the greetings of your family and friends in the following pages of this album.

I Love You
Sarah

INDEX

295